SOCIAL SECURITY

The Westerners

BRAND BOOK

LOS ANGELES CORRAL

BOOK TEN

The Westerners
BRAND BOOK
BOOK TEN

LOS ANGELES CORRAL
1963

IN MEMORIAM
1946-1963

J. J. ROLLINSON

ERNEST V. SUTTON

BRUCE KISKADDON

CHARLES YALE

J. GREGG LAYNE

A. R. VAN NOY

*HOMER E. BRITZMAN

FRANK KING

COL. WILLIAM A. GRAHAM

ROBERT A. DODSON

PERCY L. BONEBRAKE

DR. ROBERT G. CLELAND

DR. FREDERICK W. HODGE

ROGER SUMNER

FRANK S. DOLLEY, M.D.

CLARENCE ARTHUR ELLSWORTH

WILLIAM L. WRIGHT

FRED VAILE

First Sheriff of the Los Angeles Corral.

BRAND BOOK X
IS DEDICATED TO

CLARENCE ELLSWORTH
1885 - 1961

WHO CORRALED THE
WEST ON CANVAS AND
MADE THE EVENING
CAMPFIRES BRIGHTER
WITH HIS PRESENCE.

CONTENTS

LIST OF ILLUSTRATIONS

THE WESTERNERS · LOS ANGELES CORRAL · 1963

Active Members

ED AINSWORTH
JAMES N. ALGAR
PAUL D. BAILEY
NOAH BEERY
COL. C. B. BENTON, Ret'd.
DONALD E. BOELTER
HOMER H. BOELTER
LORING CAMPBELL
ARTHUR H. CLARK, JR.
DWIGHT L. CLARKE
HENRY H. CLIFFORD
IRON EYES CODY
GLEN DAWSON

CARL S. DENTZEL
EDDIE I. EDWARDS
JAMES S. FASSERO
EARLE R. FORREST
CARROLL FRISWOLD
GEORGE E. FULLERTON
PAUL W. GALLEHER
JOHN B. GOODMAN III
DUDLEY GORDON
EVERETT G. HAGER
A. STEVENS HALSTED, JR.
DONALD W. HAMBLIN
COL. C. W. HOFFMANN
HOLLING C. HOLLING
ERNEST M. HOVARD

LONNIE HULL
HARVEY S. JOHNSON, M.D.
WEBSTER A. JONES
JOHN H. KEMBLE
WILLIAM T. KIMES
RUSS LEADABRAND
ALAN LEMAY
WARREN F. LEWIS
DON C. MEADOWS
BEN H. O'CONNOR
BERT H. OLSON
DON LOUIS PERCEVAL
SID PLATFORD
PHILIP J. RASCH
JACK E. REYNOLDS

W. W. ROBINSON
CHARLES N. RUDKIN
AUGUST W. SCHATRA
HARVEY E. STARR, M.D.
ERVIN STRONG
HARLAN H. THOMPSON
WM. B. UPTON, JR.
ROBERT J. WOODS

Honorary Members

EDGAR N. CARTER
DR. M. R. HARRINGTON
LEE SHIPPEY
ARTHUR WOODWARD

In Memoriam – 1962–1963

FRED VAILE   ·   WILLIAM L. WRIGHT

OFFICERS

OFFICE	1962	1963
SHERIFF	JAMES N. ALGAR	JOHN H. KEMBLE
DEPUTY SHERIFF	JOHN H. KEMBLE	CHARLES N. RUDKIN
ROUNDUP FOREMAN	WILLIAM L. WRIGHT	SID PLATFORD
ASSISTANT ROUNDUP FOREMAN	ERVIN STRONG	AUGUST SCHATRA
LIBRARIAN	CARROLL FRISWOLD	CARROLL FRISWOLD
REPRESENTATIVE	FRED VAILE	DUDLEY GORDON
REGISTRAR	CHARLES N. RUDKIN	ERVIN STRONG
ASSISTANT REGISTRAR	SID PLATFORD	RUSS LEADABRAND
KEEPER OF THE CHIPS	BERT H. OLSON	BERT H. OLSON
DAGUERREOTYPE WRANGLER	LONNIE HULL	LONNIE HULL
CHIEF OF SMOKE SIGNALS	IRON EYES CODY	IRON EYES CODY
WRANGLERS	DUDLEY GORDON AUGUST SCHATRA RUSS LEADABRAND	JAMES S. FASSERO ERNEST M. HOVARD WARREN F. LEWIS PHILIP J. RASCH

EDITORIAL STAFF — BRAND BOOK NO. 10

Editor
EDDIE I. EDWARDS

Associate Editors
JAMES N. ALGAR, HOMER H. BOELTER, ARTHUR H. CLARK, JR., GEORGE E. FULLERTON, PAUL W. GALLEHER
JOHN B. GOODMAN III, WEBSTER A. JONES, JOHN H. KEMBLE, DON C. MEADOWS, W. W. ROBINSON

FOREWORD

Brand Book Number Ten claims the distinction of being exclusively a Los Angeles Corral production. Its contributors are members of the Corral; its central theme is in the nature of a memorial to a distinguished artist and beloved Westerner, the late Clarence Ellsworth; its Art Editor, responsible for the decorative artwork, is our own competent member — John B. Goodman III; its designer and printer is the talented Homer Boelter, a former Sheriff of the Corral and a former *Brand Book* Editor.

The function of *Brand Book* literature is to capture and record neglected segments of Western history while yet there is time and opportunity. Each *Brand Book* Editor is dedicated to the accomplishment of this purpose. With the cooperation and council of the Editorial Staff, his responsibility is to evaluate, select, and edit the material submitted in the effort to achieve this essential objective.

Each successive Editor profits from the experience of those who have served before him; and he derives substantial benefit from the books they have edited. It is the hope of the present Editor that *Brand Book Number Ten* will prove helpful to those who follow him, and will find acceptable place among the books of these other Editors who firmed the pattern and set the standard of good workmanship.

BANCROFT'S
MAP
OF THE
COLORADO MINES
PUBLISHED BY
H.H. BANCROFT & CO.
San Francisco, Cal.
1863

Entered according to Act of Congress A.D. 1863 by H.H. BANCROFT & COMPANY in the Clerk's Office of the District Court of the United States for the

FORGOTTEN ROAD TO GOLD

By HAROLD & LUCILE WEIGHT

Much has been written and told of the Butterfield Stage Line. Few know of this other, and perhaps equally romantic, pathway of travel across the Colorado Desert. Bradshaw attempted the rather obvious route that Butterfield rejected. His wagons rumbled through the San Gorgonio Pass and across the desert to Ehrenberg. In this narrative the well known Western authors have salvaged a vital fragment of California history, and have secured it for all time to come. (Note: Any attempt to retrace the dimly marked course of the Bradshaw Trail should be made in a 4-wheel drive car.)

ONCE THERE WAS A CITY CALLED LA PAZ—Queen City of the Colorado River—destined, it believed, to become the first capital of Arizona Territory, which it had helped create. Laguna de la Paz—Lake of Peace—to give its full name, located on the east bank of the river 125 miles upstream from Fort Yuma.

And once the golden placers of La Paz and of the desert beyond drew the boldest miners, boomers, adventurers and gamblers from all the West. Lodestones for a wild and exuberant stampede that changed the history of what was originally New Mexico Territory, for a time they even threatened to depopulate Los Angeles.

And once there was a wagon trail called the Bradshaw Road which crossed the deserts of southeastern California to La Paz. Born of the gold rush, familiar on the lips of thousands of goldseekers and merchants, its every landmark and waterhole was logged minutely by special correspondents of the great daily newspapers of San Francisco and Sacramento.

But this was a hundred years ago. There is no city of La Paz on Arizona maps today. On most not even the site is shown, nor the place-name remembered. Ferra Gulch, Oro Fino, Campo en Medio, Las Chollas, American Camp —all have been winnowed of their golden grain. All have vanished with La Paz.

And what of the Bradshaw Road? More important, more lasting than the rush, the city, and even the placers that created it, the Bradshaw Road became, and for decades remained, the principal freight, passenger and mail artery between Southern California and central Arizona—Prescott, Wickenburg, the gold camps of the Walker-Weaver boom, the Vulture mine. Became for a while one of the paths of emigration from East to West. Then one day there were other roads, and it was forgotten by travelers. It, too, vanished from the maps.

But not from the annals and legends of the building of the desert West. There its ruts run deep and clear.

FORGOTTEN ROAD TO GOLD

The Bradshaw Road follows hard upon an ancient Cocomaricopa Indian trail (one that Mexico attempted to develop, in the 1820s, for travel between Tucson presidio and Alta California). But the route became important only after discovery of the Colorado River placers. By most accounts that occurred in early January, 1862. Father Paul Figueroa set it on January 12, "Feast day of Our Lady of Peace"—hence the name, La Paz.

But since supposedly the strike was made by Captain Paulino (or Pauline or Powell) Weaver, famed Arizona Mountain Man and army scout, and two of his fellow trappers—Pappan (or Pap Hahn) and "a Frenchman known as Frederico"—such a christening seems unlikely. If the date and reason for naming have any validity, they probably apply to arrival of the first working miners in the placers—José Redondo and his fellow Sonorans who hastened up from the Gila City diggings, northeast of Yuma, where Weaver had shown Redondo the quill of golden dust he had gathered on the Colorado.

When the first rumors spread, there was no mention of the name "La Paz," but only the racing whisper that gold had been found across the Colorado. In California, not even *that* rumor could be pinned down. The men who came to the placers in the early weeks were almost without exception of Mexican birth, chiefly from the Fort Yuma area. When these first ones wrote "drop-everything-and-come" letters to friends and relatives scattered from San Francisco to Sonora, they evidently stressed that the matter should be kept strictly family.

In Los Angeles, at any rate, a sizeable portion of the predominantly Mexican population had quietly drifted away for the river while the *gringos* there still had no more than a suspicion that something was afoot. And when the first groups of Americans reached the Colorado, alerted by a few broken threads in the network of silence, hundreds of native Californians, Arizonans and New Mexicans, and even Sonorans and Yaqui Indians from Old Mexico, were already working the rich gravels.

From March 15, 1862, the Los Angeles *Star* and *News* carried repeated rumors and "confirmations" of placers discovered at various distances up the Colorado. But not until May 17 did the *Star* give approximately the correct location, together with the fact that at least $12,000 in gold—including a nugget as large as a hen's egg—had reached Los Angeles. Then, day after day California papers carried stories of the Colorado River placers and their fabulous richness. In response, men poured into Southern California—by coast steamers, on horseback, by wagons and stagecoaches. They swarmed in Los Angeles, outfitting themselves, and clamored for directions for reaching the mines.

FORGOTTEN ROAD TO GOLD

In the beginning there was one known route—the long way around. Los Angeles via Warner's Ranch to Fort Yuma, about 300 miles by the old Butterfield stage road. Across the Colorado on Jaeger's ferry from the fort, still following the stage road, to a point on the Gila River about 25 miles northeast, where a poorly marked pack trail led north. The pack trail was a long 90 miles—with Horse Tanks the one sure watering place—up Castle Dome and La Posa plains, through Weaver Pass and across the Colorado River Valley to the new gold fields.

From Los Angeles directly east to the placers, the distance was only 225 miles, but by this established route it was well over four hundred. Too far for the eager would-be millionaires who had to carry food for themselves, fodder for their animals, and for long stretches water for both. Much too far for Los Angeles merchants, who had not fared well in the rush of 1849, but hoped to do better with a new El Dorado almost on their doorsteps.

Could a direct road be opened? Leading citizens of Los Angeles and San Bernardino—the latter on a straight line with the placers and 60 miles closer—were certain it could. A trail from San Bernardino through San Gorgonio Pass and down the Salton Sink to Yuma crossing already existed, although almost without water for the last 85 miles and only a few miles shorter than the Warner route. But from the last good watering place on that Yuma trail, which was known both as Dos Palmas and Warm Springs, it was less than 75 miles almost due east to the river near the gold placers.

Not only that, but in 1855-57, Colonel Henry Washington's surveyors had run the San Bernardino Base Line and its South Standard Parallels to the Colorado, and supplies had been freighted to them from Dos Palmas almost to the river. L. R. Frink, who had done the freighting, was a cattle rancher in San Timoteo Canyon at the west entrance to San Gorgonio Pass. Also, undoubtedly, early settlers knew about the ancient Indian trail across that same stretch. And the expeditions along this trail in 1823 and 1825-26 by Captain Romero and Lieutenant Estudillo—the first a failure, the second touching and crossing the Colorado—should have been alive in the memory or traditions of the older Mexicans. There is good reason to believe, in fact, that some of those Mexican "earlybirds" in the placers took this trail.

But all this was hazy, uncertain and undetailed. So on May 16, William David Bradshaw left Los Angeles with eight men, bound for the river via San Bernardino not only to reach the mines, but expressly to see whether this route would make a satisfactory road to the Colorado and report on what he found. Bill Bradshaw would find death instead of fortune in his

FORGOTTEN ROAD TO GOLD

Arizona adventuring, but he also would affix his name forever to the desert road he helped open and make known.

Bradshaw was only about 36 when he joined the Colorado River rush, but already he had helped make California history. A long-time friend, Major Horace Bell, described him as "a natural lunatic"—but also "one of nature's polished gentlemen." Eccentric, nervous in temperament, brave, generous, perfect in "manly form and physical beauty," a giant in muscular strength, unequalled in fleetness of foot and endurance—that was Bradshaw as Bell saw him, and other friends agreed.

But another pioneer pinpointed the great failing that would so soon bring his needless death, remembering him, shortly and sharply, as an "old Fremont scout who struck it rich and drank it up."

Military records show Bradshaw did serve with Fremont's California battalion in the Mexican War. Before joining it, he took part in the Bear Flag Revolt in Sonoma in 1846. In 1847, as first lieutenant in Company D, he participated in the American capture of Los Angeles. He mined in the Mother Lode country after the gold discovery. By 1855 he was hunting placer gold and grizzly bears on the headwaters of the Kern River.

Probably Bradshaw came south into the San Bernardino Mountains in the rush which followed discovery of gold in Holcomb Valley on May 4, 1861. At any rate, the Los Angeles *Southern News* reported in April, 1861, that "a Mr. Bradshaw" had just found rich gold and silver quartz on the east side of those mountains.

That same April marked the outbreak of the Civil War. In 1861-62, Confederate troops under General H. H. Sibley were operating in New Mexico and Arizona. They captured and garrisoned Tucson. Holcomb Valley became a stronghold of California Secessionists, and a rallying point for Southern sympathizers trying to make their way to join the rebel forces. The only road they could take was that past Fort Yuma, where Federal forces did their best to block reinforcement of the rebel cause.

Whether this had anything to do with Bradshaw's eagerness to open a new road to the Colorado is an interesting question. Not only was he a Southerner (Bell says he was born in Buncombe County, South Carolina, while the 1864 Arizona census says Tennessee) but he was a friend of such strongly anti-Union men as Editor Henry Hamilton of the Los Angeles *Star*. And on his very first trip Bradshaw did bring back information about a continuation of the Cocomaricopa trail from La Paz to the Butterfield Stage road, which would cut ten days, he said, from the travel time to Tucson. It also, perhaps not

FORGOTTEN ROAD TO GOLD

incidentally, would by-pass Fort Yuma. By August, 1862, he actually had traced out that route, although by then the Confederates had long since retreated from Tucson.

Bradshaw's progress on his first trip to the river was reported in the *Star* on May 31: "The Cutoff—Parties who have left town for the Colorado placers, intending to take a cut off by way of San Gorgonio Pass, thence on a straight line to the new diggings, have sent back word to the effect that the new road is in first rate condition, and perfectly practicable."

The gold excitement, in the meantime, had reached furnace heat. Said the *Star* on June 7: "Our city is now in the throbs and throes of a violent fever to procure the yellow dust said to be so plentiful on the banks of the Colorado River. This fever has proved quite fatal during the past two weeks, carrying off a large portion of our population, and its effects are, if anything, becoming more widespread. Every branch of business has sent its representative to the mines; almost every household has sent its delegate—and if information shall arrive putting an end to all doubts as to the extent of the new placers, business in this city will be pretty much suspended in the rush to the gold fields."

That information was provided when Bill Bradshaw returned to Los Angeles on the afternoon of June 11. He had left La Paz the morning of June 5 and had reached San Bernardino the evening of June 9, despite the fact that he had trudged the last 70 miles on foot, after losing his horse "in consequence of an Indian difficulty."

June 14, the *Star* published the first log of the La Paz road, with distances as Bradshaw had measured and compiled them. With a few variations in stopping places and many variations in place-name spelling, this was to remain the basic log for the life of the trail.

TABLE OF DISTANCES	MILES
Los Angeles to San Bernardino	60
To San Timoteo	18
To White River	25
To Agua Caliente	6
To Sand Hole	12
To Toro Village	14
To Martin's House	4
To Lone Palm, or Soda Springs	12
To Dos Palmas	7
To Canon Creek	10
To Tabisaca	7
To Chu-cu-wallah	18
To the River	36
Total Distance	229

FORGOTTEN ROAD TO GOLD

Tied to present map names, the route which Bradshaw followed after leaving San Bernardino would pass west and then south of Redlands through San Timoteo Canyon, keep not far from the freeway through San Gorgonio Pass past Beaumont and Banning, angle southeast over to Palm Springs (then Agua Caliente), continue past Palm Desert to Indian Wells (which with the same name was one of the original waystops), down Coachella Valley west of Indio and Mecca to Torres and over to Martinez Indian Reservation (just east of Oasis) and on across near the head of Salton Sea (then Dry Lake) to Dos Palmas Springs, close to Coachella branch canal east of Salton Sea State Park.

From the point of departure from Highway 101, a few miles before reaching Dos Palmas, until paving is reached again in the Palo Verde Valley south of Ripley the old La Paz road roughly parallels U.S. 60-70, but lies south of it on the other side of the Orocopia and Chuckawalla Mountains. From Ripley the road swung northeast across Palo Verde Valley, through or close to Blythe, crossed the Colorado River on Bradshaw's Ferry, probably located just opposite Ehrenberg, and continued upriver four or five miles to Ehrenberg.

With his log, the *Star* published Bradshaw's comprehensive account of the placers and the route to them. Editorially, it declared: "As he is a reliable, intelligent and experienced miner, his report is considered as definitely settling the question—that the mines are rich and extensive."

Some of the large group of palms which now marks the site of old Dos Palmas stage station.

FORGOTTEN ROAD TO GOLD

Said Bill Bradshaw:

Left Los Angeles on 16th May, traveling by way of San Bernardino, thence through San Gorgonio Pass to White River—to Agua Caliente—to Toro Indian Village—to Martin's house, of the Toro tribe. Here met a Maricopa [Cocomaricopa] Indian who had joined Cabezon and had been to the river where the mines are. He made a map of the road, which proved to be correct, and we proceeded on our journey: From Martin's house to Lone Palm—to Dos Palmas—to Canon Creek—to Tabisaca, point of Mountains—to Chu-cul-wallah—thence to the Colorado river in front of the mines, at the point where has been established the Providence Ferry.

Found the river high, but at this point narrow, caused by the projection of two high sand bars, the current running at the rate of at least six but not more than eight miles an hour. Above and below this point, the river opens up, in flats and bayous, four or five miles wide. Made a raft and passed over the party, nine in number, with baggage, swimming the animals—from three-fourths to a mile and a half.

The Mines—Arriving on the East side of the Colorado, traveled up four miles to Lagoona [sic]. Here found 250 or 300 persons living, engaged in most kinds of trading, one concern owned by an American (the only one) and a Mexican (probably Warringer & Redondo). Remained at Laguna de la Paz for three days,

The Bradshaw road once followed up Salt Creek Wash, shown here just above the point where the Kaiser Eagle Mountain railroad now crosses it. Salton Sea in the distance. Left foreground is what is left of Clemens Well, dug by the county, which for a considerable time replaced Canyon Springs as a watering place on the later road through the wash.

FORGOTTEN ROAD TO GOLD

conversing with the people and making observations. Everyone gave a good account of the mines, some having obtained as much as six ounces in a day, but others nothing. There was, however, no complaint—not a solitary grumbler was met with, what had not been ever before experienced in any mining camp.

Went to the mines, nine miles distant, and returned same day. Saw a Mexican dry washing about seven dollars out of one pan of dirt; also, others washing out with various results, from two bits upward; saw a piece weighing seven ounces, and was informed that one piece was taken out worth $700.

The diggings were discovered in the most unlikely place, in a crevice in the bare bed rock, and by mere accident; afterward, gold was found in the gulches, and now the diggings are being traced down to the flats and plains; holes have been dug 15 feet deep and still gold is found. On the hillsides, the gold is found only in the crevices of the rock.

Miners are at work from six to ten miles from where the gold was discovered. There has been very little prospecting. No claims, so-called, are allowed. A man is allowed enough space to use his pick or crowbar, or any other mining implements, nothing more. Another may pitch in right alongside . . .

The mines are dry diggings, especially and emphatically so, being destitute of water . . . The mode of separating the gold from the sand is by the Mexican style of dry washing.

Water—Water for domestic use is hauled or packed from the river, and from the number of persons who have lately engaged in the business, prices are greatly reduced, it being sold at the nearest station for 12½c, and at the more remote for 25c, a gallon.

Provisions—There had not yet been opened anything in the line of a hotel or eating-house; nor, strange to say a drinking shop. There was no liquor at either camp. One man had brought in a 20 gallon cask of whiskey, and sold it out at $6 a bottle.—Flour sells at $25 a hundred; sugar, 75c and beef 25c per pound. Nothing else in market.

Population—The population is estimated at 75 to 100 Americans, with from 300 to 500 on the way; and from 700 to 800 Sonoranians and Yaquis, with the whole adult male population of that State expected.

The Road—Wood, Water, Grass—About one-third or one-half the distance from the last water (Chu-cu-Wallah) quail, doves and rabbit, were seen in great numbers—an infallible sign of water in the vicinity. There was no time to camp and prospect the place, but it is determined to take an opportunity to explore the locality, when water is sure to be found there; and doubtless on other portions of the road, on further investigation.

There is plenty of grass for animals on the whole route. After passing White River, it is recommended to travel at night, or early in the morning to avoid heat; although no hot weather was experienced going or coming, except a few hours one day in going down the Cabezon or White River Valley— it was sultry.

The face of the country is generally a plain, with occasionally a low hill

FORGOTTEN ROAD TO GOLD

rising up abruptly. There is also plenty of wood, greasewood, mesqueit [sic] and greenwood [palo verde] . . .

The Apache Indians claim the country lying back of the mines, on which account it has not yet been prospected. The mines are due east from Los Angeles, between the base line and second standard . . .

Providence Ferry—At the crossing of the river, now about three-fourths miles wide, Messrs. Wm. A. Warringer and W. D. Bradshaw are to start a ferry, and to have a boat on the river by the 16th, sufficient to carry over passengers and freight. Meanwhile Indians are employed in passing over with a raft, and swimming the animals.

As a result of Bradshaw's expedition and his report in the *Star*, the entire length of the La Paz route, from San Bernardino to the Colorado, became known through the West as the Bradshaw Road. But only for the stretch from Dos Palmas to the river could he possibly be called the pioneer. Even there (and even excepting the Indians and Mexicans who preceded him) probably he was not first. Other parties intending to try the same general route were scattered out behind him, and some may well have been ahead.

Most of these, however, would use the cutoff only to reach the gold fields; they were not scouting it so others could follow. But one person—James Grant of San Bernardino—apparently had that same purpose in mind. Not only that—Grant signed the first description of the La Paz cut-off to appear in print. Grant's letter was in the Los Angeles *Southern News* on June 13, beating Bradshaw, in the *Star*, by one day:

NEW ROUTE TO THE COLORADO MINES

San Bernardino, June 10th, 1862

Editors Southern News—About four weeks ago, I left this place for the purpose of securing a more direct route to the newly discovered gold diggings on the Colorado river, about 130 miles north of Yuma. In this I have been very successful, and on the morning of the 12th instant I intend starting from this place with fingerboards, etc., to be placed along the road for the benefit of the traveling public.

There are several wagons now on their way to the river over this road, which, with little labor, will answer for heavily loaded teams to pass over. The distance from this place to the river, opposite the mines, is about 180 miles, with grass and water, beyond expectation; the last stretch, from a spring to the river, being about 40 miles, and no other stretch of over 20 miles without water; all other distances from station to station with plenty of water and grass, and a far better route than via Fort Yuma for heavily loaded wagons, with little sand to pull through.

Yours, respectfully,

JAMES GRANT

FORGOTTEN ROAD TO GOLD

This Grant was as important in the history of the La Paz cut-off as was Bill Bradshaw, and at least as much of a pathfinder along it. In the early days of the rush, the two were looked upon as co-pioneers of the road. Both were traveling it at about the same time in May, 1862, and not in the same party. Therefore, if Grant is accurate in his starting date—"about four weeks ago" —he probably led Bradshaw all the way. It is interesting that he said in his letter *"I have been very successful,"* not mentioning Bradshaw at all, although the very day he wrote it Bradshaw was in San Bernardino, telling all interested parties the facts about the road which would appear in the *Star* story.

Both in the beginning and later on, Bradshaw did more than Grant to publicize the new route, and he guided more men across it. On the other hand, Grant did much more than Bradshaw to turn the old Cocomaricopa trail into a usable road. He put up signposts, improved bad spots, developed water supplies, set up stations. He conducted pack trains along it, and drove freight wagons and operated stages. He continued to use and improve it for years after Bradshaw was dead.

But always it remained the "Bradshaw Road" that Grant used and improved. This might have been because Bradshaw was more widely known than Grant. But it is more likely that it was due to the difference in impact between Bradshaw's initial informative report, containing just what the gold-seekers wanted to know, and Grant's brief letter. The one was widely copied and reprinted, the other apparently did not make a ripple. It might even be that, had Grant written a long letter, or had he been interviewed by the *News*, the La Paz cut-off would have been known then, would be remembered today, as the Grant Road.

Certainly it was Bradshaw's story and the information he broadcast in San Bernardino that triggered the first great rush along the La Paz road. With his waybill in their hands, throngs streamed east out of Los Angeles for San Bernardino and the promised land. Those who had gathered in San Bernardino started even earlier, large numbers leaving on June 13. They had listened to Bradshaw and they had talked to Grant, and they swarmed out across the Santa Ana River, past ruined San Bernardino mission *asistencia*, up San Timoteo Canyon, heading for San Gorgonio Pass.

Among these Friday-the-thirteenth starters were special correspondents for San Francisco's *Alta California* and *Evening Bulletin*, the former J. H. Riley, the latter probably Henry DeGroot. Both were good writers, but they certainly had an eye for the hardships and uncertainties of the enterprise. Possibly their

FORGOTTEN ROAD TO GOLD

editors had hinted that a little cold water on this Southern California excitement would not be unwelcome.

A rather complete log of waystops early travelers such as these found along the Bradshaw was printed in the San Bernardino *Guardian* later in the 1860s:

SAN BERNARDINO TO LA PAZ	MILES
Old San Bernardino Mission	8
Frink's	7
Dr. Edgar's	8
Chapin's Sheep Ranch	6
Antonio Creek	4
Grant's Creek	3
Indian Run	5
White River	2
Agua Caliente	10
Sand Hole	11
Old Rancheria	6
Toro's	9
Martinez	5
Palma Seca	12
Dos Palmas	7
Brown's Pass (Canyon Springs)	10
Tabassacco	8
Chucowalla	18
Slough	35
La Paz	16
Total	190

Caught by a rainstorm a few miles up San Timoteo Canyon, Riley spent the first night at Frink's big stock ranch. Along with valuable information, he acquired a tinge of prejudice against Bradshaw and Grant, due to Frink's positive statement that he had freighted over, and Colonel Washington had surveyed, "the same route to the river now trumpeted forth as a *new* one." Frink also drew for him a "minute" plan of the route which, Riley said, proved to be correct.

Following San Timoteo's easy grade, they entered the wide valley of "San Gorgonia" Pass, keeping to the right of the neighboring ranches of Dr. Edgar and Dr. Smith (the latter now Highland Springs). They camped two miles beyond George S. Chapin's sheep ranch, not far from present Banning. They struggled down the sandy bed of San Gorgonio River, crossed White River (Whitewater), "a fine stream of cold clear water coming across the valley from San Bernardino Mountain," and worked through ten miles of heavy, sandy road to Agua Caliente (Palm Springs). There they bathed in the hot springs, and there they found a small tribe of "Seranos," some 200 in number, who cultivated the land and raised corn, wheat, barley and watermelons.

They started on at 2 a.m., planning to continue through to Toros rancheria. But after six hours of heavy going, they followed one of Grant's just-placed signs to the Sand Hole, 150 yards left of the road. This was a

FORGOTTEN ROAD TO GOLD

watering place only after rain had filled it, and then only until the water dried or was used up. "Old Rancheria," or Indian Wells, dug in the dry bed of the Whitewater River a few miles farther south, was the more commonly used water stop on this section of the Bradshaw.

After watering their animals at the Sand Hole and waiting under the shade of mesquites for the rest of the group to catch up, sunlight and sand reflection had made it "too hot to lie still; too hot to go on," and they did not dare to proceed until after nightfall. Then they moved on, "the road winding along the base and within the shadow of the mountain range [the Santa Rosas], with intervals of good road, but more generally heavy pulling through the sand. The moon gave just sufficient light to render objects a little distant, dim and deceptive. Several times our outriders, fearful of passing the place, went off on false scents for water and rancherias, the wagon and packs halting, of course, to receive their reports. And so wore the weary night away, from 8 o'clock of Tuesday evening until 4 o'clock of Wednesday morning, when we reached the Rancheria de los Toros."

Bradshaw, this time guiding a party of seven from Los Angeles, came into Toros an hour after Riley. After resting until 6 p.m. that day, June 19, the enlarged company moved five miles farther out into the valley to Martinez rancheria. Making only a short stop, they struck directly east near the head of Dry Lake (now Salton Sea), reaching Palma Seca or Lone Palm at two a.m. The water was almost undrinkable; the place had lost its single palm and was now known as Soda Springs.

They continued eight miles to Dos Palmas across a desert which, Riley felt, would "require the rasping down of a thousand years of winds and rains to make even a tolerably decent country for an Indian to live in." Some vandal hand had cut one of the palms at Dos Palmas. The main spring had been dug out at the foot of the remaining "noble and graceful" tree to form a tank large enough "to water a thousand head of stock"—and also to serve as a fine bathing place for his party.

Three wagons were already at these springs, and a party of Holcomb Valley miners on foot, packing their supplies on a string of burros. Gold-seekers poured into the oasis as the day wore on, until by noon there was an encampment of 150 men and 200 animals. The heat was intense from 8 a.m. until after 4 p.m.

This was the period—June 17 to 20— when, according to the *Bulletin* correspondent, temperatures in the "Cabazone" Valley (apparently present Coachella) ranged from 120 to 140 degrees. When men were giving out from

FORGOTTEN ROAD TO GOLD

heat and exhaustion and thirst all along the way, and stories of numerous deaths were everywhere afloat. Most, but not all, of these stories resulted from rumor and misinformation. James McFeely died at Dos Palmas that very afternoon and was wrapped in a gray blanket and buried in the grass plot below the spring. But his death was due as much to disease as heat.

As evening cooled, two wagons and about 30 men, including Bradshaw and party, moved out of Dos Palmas for Water in the Canyon (Canyon Springs) in Brown's Pass or Big Wash (now Salt Creek or Salton Wash). In the wash, about five miles up from Dos Palmas, Joe Fountain's wagon, with Riley's group, broke an axle. They slept until moonrise, then moved slowly on with the wagon to reach Canyon Springs early on June 21.

The travelers found three springs in the narrow gorge opening from the north into the big wash. Best drinking water was on the east side, about 200 yards from the entrance. The largest, with a pool surrounded by tules, was a mile up, also on the right. The third, heavily impregnated with copper, was in the left branch. And up the gorge by the big spring, Fountain found two goldseekers who were also blacksmiths. A shop was improvised and the wagon repaired.

About nine in the morning, after breakfast and a rest for their animals, Riley and four companions moved on ahead of the main body, heading for the natural tanks of Tabasaca, the next watering place. Following Bradshaw's instructions, they had no trouble locating the turnoff from Brown's Pass—a dry creek entering the big wash from the south. The turnoff was further identified by the fresh tracks of James Grant's wagon, clearly visible in the sandy creek bed.

"But in pursuing that course we were unwittingly at variance with Frink's chart, which would have carried us directly on through the Pass (Salt Creek Wash) and over the summit," Riley wrote. "By that route we would have reached, 20 miles from the Canyon, a natural tank of water situated between two spurs of the mountains and an abundance of good grass. Thence, eight miles further to Brown's Well, Dry Creek, and thence 35 miles over a good road to the Colorado."

Early maps which indicate "Frink's New Road" show it leading out between Orocopia and Chuckawalla Mountains, then following Chuckawalla Valley to the river along the general course of U. S. 60-70. However, by any such route the mileages given are too short, the watering places not there. To one who knows the country and has tried to trace out Frink's road, the only reasonable explanation would seem to be that it is identical with the

FORGOTTEN ROAD TO GOLD

Bradshaw except that it did not make the southern swing to Tabasaca Tank. Instead it continued almost to the head of Salt Creek Wash, then swung over to the Chuckawalla Mountains, making an arc to the north.

It is significant that early accounts stemming from Frink positively place Brown's Well and Chuckawalla Well in the bed of "the same Dry Creek" (Arroyo Seco). It should be noted also that in 1863, when Frink entered the freighting business to La Paz, he made no attempt to develop any "better" route to the north, but followed the general course of the Bradshaw Road. And if "Frink's New Road" actually did run south of the Chuckawalla Mountains, then his assertion that the Bradshaw route was not a new road is valid.

Riley continued: "The only cause I can assign for Messrs. Grant and Bradshaw having turned off this more direct route, is that they were both under Indian guidance, which naturally followed the trail to the only watering places of which they had any knowledge. (Here Riley was mistaken if he believed any white man knew even the slightest water seep unknown to the desert Indian.) It is therefore at this point of departure from the Pass that the *new route* to the Colorado, claimed by the discoverers Grant and Bradshaw, fairly commences, as the whole of our previous journey had been over the road marked out and freighted over by Col. Washington's surveying party."

Canyon Springs station on the Bradshaw road, about 1948, when the shape of the walls could still be clearly seen. The water supply was in a narrow canyon across the Salt Creek Wash, and out of sight to right of picture.

FORGOTTEN ROAD TO GOLD

Tabasaca (commonest of the early spellings) was nearly two miles south of the main Bradshaw Road, hidden in a narrow arroyo at the foot of sharp-peaked outliers of the Chocolate Mountains. (With U. S. G. S. map it took us three trips to pinpoint it.) Two of Riley's party gave up and continued for Chuckawalla Wells. Riley and the others finally struck an Indian trail and followed it over burning desert under blazing sun, until they at last caught sight of the Holcomb Valley burros grazing on a mesa ahead, reached the ravine and camped beside the gravel-filled tank. The Bradshaw party and numerous other travelers drifted into Tabasaca later in the day and into the evening.

Bradshaw is supposed to have translated "Tabasaca," an Indian word, as "Point of Mountain." Charles B. Genung, who camped at the tank in 1863, and who had even wider knowledge of desert Indian languages, wrote it as "Tabbe Sakle" and translated "Yellow Hammer Nests," referring to the yellow-shafted Flickers sometimes found in this desert. Bradshaw may have mistaken the Cocomaricopa's directions for a definition, Riley may have misunderstood Bradshaw, or Genung (later a Colorado River Indian agent) may have been wrong.

Water seeped so slowly into the overtaxed tank that satisfying the men, teams, pack and riding animals, took a long time. The *Bulletin* correspondent

Tabaseca Tanks lies not far below and to the right of the high point of the group of hills shown in the background. Even in stage days, the regular road did not go much closer to the tanks than this point—and a side trip was necessary to reach it.

FORGOTTEN ROAD TO GOLD

wrote that he sat up until midnight, taking turns and dipping up the water with a spoon. Riley declared: "It was the greatest task trying to force that little spring to 'ante' that I ever witnessed."

Tabasaca ravine was—and is—a happy home for rattlesnakes. Digging a package of tea from his supplies that night, Riley discovered one within two feet of his hand, "and in the act of making a more striking demonstration of his presence. Bradshaw, drawing his revolver, put two blue pills in the pizen surpiant's stomak before he could give a second rattle. The dose proved sufficient, as he was only a seven year old, but tall for his age, as he measured all of four feet in length."

To cap a rough night, James Grant came back to Tabasaca in the middle of it with the doleful information that there was almost no water at Chuckawalla Wells, and that the large number of men already there were suffering from its lack. Riley wrote bitterly: "Giving this as his report of his own 'well-watered' route, Grant rode off on his return to the white settlements. Notwithstanding this warning, we arose with the moon with the intention of making Chocol-walla by noon. Besides, Bradshaw was firmly of the impression that he and Mr. Grant had struck water at different points, though perhaps on the same dry creek. When pathfinders differ, who shall agree?"

After a grim 18-mile struggle (complicated by sharp encounters with the tall cholla cactus so abundant in this section—called by Riley "the most contemptible and cruel combination of inutility and ugliness that nature ever produced") they arrived on schedule, Sunday, June 22, at "Choke-for-water," as Riley libeled it. Here, north of the main road and close against the Chuckawalla Mountains, was Last Water, 40 miles from the river. It was, Riley said, "the identical spot known as 'Chocol-walla', 'Grolep Springs', or any other name, discovered by Messrs. Grant and Bradshaw." It also, probably, is the "Well of San Pasqual" of the Estudillo expedition of 1823-24.

Riley described the wells as holes dug in small ravines to the depth of six or eight feet, each sheltered from the sun by a blanket covering. And contrary to reports, this was no copious water supply, he declared, "unless a tin cup full to the man, doled out by careful guardians of a few muddy waterholes, could be termed copious." But when he and his companions followed instructions and went a mile farther along Dry Creek and dug their own waterholes in a little ravine leading into it, in time they obtained sufficient water.

From San Bernardino to the wells, no one returning from La Paz had been met. But on June 23, at least a score of ex-goldseekers poured into Chuckawalla, in full retreat from the placers and with harrowing tales of men behind them

FORGOTTEN ROAD TO GOLD

falling and dying on the "forty-mile desert" in the attempt to reach this water. It was a shattering blow to the already shaky morale of the new wave of goldrushers. These unhappy, mosquito-bite-swollen, battered and generally impoverished men had actually "seen the elephant"—and were trying to escape from it. The new wave hesitated and broke, and most of it rolled back from Chuckawalla Wells, carrying with it practically all later travelers met with in the retreat along the Bradshaw Road. Even the teamsters turned back, refusing to honor their contracts to carry goods to the river, saying their horses were worth more than the freight.

Riley, interviewing a number of the returnees, noted along with the complaints that some of them had found gold and that many intended to return to the placers with cooler weather. However, the correspondent felt that he had too good a picture of what the mines were like and, on the morning of June 24, he turned back with the majority. The *Bulletin* "Special," made of sterner stuff, continued on to the river with the small group of stalwarts Bradshaw led out onto the 40-mile waterless stretch on the evening of June 23.

But before he left, Riley was impelled to send back a warning: "I cannot close without expressing my firm conviction that not another man should ever leave San Francisco for these mines. It is utter madness to think of doing

Tabaseca Tank is located in the streambed, left, below the little fall. The shelter at right, in the canyon wall, was used even before the La Paz gold rush by Indians. The canyon, however, was so notorious for the rattlesnakes at the time of the Bradshaw road that it was called Rattlesnake Canyon. The reptiles are still around.

anything in them at this time of year, and I much question if they will ever pay for white men to work them. There is not the least reason to believe they are either rich or extensive."

There seems to be little detail available about those last 40 miles to the river. Probably travelers were interested only in getting through. The route continued along the same Dry Creek (Arroyo Seco today) along the southern front of the Little Chuckawallas, across the broad wash between the Little Chuckawalla and Mule Mountains (where Wiley's Well is located now) and through a pass in the Mules to the first lagoon in Palo Verde Valley. When the lagoon held water, the dry stretch was shortened.

In later years a well was dug in the wash about 20 miles east of Chuckawalla Wells—where Bradshaw and others had seen water indications—and Mule Springs Station was established. But this well was completely obliterated in a cloudburst in the late summer of 1875, and it may never have been reopened.

Bradshaw brought his party to La Paz without apparent difficulty, just as he always seemed to get through in good shape. In view of Riley's attitude, the opinion of one of the original group with Bradshaw on this trip (unidentified in his letter in the San Francisco *Bulletin*) is valuable:

"Having formed a connection with Bradshaw to act as our guide, we

Part of the old stage station at the edge of the wash at Chuckawalla Wells—the most important water source on the Bradshaw between Dos Palmas and the Laguna in Palo Verde Valley. Since this picture was taken, the stone walls have been badly tumbled.

FORGOTTEN ROAD TO GOLD

bought horses for riding and packing and started out. I will not enter into details about the trip, as it has been fully described by others in the public prints. I do not agree with them, however, as to the severity of the undertaking, for, with proper care and forethought, the trip might even be made pleasant, and certainly beneficial to those in delicate health. The intensity of the heat has been greatly magnified, for after traveling through the night, we would camp, and with a blanket raised over me for shade, the sand made a good bed, on which I never enjoyed sleep so much. Water and grass we found in plenty at various places on the road, and among the Indians, corn, wheat, barley and watermelons could be obtained in plenty."

And J. A. Talbott (so ill at Dos Palmas he had been expected to die) writing from "Chu-cu Walla Camp," declared: "Too much credit cannot be given to Bradshaw, the pioneer explorer, who, by piloting nearly a hundred men thus far and through to the river, no doubt saved many valuable lives. His indomitable perseverence and sleepless vigilance prevented a good many animals from being lost . . ."

At La Paz, the *Bulletin* correspondent developed a brighter outlook about the placers. There was sufficient gold to warrant thorough prospecting, and fair or rich diggings would be—possibly already had been—discovered. Though

Two of the recent wells at Chuckawalla Wells. However, since this picture was taken, the one on the right has been filled in by flash floods, and the one on the left, in May 1963, was badly polluted.

FORGOTTEN ROAD TO GOLD

scores of Americans had left the placers in the past week, they had reasons which had little to do with the richness of the mines:

They found the weather insufferably hot; they could not obtain water at the mines and had no kegs nor pack animals to bring it in themselves. Most had been "unused to work" or were ranchmen unaccustomed to mining. They did not know how to dry wash for gold, and the Mexicans were not anxious to instruct them, but rather magnified the poverty of the mines and the difficulty of working them. Used to the cool coast climate, wilting under a sun that "sent the thermometer up to 130 in the shade, seeing their horses getting weak from want of grass, they resolved to make their escape while they could."

But the boom had been checked by the returning goldseekers and by warnings such as he himself had sent to the *Bulletin*, and when he returned along the Bradshaw Road early in July, he found it almost deserted. There was one party at "Chu-cu-le-walla," protecting goods that the freighters had abandoned there. The wells—soon to become one of the most important stage stops on a revitalized Bradshaw Road—were overflowing, the water unused. The tanks at Tabasaca were full, the camp ground empty. Dos Palmas—"at one time quite a town"—was vacated. Toros had but one camp of whites— Los Angeles traders slowly working a large supply of goods back home. There were no travelers at Agua Caliente. Between the hot springs and San Bernardino, he met one small party of miners pressing on for the river.

And when Bill Bradshaw came to Los Angeles on August 19, he reported the placers practically deserted when he left them on the tenth, owing to lack of provisions. Hundreds of miners had lived on mesquite beans for nearly two weeks, in the hope that food was on the way. None came and they were forced to depart for Fort Yuma, Sonora, and parts of Mexico.

But the situation had changed again, abruptly. When Bradshaw reached San Gorgonio Pass, he found the road lined with a new army of stampeders, drawn into Southern California by the spreading gold rumors and impatiently daring the midsummer desert heat, bound for the placers. With them were pack and wagon trains loaded with provisions, headed for La Paz, and with *them* some of the very miners who had just left the mines, having turned back when they found supplies on the way.

Said the *Star*: "There are fully 300 persons on the way to the river; about 20 wagons, 200 head of cattle, 800 head of sheep, and a great number of pack animals. People are now returning freely from Sonora and New Mexico, as well as from Washoe, Mono, Esmeralda, Potosi, and from this section of California. From this city a large number will leave for the mines. Bradshaw

Ruins of Mule Springs station, between Chuckawalla Wells and the Palo Verde Valley. This was not a stopping place when Bradshaw made his first trips across, although indications of water were reported here. A well was opened for the stage lines. The well was completely obliterated in a cloudburst about 1876.

(Photos by Harold Weight)

started out yesterday August 22 for San Bernardino, where he expects to meet probably 150 men, whom he will conduct to the river."

This was a stampede which did not turn back, but continued to stream across to the river as the weather cooled.

And on September 8, 1862, the first coach and six, operated by Warren Hall and Henry Wilkinson, left San Bernardino for La Paz on the Bradshaw route. Ten days were taken for that first crossing, because of the time spent setting up stations and stocking them with animals. On September 18, that pioneer stage crossed the Colorado on Bradshaw's Ferry, followed a trail up the river, and appeared unexpectedly and without announcement on the main street of La Paz. It left La Paz on September 20, carrying some $5000 in gold, and arrived in Los Angeles on September 24. "The quickest and most successful trip ever made to or from the river to Los Angeles," cheered the *News*.

As for the Bradshaw route: "Mr. Hall is thoroughly acquainted with staging in California, and is experienced in traveling upon the desert, and gives his opinion that the road is the shortest and best one that has yet been discovered . . . and that the stage may be run as speedily over it and with as much success as upon any line in the state . . ."

Though this particular company operated less than a month, its suspension was not due to road difficulties or lack of business, but to the violent deaths of Hall and Wilkinson near Smith's Ranch in San Gorgonio Pass, while attempting to unravel the theft of $1000 in La Paz gold from their stage. And the successful operation of this through stage line—followed by several other companies in later years—was final proof that the Bradshaw Road was open and functioning. It would remain a used and usable road into the twentieth century.

And what of the man whose name the road bore? On December 2, 1864, Bill Bradshaw walked into a La Paz carpenter shop, picked up a drawing knife and almost severed his head from his body. He had been on a prolonged drinking bout. The news of his suicide was carried along the Bradshaw Road to Los Angeles by James Grant. "He leaves thousands of friends," said the *Alta*. "He was pursued by ghosts," commented the Los Angeles *News*.

Bradshaw was buried in the graveyard at La Paz. Today neither grave nor graveyard can be positively identified. It is difficult to locate even the adobe mounds that mark old Laguna de la Paz. The once-rich arroyos of the placer fields have been returned by summer cloudbursts almost to their original state. The site of Bradshaw's Ferry is disputed.

But the stretch of Bradshaw Road from the Coachella Valley to the Colorado River remains much as it was a century ago. The watering places are virtually as they were when the goldseekers struggled to reach them. The piled rock ruins of waystops along the Bradshaw—although weathered and vandalized—can still be identified. At places even the actual ruts of the old road can be traced across barren slope and spiny hollow.

And these are the links with those wild lost days when Western history was being made. They are also Bill Bradshaw's only memorial.

BIBLIOGRAPHY

BOOKS

BEAN, LOWELL JOHN, and WILLIAM MARVIN MASON. *Diaries & Accounts of the Romero Expeditions in Arizona and California 1823-1826* Palm Springs 1962

BEATTIE, GEORGE WILLIAM, and HELEN PRUITT BEATTIE. *Heritage of the Valley, San Bernardino's First Century* Pasadena 1939

BELL, MAJOR HORACE. *Reminiscences of a Ranger, or Early Times in Southern California* Santa Barbara 1927

DEKENS, CAMIEL (as told to Tom Patterson). *Riverman Desertman* Riverside 1962

FARISH, THOMAS EDWIN. *History of Arizona* Phoenix 1915, 1916

INGERSOLL, LUTHER A., *Century Annals of San Bernardino County, 1769-1904* Los Angeles 1904

KERBY, ROBERT LEE. *The Confederate Invasion of New Mexico and Arizona 1861-1862* Los Angeles 1958

FORGOTTEN ROAD TO GOLD

U. S. GOVERNMENT PUBLICATIONS, RECORDS

Department of the Interior.
U. S. Geological Survey. *Bulletin 451*, "Reconnaissance of the Ore Deposits in Northern Yuma County, Arizona," Howland Bancroft, Washington 1911
U.S.G.S. *Water-Supply Paper 497*, "The Salton Sea Region, California," John S. Brown, Washington 1923
Report to the Secretary of the Treasury by J. Ross Browne, on "The Mineral Resources of the States and Territories West of the Rocky Mountains" (March 1868), in *Resources of the Pacific Slope* (etc.), Browne, D. Appleton & Co., New York 1869
War Department. *Annual Report*, "Geographical Surveys West of the 100th Meridian, in California, Nevada, Utah, Colorado, Wyoming, New Mexico, Arizona and Montana," George M. Wheeler, Appen. JJ of Ann. Rpt. of the Chief of Engineers for 1876. Washington 1876
War of the Rebellion Official Records of the Union and Confederate Armies, Ser.I v.I (Extracts concerning Confederate activities in Arizona, in Arizona Pioneers Historical Society Library, Tucson)

ARIZONA TERRITORY, MISCELLANEOUS

Arizona Census 1864 (Prescott)
Acts, Resolutions & Memorials Adopted by the First Legislature of the Territory of Arizona, Prescott, 1864. (Typescript in Arizona Pioneers Historical Society Library, Tucson)

ARTICLES, HISTORICAL SOCIETIES AND PERIODICALS

The California Historical Society *Quarterly*. V. XII No. I, March 1933.
(1) "Bancroft's Guide to the Colorado Mines" (2) "A Trip to the Colorado Mines in 1862," from the "Reminiscences of Mahlon Dickerson Fairchild"
Historical Society of Southern California *Annual*, V. III, Pt. 3, 1895.
"From Arizona to California in the Early 70's," P. W. Dooner
Historical Society of Southern California *Annual*, V. XIII, Pt. II, 1925.
"Development of Travel Between Southern Arizona and Los Angeles As It Related to the San Bernardino Valley," George William Beattie
Pacific Historical Review, March 1933. "Reopening the Anza Trail," George William Beattie
Overland Monthly, V. VIII 2nd Series, July 1886. "Crossing the California Sahara," Henry De Groot

NEWSPAPERS

Alta California, San Francisco. Files, microfilm, photostats 1862, California State Library, Huntington Library.
Arizona Miner, Prescott (APHS)
Bulletin, San Francisco. Files, microfilm, photostats, California State Library, Nevada Historical Society Library, Reno; APHS, Tucson. 1862, 1863
Guardian, San Bernardino. San Bernardino County Free Library, 1867-68. Huntington Library, various, 1869-70-71-72-73
News, Los Angeles (Semi-Weekly Southern News, 1861-62; Semi-Weekly News, 1862; Tri-Weekly News 1863-64) Photostats, Los Angeles Public Library, California State Library, Huntington Library; Also Huntington, various 1863-64-65; 1868, 1870.
Reese River Reveille, Austin, Nevada. 1864, 1867
Star, Los Angeles. Files, photostats, Los Angeles Public Library, San Bernardino County Free Library; also at latter, various, 1860, 1861, 1863.
Union, Sacramento. Files, microfilm, photostats, California State Library—1862; also microfilm at APHS-Tucson. Also various libraries—1861, 1865, 1866.

UNPUBLISHED MATERIALS

Figueroa, Rev. Paul. Manuscript, reminiscences of early Yuma area. Also personal correspondence. (In Arizona Pioneers Historical Society Library, Tucson)
Sawtell, "Pioneer Sketches" (MS. C-D154 Bancroft Library, Berkeley; Concerning Wm. D. Bradshaw)
Provincial State papers V. XX pp. 287-9 287-9 Bancroft Library. Photostats of the Spanish, Typescripts of Spanish and translation (In Beattie Collection, Huntington Library). Statement taken by Santiago Arguello at San Gabriel, Feb. 28, 1821, of declaration of the Captain of the Cocomaricopas.
Gonzales, Rafael. (MS. Bancroft Library), "Experiences of a Soldier" (Photostat in Huntington Library, Beattie Collection)

ENTERING SAN FRANCISCO BAY

CALIFORNIA FLEET 1849

By JOHN B. GOODMAN, III

From his extensive collection of scarce and unusual material on Gold Rush shipping, Mr. Goodman—regarded as one of our outstanding authorities on the subject—has gathered valuable and fascinating data relating to a phase of California's Gold Rush period that certainly merits more recognition than it has received in the past. Emphasis placed upon the experiences of land parties has effectually subordinated the equally impressive drama of those who came to California by sea. Because of its historical contribution, this article assumes considerable importance.

THE TERM "CALIFORNIA FLEET," when loosely applied, refers to those vessels departing from the eastern seaboard of the United States direct for California during the period from December 7, 1848 to December 31, 1849. The following is a "potpourri" account of a few of the many sidelights regarding this "fleet" during that period.

The event that set the stage for the unprecedented assemblage of such a fleet was, of course, the discovery of gold in California in January, 1848. It was not until December of that year, however, that the full impact of this momentous event spread over the entire eastern part of the United States like a plague. By December 16, 1848 there was reported to be from 45 to 50 vessels of all sizes preparing to sail for Chagres or San Francisco direct. As early as New Years day, 1849 there was a large number of vessels of all classes in the port of New York, being readied for the voyage to San Francisco. About one-half were partially, if not entirely, unseaworthy and unsafe for a *short* voyage, much less for one around Cape Horn.

Probably even more remarkable was the effect on all classes of citizens that were soon to stampede for passage in this "fleet." The spreading gold mania, bordering on insanity, infected almost everyone in one way or another.

The voyages of the first sailing vessels and steamers to California are of great interest to us today because they brought some of our most prominent pioneers and citizens to the Golden State. However, a large majority among the hordes endeavoring to find ways and means of getting to the gold region were broken-down merchants, ruined and disgraced brokers, blacklegs and gamblers, pickpockets, thieves, prizefighters, and loafers. There were out-of-work newspaper men, printers, ex-cashiers of banks, office seekers and politicians. It is interesting to read of this period that the "venerable, sainted old Tammany" Hall,[1] at their last general committee meeting for 1848, met

---

1. *New York Herald* January 22, 1849

at 7 o'clock and waited until 9, but could not get a quorum together. Out of a quorum of 17, the secretary and 8 of the committee members were booked for California and were busy packing their belongings.

About 50 fighters, and other characters of that class, sailed for California two weeks after the Tom Hyer-Yankee Sullivan fight in January, 1849. Sullivan later became a notorious figure in the mines. The 580 ton ship *South Carolina* sailed from New York with the toughest looking party of emigrants aboard to be seen anywhere.[2] She carried 163 passengers including a company comprising 9 members of "The New York and South Carolina Mining Association." In contrast to this was the bark *Orb*, 240 tons, of Boston, with the "North Western Trading and Mining Association" aboard. This was a fashionable organization from Worcester, Massachusetts; and the members about the deck and lining the rail were in marked contrast in their neat uniforms. Many of New York's finest families were represented by those sailing on the ship *Christoval Colon*, formerly a Havana packet. The names on passenger lists were often suppressed from publication until the vessel had sailed. The ship *Pacific* hurriedly sailed from New York to escape the clutches of the law.[3]

By the end of December, 1849 the rush for California was still on the increase. The calculating minds of all classes of citizens were greatly influenced by this rise in the tide of emigration to the gold region. Whole families, rather than individual members, were making preparations to start for the land of Midas.

It was far easier for seafaring men to ship out for California than it was for any other class. In a relatively short time so many more seamen were striving to go than were required to man the vessels that the competition drastically reduced wages. For a short time, early in 1849, crews could be shipped in any quantity to man the vessels on the outward voyage to San Francisco without wages. Fifty and one hundred dollars was actually being paid ship owners for the opportunity to fill the premium jobs of cooks and stewards.

The 348 ton bark *Ann Perry*, of Salem (late of Portsmouth), sailed for San Francisco with a crew of about 20, all of whom had been masters or mates of vessels. They shipped for twenty cents per month each.[4] The crew of the 346 ton ship *Aurora*, from Nantucket, received one dollar a month each for the voyage out, with liberty to leave the ship on her arrival at San Francisco.[5]

---

2. *Philadelphia Public Ledger*   January 25, 1849

3. *Seeking the Golden Fleece* by J. D. B. Stillman, New York, 1877 (p.40)

4. *Philadelphia Public Ledger*   June 23, 1849

5. *New York Herald*   January 7, 1849

  The privilege to leave the vessel was hardly any inducement as the crew took "their own liberty" upon arriving in the port of San Francisco.

CALIFORNIA FLEET 1849

Aboard the 550 ton half-clipper ship *Tarolinta*, of New York, was a crew of 20—all negroes—and but few of them less than six feet in height; with a blustering captain and four mates.[6]

Some strange passenger complements were assembled, generally to form companies or associations. Early in January, 1849 a party was made up of railroad men from Utica, New York.[7] Much to the surprise of everyone aboard the 473 ton ship *Albany*, from New York, 20 stowaways were brought to light after the boat put to sea. And to the disgust of the passengers, the vessel returned to port and set the persona non grata element ashore, after which she proceeded on her way. It was said that one vessel carried nearly 100 passengers, all being musicians and actors. Early in 1849 a theatrical group was organized in Philadelphia to go to the gold region of California.

About this same time another association was being formed in New York for the purpose of going to the gold diggings. Fully 50 "gentleman of color" were signed up to compose this organization. No caucasians were to be admitted.[8] In New York City, in November 1849, some merchants formed an association of 10 of the most intelligent and respectable colored men of the city. They were to have sailed on the ship *Hampden*.[9]

Most of the young men, members of the "Mount Vernon Mining Association" and the "Mattapoisett Mining Company" sailing on the 388 ton ship *Mount Vernon*, were experienced whalers. They carried along harpoons and other equipment on the voyage. She sailed from Mattapoisett in April, 1849, and before they reached the Azores the whalers had taken a whale and stowed the oil to sell in California.[10] A party of whaling captains sailed from New Bedford in the clipper schooner *Rialto*.[11] Fifteen stone cutters from Pigeon Cove, Massachusetts, banded together and sailed aboard the ship *Euphrasia*. Fifty German Jews arrived in New York from Scotland on August 13, 1849 on the British ship *Sir William Molesworth*. They planned to purchase a

---

6. *To the Golden Goal* by Dr. J. C. Tucker, S. F. 1895 (p.20)
7. *New York Tribune* February 3, 1849
   The names of the members are as follow: Civil Engineer, Homer Williams; John Bell; James M. Warner; Michael Kildruff; Levi Parsons; James Carter; Mr. Potter; and William Hall.
8. *Chicago Daily Journal* February 28, 1849
9. *New York Tribune* November 21, 1849
   The *Hampden* sailed November 23, 1849, and arrived in San Francisco, April 2, 1850, 160 days passage.
10. *New York Tribune* May 3, 1849; *Argonauts of '49* by Octavious Howe, Cambridge, 1923 (p.211)
11. *New York Herald* February 3, 1849; *New York Tribune* February 10, 1849
    There were 16 forming the "Rialto Mining Company," almost all of whom were whaling captains. The *Rialto* sailed January 30, 1849 for Holmes Hole and California. She carried the first organized company from New Bedford to sail direct for California.

vessel and depart as soon as possible for California.[12]

A number of vessels carried cargoes which were valued as high as $100,000. The cargo of the Baltimore ship *Greyhound* was so valued, and her manifest was 30 feet long. Most of the cargo shipped to California by the various mining and trading associations, and by some individuals, consisted of slow-moving merchandise, bought at bargain prices.

A gentleman going to California paid $155 to freight his goods on the ship *Sweden*, from Boston to San Francisco, a 19,000 mile voyage. On arrival at San Francisco the goods were transferred to the schooner *Decatur*[13]; and for the 150 mile trip to Sacramento he had to pay $283.

Perhaps the three most common commodities shipped to California in 1849—aside from mining equipment, machinery and liquor—were house frames, building materials and small steamers. There were two French ships that passed Valparaiso, heading for San Francisco early in August, 1849. One was carrying 80,000 gallons, and the other 50,000 gallons, of brandy. [14] The brig *Elle Maria*, of Maine, took out a cargo of house frames and building materials. The ship *Decucalion* had aboard 50 houses, and the bark *Bolton* shipped only building materials. A cargo of portable houses, two hospitals, a bowling alley, etc., formed the cargo of the *Sartell*, *Laurens* and *Diadem*. Hotels (many 3½ stories high) were the sole cargo of several California-bound vessels. One was shipped completely furnished, including liquor and the bartender. South America and China also shipped hundreds of these knocked-down buildings[15] to San Francisco.

Many miniature steamboats formerly used on the various rivers for towboats or pleasure yachts were bought up, eventually to ply the waters of San Francisco Bay or the San Joaquin and Sacramento Rivers. The 460 ton ship *Levant*, of Philadelphia, carried the "Pacific Adventurers Association No. 2" to the mines. She also carried a steamboat built in 3 sections, a launch 30 feet long, and 8 other boats of smaller size.[16] The 446 ton ship *Frances Ann*, of Boston, with the "New England Pilgrims" and the "Granite State Company No. 2" as passengers, took out as freight a 15 ton yacht named *MayFlower*.[17]

---

12. *Philadelphia Public Ledger*   August 14, 1849; *Boston Transcript*   August 14, 1849
13. *Philadelphia Public Ledger*   October 18, 1849
14. *Philadelphia Public Ledger*   October 17, 1849
15. *New York Tribune*   November 13, 1849
    The seaport town of Talcahuano, Chile, by June of 1849, had sent 200 buildings to California, and had orders for 600 more. They were one story and measured 14 x 18 feet.
16. *New York Tribune*   March 5, 1849
17. *New York Tribune*   Supplement   May 3, 1849
    The *Frances Ann*, sailed from Boston, April 17, 1849, and arrived in San Francisco, Nov. 1, 1849

CALIFORNIA FLEET 1849

The ship *Somoset,* of New York, among her many other distinctions, carried a steamer. The 209 ton brig *Oniota* carried out the well known steamboat *Islander.* Brought around the Horn were the little iron steamer *Mint;* the 80 ton, side wheeler *Pioneer* (No. 1); the 60 foot long side wheeler *Sacramento* (No. 1); and many others. The ship *Mayflower* brought the 108 foot long steamer *Lawrence,* and the ship *Fanny* took out the 120 foot stern wheeler *S. B. Wheeler.* The bark *La Grange,* aside from taking out the "Salem California Trading and Mining Company," carried out the little 31 ton steamer *Commodore Jones.* The ship *Leonore,* of Boston, took out a small steam launch that cost its owners the sum of $1700. They sold her at San Francisco for $35,000. The 700 ton Cape Town Trader *Edward Everett,* of Boston, was said to have taken out a stern wheeler of 50 tons, named the *Edward Everett Jr.*[18] The flat-bottomed stern wheeler *Lady Washington* was shipped to California, knocked down, and reassembled at Sutter's Embarcadero on the Sacramento River.

Oddly enough, there was a sufficient number of steamers sent around the Horn to justify the erection of a plant in San Francisco for the sole purpose of setting up these very hulls and engines sent in knock-down form from the East coast. The Sutter Iron Works, as the plant was called, employed and staffed the plant with the pick of Philadelphia's shipwrights and engineers.[19]

It has been said (but not verified) that one vessel sailed to the gold regions with a cargo entirely of bibles. Nearly all the larger vessels of the "California Fleet" provided the passengers with a well selected library. The five months old 730 ton Baltimore clipper *Susan G. Owens* was provided with a library of 500 volumes. The 296 ton bark *Ralph Cross,* of Philadelphia, carrying as passengers the two mining companies—the "Philadelphia Commercial and Mining Company" and the "Narraguagus Mining Company"—had aboard a select library. The 186 ton brig *Forest,* from Boston, had a completely stocked library on board, partly furnished by the owner and the remainder by the American Home Missionary Society. The 150 ton brig *Pauline,* of Boston, with the "Bunker Hill and California Mining and Trading Company" aboard, was supplied with reading material by the Missionary of the Seaman's Episcopal Church of Boston. The ship *Edward Everett,* of Boston, also carried a valuable and well selected library. The "New York Mining Company," sailing on the 400 ton bark *Strafford,* had aft between decks fitted up with an

---

18.　　An item appearing in the *San Jose Pioneer,* April 15, 1895, p.4, c.5 by Albert W. Gale, of the ship *Leonore,* requires additional research. He states that the *Edward Everett Jr.* was not brought out by the *Edward Everett,* and set up in August, but: "The frame of that steamer was carried out in the ship *Leonore* and was put together by its owners, of which I was one, on our arrival at Benecia in July 1849."

19.　*Paddle-Wheel Days in California,* by Jerry MacMullen, Stanford University, 1944 (p.11)

admirably selected library of 3000 volumes. [20]

Upon the final dissolution of the "New Brunswick and California Mining and Trading Company," on the Embarcadero at Sacramento during the first week in October, 1849, the members voted to give its library, which they brought around the Horn in the bark *Isabel*, to the founding of a library in the City of Sacramento. [21]

There was at this time a United States maritime law, relative to the ventilation of passenger vessels. This law, however, did not apply to persons or vessels bound for California. So it was only natural that, in the keen competition for passengers to that far off country, advertisements like the one for the ship *Samoset* should appear. The *Samoset* was quite new, having been built only sixteen months before. It was advertised that she "was built expressly with the view to accommodation of passengers in tropical climates, being amply provided with patent port holes between decks, for light and ventilation, and also with Emerson's celebrated patent ventilators as used upon vessels of war . . ." She also had the distinction, and novelty, of carrying a stewardess to attend upon families in the first cabin. [22]

Where the vessels were company owned, the accommodations were fairly good; and, while the food was coarse, it was plentiful. The reverse was usually the case in other vessels. Ventilation was non existent, and the luckless gold hunters were jammed together like "bugs under a rug." Most of the argonauts that journeyed to California by sea suffered from cramped, damp and stale-aired accommodations, plus many other forms of hardships and inconveniences. It should be stressed here that none of these vessels smelled exactly like "floating roses."

There was a maritime law, hurriedly passed by the government early in the year 1849, regulating the number of passengers allowed in a given space on all vessels sailing to California. The 480 ton ship *Salem*, with the "New York and California Mutual Benefit Association" as passengers, made a hasty departure from New York with only a partial crew in order to circumvent this new maritime law. She carried 196 passengers, 50 more than allowed by law. She anchored near the Hook until she could complement men enough

20. *New York Herald* February 6, 1849
  The *Strafford* carried a full time librarian, a Mr. W. A. Spies.
21. *The New Brunswick Forty-Niners*, by Irving Stoddard Kull.
  Reprinted from the Rutgers Alumni Monthly Vol. IV., No. 8, May, 1925 (p.10)
22. *New York Herald* February 5, 1849
  Aboard the *Samoset* were the following mining companies: "Ithaca Mining Company," "Otsego California Mining Company," and the "Sing Sing Company."

CALIFORNIA FLEET 1849

to navigate her.[23]

Theft was a rather common occurrence aboard the many vessels sailing to California. Sometimes it was only food, or some passenger's "jug;" but other times it was more serious. A small tin trunk containing $1200 in bank bills and gold was stolen from the "Mattapan and California Mining Company," sailing on the brig *Ann* from Gloucester. The "Mattapan and California Trading and Mining Company" were also aboard the brig.

Another form of thievery was the shipping of counterfeit coins to California. Nearly 100,000 counterfeit coins were said to have been shipped from New York alone.[24] As early as January, large quantities of spelter solder were being sent to the gold regions by unscrupulous persons in the east. The scheme of the jackanapes was to sell the base metal to the gold hunters as they arrived in California to be used as spurious gold. When dropped in water, while hot, small scales would form, resembling the gold dust or scales of the Feather River.[25]

The brig *Baltimore*, advertised to sail from Philadelphia with passengers for California via Tampico, was detained in consequence of the sudden disappearance of the person who chartered her. He had gone to California on the steamer *Falcon* with the money belonging to the passengers.

Gambling aboard ship generally prevailed to a large extent. Most vessels made a pretext of prohibiting gambling and drinking during the voyage. Some of the vessels were equipped with a large quantity of gambling equipment. Among the many forms of gambling were the usual faro boards, roulette tables, sweat cloths, etc. Equally popular was poker, monte and "rattle-and-snap." Even aboard a well regulated ship, gambling would sometimes break out and reach the proportions of an epidemic.

Boxing, dancing, gymnastics and other amusements were resorted to in order to kill the monotony of the voyage. Glee clubs and literary clubs were organized, and musical and religious gatherings were enjoyed by many. Aboard the ship *Mason*, from Philadelphia, the Fourth of July celebration was attended with much levity, the shooting of a cannon, drinking, and the inevitable fighting.

Most of us think only of the forty-niner who crossed the plains as having enjoyed any extensive hunting, while those who went by sea were limited in their sport to fishing. However, this was not always true. Those argonauts

---

23. *Boston Transcript*   March 16, 1849
    This company is not to be confused with the "California Mutual Benefit Association" of New York, which sailed on the ship *Flavius*, March 25, 1849; the former company having sailed on March 13, 1849. The *Salem* became a land lubber's counting house in San Francisco.

24. *Boston Transcript*   April 26, 1849

25. *New York Tribune*   January 23, 1849

traveling to California by sea enjoyed buffalo hunting as much as did those going overland. Landing on the shores of Patagonia, in the Straits of Magellan, they explored and hunted a type of buffalo not unlike that found in North America. They welcomed this diversion from the monotony of the sea voyage. The voyagers spent hours fishing and shooting at sharks, dolphins and gulls. On Eagle Island they shot ducks, seals and geese; while at the Island of Juan Fernández (Crusoe's Island) they explored the caves and chased goats.

Profanity prevailed to an alarming degree among the voyagers and crew. Particularly was this true, as reported on the *Susan G. Owens*. Hard feelings existed between the captain and passengers in many instances. More often than not the hard feelings and difficulties were engendered between passengers and the ship's captain merely because the passengers failed to attend to their own business, and did not permit the captain to attend to his.

As if fire and wrecks were not enough to worry about, a mutiny broke out aboard the New York pilot boat, *John L. Davis No. 7*, about 80 miles east of Rio de Janeiro. The captain was shot through the foot and the mate seriously wounded with an ax and harpoon. The crew, however, were overpowered and the ship *Arkansas* tended the wounds of the injured, even providing irons to confine the cook who was the ringleader.[26] The *Albany* had a mutiny aboard; and it was stated that the captain was thrown overboard. The ship *Sweden* had aboard three of the dirtiest cooks in the entire world. The brig *Oscela*, a leaky, creaky old tub commanded by a "sea tyrant," served boiled codfish and hardtack, and rationed the water, as retaliatory measures in the running feud with its passengers.

There were many on the voyage to California who became dangerously ill, but eventually recovered; others, perhaps more unfortunate, died on the high seas. The thought of being committed to the cold depths of the impassive sea, so far from home and loved ones, was enough to make the stoutest heart quail. Somewhat different was the case of Captain William Bell of the ship *Mason*, who died at sea. His body was jammed into a barrel of whiskey to be preserved. He was carried to San Francisco where he was buried with hundreds attending his funeral. Usually this was an occasion for a drinking bout. It is wondered if the whiskey was so used in this case. The ship *Architect*, of New Orleans, had six deaths from cholera. The first seven days out they threw a dead man overboard every morning, except one, before breakfast.[27] Ship fever, dysentery, and even measles, were common causes of distress.

26. *Philadelphia Public Ledger*   October 10, 1849
27. *New York Tribune*   August 24, 1849

CALIFORNIA FLEET 1849

It is rather remarkable that, considering the number of vessels making the voyage to California, relatively few were actually lost. Many were reported shipwrecked only to appear at a later date. Quite a few were detained in various ports enroute and condemned.

Members aboard the schooner *General Morgan* reported discovering the wreckage of two California bound vessels—the *Nightingale,* of New Bedford, and the *James Leeds,* of London.[28] The 140 ton schooner *Sacramento,* of New Orleans, struck on a reef of rocks near Port Gallant in the Straits of Magellan, August 8, 1849. All succeeded in getting ashore and in rescuing some stores on which they subsisted for sixteen days on the desolate, dreary and frozen coast, surrounded by savages. They were rescued by the bark *J. G. Colley;* and, for the payment of $150 each, transported to their destination—San Francisco.[29]

On the other hand, the California bound schooner *Ferdinand,* from Baltimore, was reported lost with 39 lives. This later was proven false.[30] The bark *Ralph Cross* was reported wrecked off Cape Horn, much to the surprise of the passengers on their arrival at Valparaiso.[31] The passengers of the ship *Pacific* were greatly surprised to discover, upon nearing the port of San Francisco, that they had reportedly been shipwrecked off Cape Horn.[32]

The new schooner *John A. Sutter,* with Samuel R. Eddy as master, and with the "Warren Trading and Mining Company" aboard, sailed from Warren, R. I. on March 9, 1849. She ran ashore near Tamer Harbor, close to the outlet of the Straits of Magellan, during a snow storm on June 25, 1849. The passengers and crew were picked up by the brig *Acadian.*[33]

The ship *Robert Fulton,* of New York, was lost off the East Falkland Island. The passengers, crew and part of the cargo were saved. She was formerly of Philadelphia and engaged in the East Indian Trade.[34]

Considerable has been written regarding the various aspects of the "California Fleet" of 1849, even about many of the individual vessels; but I find the following facts rather interesting and not generally known.

28. *New York Tribune* supplement   October 20, 1849
29. *Philadelphia Public Ledger*   December 4, 1849
30. *Philadelphia Public Ledger*   August 6, 1849
31. *Philadelphia Public Ledger*   November 13, 1849
32. *Seeking the Golden Fleece,* by J. D. B. Stillman, New York, 1877 (p.115)
33. *Boston Transcript*   February 20, 1849
      This company is not to be confused with the "Warren Mining and Trading Company" that sailed from Newport, December 6, 1849, on the schooner *Charles Herbert.* Also aboard the *John A. Sutter* was the "John A. Sutter Company."
   New Orleans Bee   October 6, 1849; also the Lansing papers 103/12/2 Pioneers 1814-1849 Vol. C to G University of California at Los Angeles.
34. *Philadelphia Public Ledger*   November 13, 1849

THE WHALING-INTERESTS OF SAN FRANCISCO.

The bark "NILE", Capt. Goldsmith, sailed from Boston September 24, 1849 and arrived at San Francisco March 18, 1850, (175 days). The "CAMILLA", listed as a Mexican ship under Capt. Merchardo, sailed from Mazatlan, June 20, 1850 and arrived July 24, 1850, (35 days). The schooner "SUSAN ABIGAL" is listed as having arrived from Aukland, February 19, 1850. The schooner "TOCCAO", Capt. Cranston, sailed from New Bedford, October 28, 1849 and arrived April 13, 1850. (163 days).

(Photo Courtesy of Bob Weinstein)

CALIFORNIA FLEET 1849

The largest vessel in the "fleet" to sail in 1849, (steamers excluded) was the full rigged ship *Grey Eagle*. She cleared from the dingy docks of Philadelphia on January 18, 1849, and sailed on the 21st. Her huge bulk of 1178 tons easily gave her the distinction of being the largest *sailing* vessel for that year. Incidentally the *Grey Eagle* was the first of the "fleet" to sail from Philadelphia. Her manifest was 12 feet long and valued at $120,000. She carried 35 passengers and a crew of 40. The next behemoth in tonnage was the clipper built ship *Memnon*, 1084 tons. There were possibly not over three or four other sailing vessels in the "fleet" that came near this tonnage, these being around 800 tons.

The smallest *sailing* vessel to sail from the eastern seaboard of the United States for California in 1849 was the tiny New England pleasure yacht named the *Breeze*. She was only 14 tons, and sailed from Boston November 6, 1849. I have been unable to locate any further news regarding her fate. There is no record of her arrival at San Francisco.[35]

The vessel generally referred to as the smallest for the year 1849, to make the voyage around Cape Horn to California, was the new clipper built schooner *Toccao*. She was 28-21/95 tons. The *Toccao* was built by five ship carpenters at New Bedford. She sailed from that port on October 28, 1849 and arrived at San Francisco 163 days later on April 13, 1850. She carried a crew of 4 men and 5 members, comprising the "Toccao Company."[36] It was their intention to employ her as a freighting vessel on the Sacramento River.

Many vessels, considered to be fast sailers, were among the fleet of vessels sailing to California in 1849. However, these did not always make the record runs expected of them. Of those vessels leaving the eastern seaboard before December 31, 1849 for San Francisco, the blue ribbon winner for the fastest passage goes to the ship *Grey Eagle* from Philadelphia. She sailed on January 21, 1849 and lived up to her reputation as a fast ship. She arrived on May 18, 1849, making the passage in 117 days. The bark *Arabian* and the brig *Tecumseh* have been erroneously credited with making the voyage in the same record time.[37]

Without a doubt the unenviable distinction of having made the voyage in the *longest* elapsed time goes to the bark *Chase*, 150 tons, of New Bedford. This vessel left New Bedford on April 17, 1849 on a "whaling and mining

---

35. *Boston Transcript*   November 6, 1849? (marine news section)

36. *New York Tribune*   October 3, 27, 1849
    The *Toccao* later became a whaler, joining the Pacific Coast whaling fleet.

37. *Argonauts of '49* by Octavious Howe, Cambridge, 1923, footnote (p.59).
    Howe gives the elapsed time of the *Greyhound* and *Sea Eagle*, which is at considerable variance with my source which I believe to be more nearly correct.

voyage," and arrived in San Francisco April 7, 1850 in 355 days, or just ten days short of one year. Undoubtedly she spent a part of that time in pursuit of whales. It was not uncommon for vessels to require as many as 240 to 250 days in making the voyage. The 157 ton brig *Acadian*, for example, taking out as passengers the "Hampshire and Holyoke Mining Company" on their quest for gold, cleared February 5, 1849 from Boston, and sailed on the 11th. After a long passage of 260 days,[38] she reached San Francisco on October 29, 1849. The average passage of all U.S. vessels arriving at San Francisco up to August 1, 1849, is given as 168 days. I believe this to be somewhat on the low side.

It is difficult to establish which of the many vessels carried the greatest number of passengers (steamers again excluded). Passengers crowding the decks and cabins of the various types of vessels numbered as many as 210 on the *Capitol*, from Boston; the *Elizabeth Ellen*, out of New York, carried 200; and the *Orpheus, New Jersey, Susan G. Owens*, and others had nearly as many. Sailing from Panama the five year old Dutch ship *Alexander Von Humboldt*, late a coal vessel, is authoritatively said to have reached San Francisco with 365 passengers. The *Niantic*, a former whaling ship, carried 248; and the ship *Norman* 250. This latter was supposed to have sailed from Panama with 400 passengers.

Of course, the least number of passengers that a vessel could carry was one. Several vessels departed for the land of promise with no more than one. The new and tiny clipper-built schooner *Sea Witch*, of New York, was built as a fishing smack with an open well. This was calked for the voyage, and she was advertised to carry passengers; but apparently only one person was brave enough to undertake the venture. She picked up another passenger at Borja Bay, in the Straits of Magellan, and arrived in San Francisco on June 15, 1849 with two passengers. Five days later, however, she continued her voyage to the port of her destination, Sacramento, with a total of 145 persons aboard.

The 370 ton ship *Othello*, with Captain Galloway and 60 passengers, was the first vessel to sail from the south. She cleared for California from Charleston, South Carolina, on January 30, 1849, arriving in San Francisco on November 13, 1849. This was a near record—286 days— for the longest passage of 1849. She did not reach Rio de Janeiro until June 26, nearly five months after her departure. The captain took his family with him.

The first vessel to arrive in San Francisco from the east coast, as recorded in the San Francisco list kept during 1849 by Edward A. King, Harbor Master,

---

38. *Argonauts of '49* by Octavious Howe, Cambridge, 1923.

Howe gives the time as 267 days, and the sailing date as February 4, 1849.

CALIFORNIA FLEET 1849

was the brig *Mary & Ellen*, of Salem, which arrived March 26, 1849.[39] The last to arrive at that port (from the same list) was the 348 ton bark *Ann Perry*, also from Salem. She made the passage in 184 days, arriving December 29, 1849, along with five other vessels.[40]

Compared to the overland route, the distance by way of Cape Horn was many miles farther. The trip via the Isthmus of Panama, however, was about the same distance as that by the overland.

New York to Valparaiso via Cape Horn	12,000 miles
" Callao " " "	13,500 "
" Guayaquil " " "	14,300 "
" Panama " " "	16,000 "
" San Blas " " "	17,800 "
" Mazatlan " " "	18,000 "
" San Diego " " "	18,500 "
" San Francisco " " "	19,000 "
New York via the Isthmus of Panama	4,000 "

The brig *Osceola*, upon arrival at Rio de Janeiro, had logged 6,088 miles and was 49 days at sea. She arrived at Talcahuana, Chile, sailing 6,156 miles with 57 days at sea. On her arrival in San Francisco, she had logged an additional 7,064 miles, and at sea another 70 days. Her total number of days from Philadelphia to San Francisco was 201—176 days at sea and 25 in port. Her total number of miles sailed was 19,308 between these two ports.[41]

There have been several estimates, all at variance with one another, as to the number of vessels sailing from the eastern seaboard direct to California. It is somewhat difficult to estimate the exact number of vessels in the "California Fleet," as many that sailed cleared for Rio de Janeiro and other South American ports, and even Oregon. They were chartered upon arrival at these ports to take passengers and cargo to California.

It has been estimated that upwards of 400 ships with merchandise and passengers sailed for California during the first six months of 1849, with an

39. "Essex Institute Historical Collection" Vol. XII, Part II, April, 1874, pp.124-131: Account of the voyage of the *Mary & Ellen*, by Captain Eagleston.
    The brig *Mary & Ellen*, Captain John H. Eagleston, technically was the first to depart. She was loading for the Hawaiian Islands when the gold discoveries were confirmed. She changed her destination to those Islands *via San Francisco*. She sailed from Salem, Massachusetts, October 28, 1848, with the captain, 2 mates, 6 crew members and 2 passengers. She arrived in San Francisco, March 28, 1849. She was sold soon thereafter for $1500.

40.   The list of vessels arriving in San Francisco, published from time to time in the *New York Herald*, and possibly copied from the *Alta California*, cannot in my opinion be entirely relied upon. It is at variance with the list regarding the last arrivals in 1849. However, for want of a better list of arrivals during 1850, it must be consulted.

41. *Notes of a Voyage to California—in the years 1849-'50* by Samuel C. Upham, Philadelphia, 1878 (p.217)

outlay of some 15 or 20 million dollars of capital.

One estimate gives the number of vessels that cleared from Boston for California, during the year 1849, as 151—ships 58, barks 37, brigs 41, and schooners 15. There were no steamers.[42] This coincides with my own figures. Octavious Howe states that, from the State of Massachusetts in 1849, the number of vessels sailing totaled 250.[43] From New Bedford the total is given as 42; Nantucket 8; Newburyport 6; Gloucester 6; and from other ports in Massachusetts 38. From my own list of vessels departing from the eastern seaboard in 1849, I arrive at the following figures: New Bedford 70, with possibly 72, departing; Nantucket 10; Newburyport 8; and Gloucester 8. From all New England there sailed direct for the gold regions, during the year 1849, approximately 429 vessels of all types except steamers. (Actually my list indicates that the steamer *Narraguagus*, of Cherryfield, Maine, sailed from Boston for California. But I have no record of her arrival.) Also, from my list, I estimate that 228 vessels sailed from New York City in 1849, with possibly 10 additional subject to question. Another account claimed that in 1849 there cleared from Philadelphia for California 11 ships, 8 barks, 8 brigs, 3 schooners, and no steamers; a total of 30. This latter figure checks with my estimate.

Considerable material has been omitted from this potpourri account, and much has been glossed over or slightly touched upon. In closing, I think the sage advise of one of the passengers aboard the ship *Susan G. Owens* may well be stated:

"1st. Pay your own way, and don't give $200 for your passage to one who gets it from the ship for $125 and a share of your earnings besides;

"2nd. Go in a ship where there are neither ladies, or women, unless of your own family or with their families;

"3rd. Be sure your captain is not only respectable, but a good navigator...;

"4th. *Go by land* and not without plenty of means."

42. *Philadelphia Public Ledger* January 8, 1850
43. *Argonauts of '49* by Octavious Howe, Cambridge, 1923, (p.174)

The diversity of data laboriously compiled from the shipping records of 1849 and 1850, is substantial. That errors and mistakes crept into the records is understandable. The hand writing of many of the agents at the ports of entrance or departure can scarcely be deciphered. The tonnage as given cannot entirely be depended upon. Sometimes it is stated as net, other times as gross, while the newspapers generally omit both terms. The names of the captains are often misspelled or transposed. The use of "sea time" in the marine news, by which the date of departure and arrival was frequently advanced an entire day, is copied by writers not familiar with the marine time quotation. The arrivals at San Francisco were sometimes not entered into the records until the following day.

I am aware that errors in an article such as this are inevitable. Therefore, I wish to take refuge behind the fact that much of the contemporary source material is often conflicting, and time does not permit a thorough check. I can only ask for indulgence on the part of the reader should any errors come to light.

"The first vessels to depart direct for California in 1849, from the following east coast seaports, as near as can be determined. December 7, 1848 - December 31, 1849."

PLACE OF SAILING	SHIP	BRIG	SCHOONER	BARK	NAME OF VESSEL	MASTER	TONNAGE	DATE OF SAILING	DATE OF ARRIVAL S.F.	DAYS PASSAGE	NO. PASSENGERS	CREW	MISCELLANEOUS
BEVERLY, MASS.	X				STERLING	GALLOUP	201	JAN. 3,'49	JULY 1,'49	180	7		
BOSTON	X				JOHN W. COFFIN	CHAS. C. MARTIN ?	218	DEC. 7,'48	JULY 30,'49	235?	10		
EDGARTOWN		X			VESTA	MAYHEW	155	APR.10,'49	DEC. 1,'49	229?	19		WINNEGAHEE MINING CO.
FAIRHAVEN	X				WM. & HENRY	JOHN CHURCH	260	FEB. 22,'49	SEPT.16,'49	206?	70		WILLIAM & HENRY MIN. CO.
FALL RIVER	X				MARY MITCHELL	JOSEPH BARNARD		AUG. 24,'49	APR.11,'50	230	40		
GLOUCESTER			X		PARAGON	TIMOTHY HALEY	92	FEB. 20,'49	SEPT.21,'49	213	5		GLOUCESTER FISHING MIN. & TRAD. CO.
HYANNIS			X		ELIZABETH B.	BACON	98	DEC.12,'49	MAY 6,'50	135	11		HYANNIS GOLD CO.
MARTHA'S VINEYARD			X		RIALTO			JULY 3,'49		135			
MATTAPOISETT	X				MOUNT VERNON	ATTSATT	388	APR.17,'49	OCT. 2,'49	164	67		MOUNT VERNON MINING ASSOCIATION / MATTAPOISETT MINING COMPANY
NANTUCKET	X				AURORA	SETH M. SWAIN	346	JULY 1,'49		169	22	24	
NEW BEDFORD			X		FAVORITE	FRANCES LePARKER	38	JUNE 3,'49		172	8	8	
NEWBURYPORT				X	CHARLOTTE		170	JULY 24,'49		180	43		
PLYMOUTH				X	ELENA			OCT. 1,'49		198			
SALEM	X				ELIZA	PERKINS	240	MAR.17,'49		181	2		
BANGOR, MAINE			X		MONTANO	AUSTIN	365	DEC.23,'48	JUNE 2,'49		7	12	
BATH		X			FAWN	PATTEN							NOT THE BR. FAWN THAT SAILED 10/10/'49
BELFAST	X				SULTOTE	SIMPSON	264	JAN.30,'49	JULY 18,'49	169	50		
CAMDEN	X				PERFECT	JAS. STACKPOLE	156	NOV.12,'49	APR. 7,'50	125	36?		CALIF. & THOMASTON PROTECTION CO.
CHERRYFIELD			X		BELGRADE	PLUMMER	252	NOV.27,'49	MAY 28,'50	203			[SACRAMENTO MINING] & [...] STACKPOLE MINING & NAVIGATION COMPANY
EAST MACHIAS				X	ORIENTAL	TALBOT	140	SEPT.19,'49	NOV.26,'49	182			NEVER REACHED SAN FRANCISCO
(EASTPORT) MACHIAS				X	TALBOT	JOHNSON	194		MAR. 4,'50	148	13	11	
FALMOUTH	X				AGATE								APPARENTLY DID NOT ARRIVE IN S.F.
KENNEBEC		X			COM. MORRIS	LAWRENCE	225		MAY 16,'50	172	40		
PORTLAND			X		SARAH MOOERS	C.M. SCAMMON		AUG.16,'49	FEB.21,'50	186	20		
SEARSPORT				X	OXFORD	SUCHET MAURAN	286		AUG.22,'49	222	63?		
SCARSPORT				X	FRANKLIN ADAMS	FELKER	248	OCT.29,'49	APR.28,'50	152	27		
BRIDGEPORT, CONN.	X				J. MERITHEW	FREEMAN McGILVERY							
MYSTIC	X				EMPEROR	BOLLES		DEC. 1,'49	JULY 8,'50				
NEW HAVEN			X		TRESCOTT	MALLORY	341	FEB. 4,'49	AUG. 7,'49	184	58		
NEW LONDON			X		G.H. MONTAGUE	G.H. MONTAGUE ?	167	JAN.23,'49	JUNE 27,'49	158	40		MONTAGUE MIN. & TRAD. CO.
NORWICH			X		MARY TAYLOR	SWEET	84	JAN.13,'49	AUG. 3,'49	202	3		
STONINGTON	X				BOSTON	NASH		NOV.21,'49	JULY 29,'50	250			
BRISTOL, RHODE ISLAND	X				CALUMET	HUBBARD	317	AUG. 1,'49	FEB.26,'50	208			
FRANKFORT		X			ANNE	COBB	222	FEB.21,'49	AUG.29,'49	189	57		
NEWPORT			X		EUDORUS	WIGGIN	144	FEB.13,'49	SEPT. 5,'49	214	29		NEWPORT & CALIF. EXPEDITION
WARREN			X		AUDLEY CLARK	DENNIS			SEPT. 1,'49	196	70		
GREENPORT, N.Y.				X	MARY FRANCES	SMITH	331	JAN. – ,'49	MAY 3,'49	123	127		THIS VESSEL IN THE S.F. LIST IS LISTED AS AN HAWAIIAN BARK, SAILED VIA HAWAII
NEW YORK CITY	X				BAYARD	GRAHAM	280?	AUG.21,'49					VIA VALPARAISO. THE S.F. LIST SAYS 170 DAYS PASSAGE
SAG HARBOR			X		FLORENCE		360	DEC.14,'48	AUG.26,'49	256	10	20	
PHILADELPHIA, PA.	X				IOWA	HOWES	133	JAN. 5,'49	JULY 7,'49	183	4		
BALTIMORE, MD.	X				LOUISIANA		300	DEC.23,'48	JUNE 2,'49	214			VIA VALPARAISO
NORFOLK, VA.	X				GREYHOUND	CLAYPOOL	536	JAN.10,'49	JUNE 3,'49	161	40	12	
RICHMOND	X				JOHN PETTY	FLAVEL	179	JAN.13,'49	AUG 29,'49	144	56	20	
CHARLESTON, S.C.	X				MARY ANNA		385	MAY 24,'49	SEPT.30,'49	228	20	10	
MOBILE, ALB.			X		OTHELLO	GALLOWAY	370	JAN.30,'49	NOV.13,'49	190	121		
NEW ORLEANS, LA.			X		REPUBLIC	BLIVEN	214	JUNE 19,'50	JAN.29,'50	286	60		
	X				ARCHITECT	GRAY	520	JAN.19,'50	JUNE 28,'49	160	60		

(JOHN B. GOODMAN)

Graph, showing interest in the California Gold Rush December 1, 1848 - December 31, 1849; giving the number of vessels to sail with gold seekers from the Port of New York, Boston and the New England States, by months. The sharp rises generally follow exciting news from California.

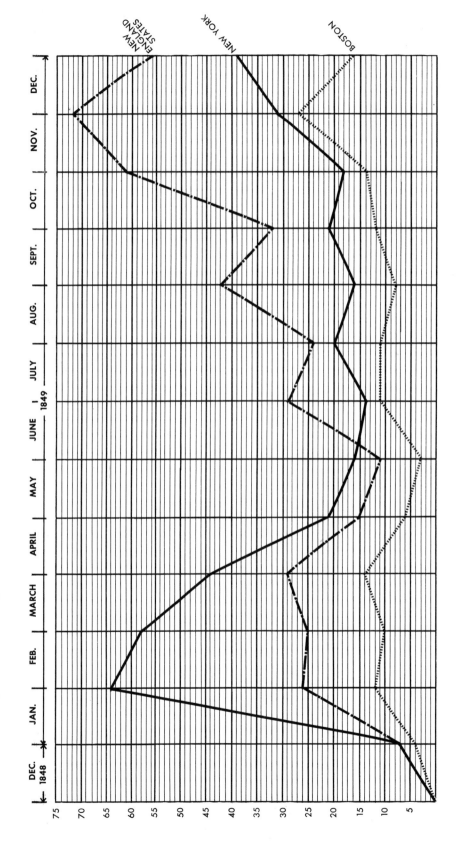

A large part of the sailings from New York was from Vera Cruz, La Vaca, Tampico and Chagres. Except for the early months, most of the sailings from Boston and New England was via Cape Horn.

(JOHN B. GOODMAN)

BETWIXT THE DEVIL AND THE DEEP

By GEORGE KOENIG

"Near camp are some soft rocks on which I cut the three first letters of my name and the date." — So wrote Henry W. Bigler, on November 3, 1849. Recently, Mr. Koenig journeyed into the wilderness country of southwestern Utah in the effort to locate these initials, carved by the Mormon Bigler well over one hundred years ago. The author did not do his exploring from the front seat of a car. He fought his way on foot over this difficult terrain; worked his course down the steep slopes of "Mt. Misery," even as Bigler had done before him. He tells all about it in this exciting article.

JUST AS THE EPIC CROSSING OF DEATH VALLEY by the intrepid '49ers has gained in familiarity, the approach route across Nevada has been slowly obliterated by the swirling sands of time. Yet Death Valley was not *the great obstacle* in itself. It was merely the climax of a month and a half of desperate struggle across Central Nevada's sun-scorched wastelands.

The die had been cast for the emigrant train, moving south from Salt Lake, since early October of 1849. And despite the protestations of Captain Jefferson Hunt, who had round-tripped over the main trail from Salt Lake to Chino a year and a half before, the temptations of a shortcut were too great to resist.

It was "About 3 days journey on the new trail," according to Lewis Manly, when—

> "Immediately in front of us was a cañon, impassable for wagons and down into this the trail descended. Men could go, horses and mules perhaps, but wagons could no longer follow that trail, so we proposed to search a pass across this steep and rocky cañon. Wood and bunch grass were plenty but water was a long way down the trail and had to be packed up to camp."

Later, in voicing the emigrants' despair and discouragement, he added, "They named this place Mt. Misery."

Altho the various accounts of the emigrants may appear to differ as much as they agree, Mt. Misery and its promentory—Poverty Point—left indelible impressions to be recalled with singular consistency.

Nusbaumer (whose party of six included Captain Culverwell—the only member of the '49ers to perish in Death Valley), logged—

> "All went well for 2 days, until on the third we came across nearly all the other parties camping on knolls without water and without food for the cattle, on the edge of a deep and rocky canion which we were unable to cross."

BETWIXT THE DEVIL AND THE DEEP

Colton, who was later to act as general secretary and historian for the surviving Jayhawkers, recalled—altho in doing so he misplaced the Wasatch Range—

> "... we reached what we called Poverty Point and which we all agreed must be the jumping off place. It was in the Wasatch Mountains and as far as the eye could reach in either direction there was a sheer precipice of a thousand feet or more."

At a distance, Mt. Misery's crags and crevices flattened deceptively. Its knolls, saddles and ravines blended into the illusion of a mesa extending hazily westward. Even its 6000 feet heights, lost in the expanse of similar surrounding ridges, gave little hint of the encircling canyons ahead. Gradually narrowing, the prow of this mountainous ship of stone poised above the dizzy depths, immobilized by the sandy gorges of Beaver Dam Wash.

Forced to an abrupt halt, the wagon train camped, wracked by uncertainty and doubt. There was some grass, but the meager supply was soon exhausted. Water was frustratingly far below. Those with agility and ability laboriously hauled the water up by bucket. According to J. W. Brier, Jr., in his "Grizzly Bear" article of June 1911, "the Frenchman did so for others for a dollar a bucket." And Mecum, with the Jayhawkers, recalled "the deep canion where the little Frenchman hauled up so much water"—later noting that the little Frenchman "perished" along with Robinson as they approached the San Francisco Rancho.

The need for grass and water forced the emigrants to forage over a wide area. The more venturesome descended into the wash bottom, scouting for a way out. Here, according to Haynes, whose diary provides a cryptic key to the emigrant route, there was "a small valley where there was plenty of water and grass" tantalizingly beneath the wagon train stranded on the summit. Whatever the choices and chances for escape, they were neither obvious nor easy.

Unencumbered by wagons, the "horse and mule" packers—including the Smith, Flake-Rich, Stover and Savage-Pinney parties—precariously switchbacked their way down into the canyon and on through the narrow and rugged defile to the south. Unable to follow, the majority of those with wagons turned back in an endeavor to rejoin Captain Hunt. Of those still in camp, when scouts reported finding a pass, were some 95 men, women and children with perhaps 27 wagons. Indeed, trapped atop scrub-covered Mt. Misery, it is surprising that even these few remained. But, reluctant to turn back, unwilling to abandon their wagons and possessions, the Jayhawkers, Bennetts-Arcanes, Briers, Wades, Young and Nusbaumer groups held resolutely to their westward course.

BETWIXT THE DEVIL AND THE DEEP

Of all the pivotal points in their famed trek, few were more fateful than Mt. Misery. It is here that the story of the Death Valley emigrants of '49 really began. For the steps taken here determined the outcome of the days ahead. Not only in *where* they went, but *why*. Not only in their physical, but also their psychological disintegrations.

* * * *

But just where is Mt. Misery? Offhand, somewhere west of Enterprise, in southwestern Utah, in the vast cedar-covered hills straddling the Nevada border.

What does it look like? Few know.

What of the wagon irons, the Bigler initials, and the rumored "Osborn 49" inscription? Do they still remain? Few, if any, could be sure.

Insatiably curious, I ventured into the pristine wilderness encompassing Nevada's Beaver Dam Wash area with my twelve year old, desert-wise son Steven.

Altho all maps—including those of the USGS and even high altitude aerial photos—proved woefully inadequate for the task at hand, we were not entirely unarmed. Backpacked was a copy of Charles Kelly's *Desert Magazine* (February 1939) article, along with some helpful hints and a few photos from the late John W. Beck who prowled this area, back in 1940, in pursuit of the '49er trail.

Unfortunately, time had taken its toll even since then. The old timers who guided both Kelly and Beck were gone. Their routes were uncertain and unseen in the labyrinth of ridges and washes. Hesitating at the bewildering expanse from the crest, we snaked our way down a dimly-marked road into Beaver Dam State Park. Our best bet seemed to be in orienting ourselves from the old Hamblin ranch about a mile or so beyond the ill-defined confines of the Park.

Normally a paradise of colorful cliffs, verdant greenness and cobalt skies, we literally *moored* ourselves the first night along the edge of the Beaver Dam stream bed, with a sea of red mud cascading down the road under a torrential downpour. But hope blossomed with the dawn—clear, dry, intoxicating. Abandoning the car we set out from the handhewn log cabin and old corral of the Hamblin ranch.*

"Be sure," admonished Mr. Beck in his notes, "to use a compass, for the country is deceptive with its twists and turns."

---

*Edwin Hamblin, brother of Jacob, settled in Beaver Dam in 1869. The cabin is not to be confused with the two story frame house built at the turn of the century and which burned in 1919, leaving only a stone fireplace standing.

BETWIXT THE DEVIL AND THE DEEP

Conscientiously, we took two. Both were useless. The mountain directly ahead must have been impregnated with magnetite for the needles spun drunkenly. When they did stagger to a sobering stop they pointed North into the rising sun.

More by guess than by rationalization, we started in a general direction that seemed to us to be north. The sun, with sudden bashfulness, hid behind a screen of clouds and was of little help in our hour of need.

A few hundred yards and the stream bed forked—both branches cleaving their way in a northerly direction. With fingers crossed we picked what we hoped would be the right course.

"Continuing north," Beck directed, "about 20 minutes will take you to the old Bauer cabin. We drove it quite easily."

Grateful that we were afoot, we criss-crossed the recent rain-swollen stream time and time again. To our right the cliff rose seemingly "a thousand feet or more." But was it Mt. Misery? As far as the eye could see, similar cliffs rose just as impressively.

Periodically the wash widened to form tree-clumped shelves that *might* have curtained the Bauer ranch. Each had to be checked. So it was that an hour—two hours—passed. Surely we must have taken the wrong fork.

With welcomed suddenness the wash widened into a small meadow. The stream angled sharply east and strained through narrowing cliffs to burst into another meadow beyond. But through the waist-high tules and dense thickets about us there was no sign of structures or even of their remains. Yet—surely the cliff profiles *looked* like those in the Beck photos. But, for that matter, so did a hundred others. In any event, it was a lunch stop with trees affording both shade and shelter from a sky that seemed uncertain of sun or shower.

It was while searching for something to sit on that we found the broken boards. These, surely, were of man; not of nature. Scurrying around we turned up the remnants of tubs, pails and other unmistakable evidence of human habitation. Climbing into a rocky cul-de-sac we observed a rail, still in place, that helped to form this handy natural corral. Beyond this was a hewn log storage shed. Eureka! We had found the Bauer ranch!

After lunch we shed our packs and, with soaring spirits and only cameras and canteens to weigh us down, set forth for the next clue on our treasure hunt.

Kelly's article seemed less specific than Beck's directive—

"East from Bauer's, the Bigler initials are in the second alcove along Mt. Misery. They are in the first light sandstone facing that you'll find."

Simple. Besides, Kelly had noted that the inscription was "seven feet

BETWIXT THE DEVIL AND THE DEEP

from the ground." Alas, to anyone unfamiliar with this country, such simplicity can become incredibly complex.

The main body of the mountain to the southeast, now on our right, was *laced* with alcoves—high, low, small, and large.

"Light sandstone"? Take your pick of any hue. They were all there for the choosing.

"Seven feet from the ground"? How much had twenty-two years of washed-down debris and erosion changed that loose measurement?

There was but one thing to do—keep the main mountainous mass to our right and scrutinize every sandstone shading within a reasonable distance of the ground. Mile after mile, gully after gully, facing after facing, we stubbornly checked out every possibility, however remote, until we finally dead-ended at an insurmountable wall of rock. 'Twas enough to drive the strongest to the brink of tears. With desperate obsession we rechecked every nook and cranny along the return. Perhaps the Bigler initials had been concealed by brush. Possibly they had weathered away. On the other hand, a few more steps might turn the trick. There had to be some sign of them. There *had* to be.

Retracing our way across the thistle-thick meadow, heading back toward Bauer's, we paused at the meandering stream. Why, oh why, weren't Kelly and Beck more explicit? Then the hours would have been but minutes. By now the sky was blackening, and the thunder rumbled ominously.

Wait! Beck and Kelly were in tow of those who knew the area well. With no abortive searches, there was little need to detail time and distance as points of importance. What about forking *north* from the meadow instead of east? Perhaps to the distant cliff edgings where the cedars dimmed the view?

Hopefully we made our way to a large opening at the base of the cliffs. It was indeed an "alcove" of sorts. Larger than anticipated, to be sure; but a certain allowance had to be made for personal geological definitions. And the cliff walls were light. White, in fact; and against them the brush and trees stood out in stark contrast.

Circling from left to right, I had progressed only a few yards when suddenly, with no conscious warning, I was staring directly at them. The initials! The identical initials Bigler had carved over a hundred years before!

Here, then, was that historically-hallowed ground where Bigler, on—

"Nov. 2. crost over into a Canion Running about S.West. . . the Road generally today was rough. we are now encamped in the Canion on a level spot of grass about 50 acres, wood and water plenty.

Sat 3d Laid by until nearly noon for our animals to rest and eat grass. I cut the 3 first letters of my name on a Rock & the date."

OSBORN

HWB

MT. MISERY

TO RENO

ELY

TO SALT LAKE CITY

N

TO BISHOP

6

93

91

UTAH

KANOSH

TONOPAH

PIOCHE

ESCALANTE DESERT

NEVADA

CALIENTE

CEDAR CITY

"MT" MISERY

SANTA CLARA RIVER

95

BEAVER DAM WASH

MEADOW VALLEY WASH

RIVER

VIRGIN

LITTLEFIELD (BEAVER DAMS)

LAKE MEAD

DEATH VALLEY

TRAIL

LAS VEGAS

COLORADO RIVER

ARIZONA

CALIF.

SALT SPRING

1849

TO KINGMAN

91 93

BARSTOW

TO LOS ANGELES

0 25 50 75 100

10

(Map by John B. Goodman III.)

MOUNT MISERY—(*right*) along the Pine Ridge side.
For the '49ers a—"sheer precipice of a thousand feet or more."

HENRY W. BIGLER'S INSCRIPTION, Beaver Dam Wash.
"I cut the 3 first letters of my name . . ."

BETWIXT THE DEVIL AND THE DEEP

Quarrel as one will with any theorizations of emigrant routing, here was a definite anchor point, not only for the parties that threaded their way south but for those emigrants who persisted on continuing west. For here was one of the few, if not the only, feasible escape routes from the heights of Mt. Misery—angling north to skirt the canyon we had first explored, thence to where the slopes now gentled less precipitously in forming the Bigler alcove. This indeed was the birthplace of the exodus that was to grace the lore and legends of the historical West for a century and more.

Surely my proverbial cup should now be running over. And it would have, save for the disquieting realization it was only one-half full. There was still to be found that rumored "wall of inscriptions," with its coveted "OSBORN 49".

Recuperating at the Bauer ranch, and taking stock of time, weather and film, I re-read Beck's instructions:

> "Round the granite knob to the *east* of Bauer's and you will find a narrow canyon. It is a steep climb. Very steep. To the right are Indian caves in which I found firemaking tools, etc. A short way beyond, to your left, at the foot of a yellow cliff wall, probably hidden by brush, are a number of names, initials and dates. Take flashbulbs for the place is narrow, deep and dark. Unfortunately I didn't have any with me and time precluded a second try the next day."

Alas, we were equally as wanting as was Beck, both in flashbulbs and in time. But at least we could make notes. Even *seeing* the inscription would give fact to the fable. So we rounded the granite knob to the East, tho it risked a drenched haul back to our Hamblin ranch base in the threatening storm.

As with the poor, God must surely have loved canyons, washes and ravines —for He made so many of them. It was an abundance we were soon to regret. Trails may no longer look like trails after the lapse of twenty years. Underbrush can grow with a bit of sun, rain and protective sheltering. Boulders will wash down from higher slopes to create a shambles of what once was a passage. But caves there were; and to these we clawed our way up the soft slopes. They were soot-smudged and bone-littered, but disappointingly destitute of more tangible signs of man.

No needle in a haystack was ever sought more diligently. Finally, in utter despair of achieving our goal, we turned back, bitterly disappointed. It had been a long trip and foreseeably we would not pass this way again. Nor did we know of any to whom we might fling our torch to carry on with any more information than we had already exhausted. Perhaps we should have utilized Kelly's entry route from the northwest rim and across the meadows from Mt. Misery. At least we could have *endeavored* to follow—

BETWIXT THE DEVIL AND THE DEEP

"...on a very dim trail which soon led us to the brink of the wash. Straight down it ran, apparently into the bowels of the earth, the longest, steepest, narrowest trail we had ever encountered in many years of desert travel. Down, down and down we went at a snail's pace, finally reaching a small meadow containing an abandoned cabin. Walls of the canyon were of white volcanic ash so we scrutinized them closely for names. At last to our joy we found deeply engraved the name "OSBORN 49."

Scrutinizing the walls of the ampitheatre almost encircling the Bauer homesite we could discern no tell-tale signs of any trail up—east, behind or beyond. Anything even hinting of possibilities had already been tried. It would take days of deeper digging; days that, unfortunately, we did not have. So we shouldered our cached packs and turned south.

The next day was spent fishing in the reservoir lake into which Beaver Dam emptied a quarter mile away, rock hunting along the wash, and loafingly savoring yesterday's triumph and heartbreak. Reconnoitering climbs were made for photos and for mapping along the Pine Park side of enigmatic Mt. Misery, now to our north. Guy Hamblin, who still visits the old homestead, had reported the emigrant wagon irons they gathered on top of Mt. Misery had long since been salvaged for use at the ranch. What they missed, if any, John Beck failed to find in his foot-by-foot search. If any pieces remained they had by now settled twenty years deeper into the sands of time. The sheer cliffs and chaparral-covered ridges had been weighed and found wanting of any conclusive rewards for still another fine-tooth combing.

The next morning we drove out of the depths of Beaver Dam Wash, past the Hamblin ranch and on toward the crest where we paused at the faint signs of what could have been an old road, or a firebreak, or perhaps a short workroad from the Park development activities. But there is something heady about a clear morning on the high desert that rolls away the years and dulls the fears of efforts that will probably not pan out. So off we swung, optimistically trusting that the road led *somewhere* and without too many car-jarring jolts.

The road, such as it was, stayed surprisingly passable and we seemed to be skirting the canyon rim, glimpsed now and then through the undulating cedar, juniper and scrub-covered slopes. If there is any consolation for the lonesomeness of such a land it is that one doesn't find himself torn with decisions over what road to follow. And so it was that two faint wheel tracks easily lured us onward towards the rim. Just for one last, longing look from the top of Mt. Misery!

A short walk; and then we peered down, deep down, and beyond to the

BETWIXT THE DEVIL AND THE DEEP

Bauer site and the scene of our searchings two days before. It was a long haul down. The trail was uncertain. It also emptied *west*, not east, of Bauer's. And obviously, having searched so thoroughly once, there was little need to hoof it down and huff it back up again just for the exercise. If Kelly, in progressing west to east, had—in sequence—passed (1) a meadow containing an abandoned cabin and then (2) found the Osborn inscription, it chronologically must have been the area we had already covered in our vain attempt.

Almost certainly it would be a waste of time. And, while the trail didn't look so steep as Kelly had described, it would still be hard work. It would also be futile. Even downright foolish.

Besides, I did not know then what I was to learn later from Kelly—

"I remember the dugway going down into the wash because it was so steep that I had to make three runs at it *with a Model A Ford*, assisted by two men in order to get back up."

But ignorance is bliss; so we yielded to temptation, buckled on canteens, shouldered cameras, and abandoned the car.

The wheel tracks we had followed soon faded out. Following what was a path in name only, we hooked our way downward, hemmed in by cliffs on both sides. While it wasn't unusually steep, we were mindful its angle would increase a hundred fold coming back up. Whether it had been a road at one time was anyone's guess. It was certainly gutted and boulder strewn now, although not impassably so for anyone attempting it on foot.

Interpreting Kelly's article literally, a cabin or cabin site would be our first big clue. I mused that, descriptively, it couldn't be Bauer's place out in the flat. But why *wasn't* their cabin mentioned? It had to be passed on the way to the Bigler initials. I also pondered over Beck finding Mr. and Mrs. Bauer living there in Spring of '40, wondering how it tied in with the cabin Kelly found abandoned in the Fall of '38. I was still half lost in these thoughts as we neared the bottom of our narrow canyon trail. Then suddenly we saw it. A red and yellow, black-streaked wall of sandstone covered with inscriptions!

Protected by an overhang they stood out with time-defying clarity. Most of them dated from the 1920's. Among those half obliterated by age were such early pioneer names of the area as Hamblin, Pulsipher and others. *And there, too, was the elusive "OSBORN 49"!*

However triumphant, our finding of the Bigler inscription did not now seem half so sweet as the reward for our impulsive *second* search after that for which hope had once been abandoned. Magnanimously, ecstatically, we forgave Fate for her earlier fickleness.

OSBORN INSCRIPTION WALL, Beaver Dam Wash.
Pointing the escape west from "Mt. Misery".

* * * *

Questionable as the "OSBORN 49" inscription may be, for the figure "49" appears to belong less to OSBORN than to the indecipherable name alongside, it and the other inscriptions disclosed the only practicable route up the westward rim, even as Bigler's initials had revealed the route down from Mt. Misery.

As Kelly wrote, in concluding his article—

"The finding of Bigler's initials . . . provides a starting place for anyone who cares to finish tracing the old trail of '49."

So, too, does "OSBORN 49" tell us how, twixt the devil and the deep, the depths of Beaver Dam were defeated. From the heights of their "misery" the '49ers' wagons again rolled westward. *Westward into destiny. Westward into history.*

DEADMAN'S ISLAND

By Everett Gordon, &
Anna Marie Hager

Few remember, and many have no knowledge of, the rather lonely and pathetic little island that—until recently—proudly occupied its conspicuous position in San Pedro Bay. In our knowledge, no comprehensive account has ever before been written of this desolate, dramatic, and historically prominent little island. Yet Dana, in his classic *Two Years Before the Mast* (1840), tells us "it was the only thing in California from which I could ever extract anything like poetry." The capable authors have researched material extending over a three hundred and seventy-two year period.

Deadman's Island—a small, wave-beaten, rocky island prior to 1928—served as the sentinel at the gate to the inner harbor of San Pedro Bay. Records indicate it was approximately eight hundred feet long, two hundred and fifty feet wide and over sixty feet high. Separated from the mainland, opposite Timms Point, this conical-peaked islet once served as the anchor end of the first breakwater built in the harbor. Better known as the 'home-port' or base for numerous legends of buried men, wealth and scientific lore, the island continues, in memory, as a romantic and historical landmark of yesteryear.

Pious Spanish explorers did not deem the island worthy of a saint's name, and for nearly two centuries it was nameless until crowned with the mournful and gloomy soubriquet, *La Isla de los Muertos, El Morro*, later Americanized to Deadman's Island.

For many years the island served a most prosaic humane need as a cemetery to protect the dead placed there from the ravages of the "robbers of the plains"—the prowling coyotes. After the 1850's, the island no longer provided the hoped-for sanctuary for the interred.

When surrounding rocks which provided protection against erosion were removed for construction of the first jetty in the harbor in 1872, Deadman's Island began to deteriorate from the battering of the waves against its clay-ey sides.

Other destructive forces to which the island fell heir were fortune hunters, lured by tales of hidden piratical plunder. These literally honeycombed its surface. Not all those drawn to the island, armed with pick and shovel, searched for mythical treasures; conchologists sought the rare fossil shells with which the island was so richly endowed.

The rapid growth of the Harbor of Los Angeles marked Deadman's Island an obstruction to navigation and led to its eventual obliteration by man, dredger and dynamite.

DEADMAN'S ISLAND

Historically, Deadman's Island has been identified with the taking of the capital of California, at that time (1846) the Pueblo de Los Angeles. Scientifically, it achieved importance because of its rare fossils.[1]

This chronological narrative spans a three hundred and seventy-two year history of the picturesque and grotesquely-named vanished landmark.

An early reference will be found in the writings of Fray Antonio de la Ascension to a small nondescript island, later to be called Deadman's Island: "From the *Punta de la Conversion*, the coast trends east for more than fourteen leagues, very rough and rugged without any trees to a point which the land makes extending north-south, and with a hill of medium height bare on top, which from afar looks like an island (Pt. Vicente). To the east of this is a very good ensenada with shelter from the northwest, west and southwest winds. It is named the *Ensenada de San Pedro*, in thirty four and a half degrees, and in it there is a small island."[2]

Many legends claim that members of scurvy-ridden crews from Spanish sailing vessels were buried on the little island.[3]

George Vancouver described the Bay and named the two points extending from it. He included mention of the "supposed bay of San Pedro about a league . . . having a small island lying off their northern extremity."[4]

Alfred Robinson, Captain John Hall and Alexander Forbes were among many who noted the lonely little island.[5]

The use of the island as a repository for the dead supposedly began in 1810 when some fishermen happened to find on its shore the body of an unknown white man who had perished from hunger, thirst and exposure. The pious fishermen buried the white stranger on top of the isle to which they gave the name *Isle del Muerto*, or Deadman's Island.[6] In the years that followed, the sad fate of this sailor was made much of in song and poetry and the island became historic.

J. J. Warner mentioned that, upon his arrival in Los Angeles in 1831, the sland was referred to as *La Isla del Muerto* and had been known by that name since 1810.[7]

---

1. Williamson, Mrs. M. Burton, "Isla de los Muertos," *Historical Society of Southern California*, IV, part 1 (1897) 64-69

2. Wagner, Henry Raup, "Spanish Voyages to the Northwest Coast in the Sixteenth Century," California Historical Society *Quarterly*, VIII, (March, 1929) 48

3. Bancroft, H. H., *History of California, 1542-1800*, Vol. I, 130

4. Wilbur, Marguerite Eyer (Editor), *George Vancouver in California, 1792-1794*, (Los Angeles, 1954) 177

5. Robinson, Alfred, *Life in California* (Oakland, 1947) 24; Forbes, Alexander, *California: a History of Upper and Lower California*, (San Francisco, 1937) 103

6. Sten, Pod, *Sails and Rails* (thesis, no date, not submitted)

7. Williamson, Mrs. M. Burton, *opus cited.*, 64

DEADMAN'S ISLAND

It was a Christmas day in 1824, that the American brig *Danube* lay off *La Isla del Muerto* with most her crew given shore leave. Suddenly a dread *Santana* storm caused the brig to drag her anchors and, despite the efforts of the small crew on board, was smashed upon the rocks inside Point Fermin to become San Pedro's first shipwreck.[8]

A happier appellation, "Anniversary Island," was bestowed by DuHaut-Cilly in 1827, who wrote: "Before regaining the ship, we went to visit a small island, to which we had allowed ourselves to give, on our arrival, the name *Anniversary Island*. When upon coming to the bay at San Pedro, we had noticed this rock which had no name, it was just a year since we had left France. We found upon its topmost point a sea-eagle's eyrie, with two eaglets lying in the midst of some disgusting remains of fish." His survey of the anchorage included the newly named island.[9]

Dana's *Two Years Before the Mast* has pictured the island so vividly that many who had never ventured to the Pacific Coast knew the island most intimately from his unique descriptions. Says Dana: "The only thing that broke the surface of the great bay was a small desolate-looking island, steep and conical, of clay-ey soil and without a sign of vegetation on it. It was always a solemn and an interesting spot to me. There it stood, desolate and in the midst of desolation; and there were the remains of one who had died, friendless and alone—it was the only thing in California from which I could ever extract anything like poetry."[10]

The prophetic observations of G. M. Waseurtz af Sandels in 1843, foresaw: "A splendid harbor might be constructed or formed by blocking up one place between a small island and the mainland and give the sea lead to dig itself a more ampel(sic) channel up toward a kreek(sic) deep enough for any vessel."[11]

Intrigued by the island in the bay, Charles Nordhoff took time to scramble over its rocky sides and, in *Nine Years a Sailor*, said: "The most interesting spot in the entire neighborhood to me, was the island fronting the harbor, to seaward. This was the abode of numberless sea-fowl which had their nests thickly studding the ground and which when suddenly disturbed rose up in vast crowds almost hiding the sight of the sun, and filling the air with discordant cries."[12]

---

8. Robinson, W. W., "Rancho Los Palos Verdes" *Historical Society of Southern California Quarterly*, (September, 1954) 248
9. Carter, Charles F., trans., "DuHaut-Cilly's Account of California in the Years 1827-28," California Historical Society *Quarterly*, VIII, (June, 1929) 164-166
10. Dana, Richard Henry, Jr., *Two Years Before the Mast*, (Boston, 1911) 128
11. Waseurtz af Sandels, G. M., "The King's Orphan's Manuscript," *Quarterly of the Society of California Pioneers*, III, (June, 1926) 84
12. Nordhoff, Charles, *Nine Years a Sailor*, (Cincinnati, 1855) 244-245

DEADMAN'S ISLAND

The island loomed up importantly when the Battle of Dominguez marked the year 1846. J. M. Guinn's account, taken from the log book of Lieutenant Robert C. Duvall, seems inclusive of all published accounts of this incident: "On the following morning we buried the bodies of William A. Smith, Charles Sommers, David Johnson and Michael Hoey on an island in the harbor.

"Entry in the log Sunday 11th: William H. Berry (ordinary seaman) departed this life from the effects of wounds received in battle. Sent his body for internment to Deadman's Island, so named by us. Mustered the command at quarters, after which performed divine services.

"From this account it will be seen that the number killed and died of wounds received in battle was four; number wounded six, and one accidentally killed before the battle. On October 22nd, Henry Lewis died and was buried on the island. Lewis's name does not appear in the list of the wounded. It is presumed that he died of disease. Six of the crew of the *Savannah* were buried on Dead Man's Island, four of whom were killed in battle."[13]

José Palomares, an observer of the burial party, described the sad ritual: "The next day some of the spies came to report that boats were making from the ship for an island which is in the middle of the roadstead, facing the port. At that moment several boats were reaching the island, called *El Morro* by the natives, and about fifty men were landing on it, carrying their dead with the object of burying them at that spot. They finished landing about eight-thirty in the morning.

"Afterwards, while some busied themselves in opening a large hole or grave, the others placed a piece of artillery of small caliber on the highest point of the island, and pointing its muzzle towards where we were, fired. And so they kept their spy-glass on us, firing and burying their dead, until one in the afternoon, hour in which they finished their task and returned to the ship in the same way in which they had come."[14]

Lured West by the 'Boom of the '80s,' to prowl through southern California, Emma H. Adams in "To and Fro in Southern California," wrote: "Deadman's Island just before us, and containing less than an acre of ground, received its name, it is said, from the circumstances that when on the march towards Los Angeles, the troops above mentioned had an engagement with the Mexican force and suffered a loss of fifteen men. The bodies of the slain were returned to San Pedro and interred near this (Timms) point. At this the natives were much incensed and declared that if the bodies were not removed

13. Guinn, J. M., *Historical and Biographical Record of Los Angeles and Vicinity*, (Chicago, 1901) 89
14. Temple, Thomas W., II, trans., *Memoirs of José Francisco Palomares*, XXXIII, ECTS (Los Angeles, 1955) 51-52

they should be thrown over the high bluff into the sea. Thereupon the dead were exhumed and re-buried on this little hillock, rising out of the water."[15]

Somewhat divergent from these three accounts, yet lending support to Mrs. Adams' narrative, is one by W. A. Corey which appeared in the Los Angeles *Times*, 1898: "The Americans lost five men killed and several wounded, one of whom soon afterwards died. The dead and the wounded were loaded upon ox carts and taken to San Pedro, from whence the dead were transported to Deadman's Island, and interred. Burial elsewhere being refused by the mission authorities, on the claim the mainland was consecrated ground, in which none but Catholics could be buried."[16]

Major Horace Bell portrayed a notable event in which the island played a major role, the July 4, 1853 celebration: "Captain Sepulveda mustered and embarked his command on a large boat and proceeded up Wilmington Bay, where he embarked his artillery and sailed for Deadman's Island, where, after infinite labor, he succeeded in mounting his battery on the highest point of the island, and all being ready, we let loose such a thunder as was never exceeded by one gun. It seemed that we would wake the seven sleeping heroes who so quietly reposed on the little barren rock. Don Juan said the firing would serve a triple purpose; it would dissipate the last vestige of unfriendly feeling that may have lingered in the bosoms of the sons of the country towards the United States; that it would serve to express our gratitude to the great founders of modern liberty; and it would be an appropriate salute to the seven brave marines who lost their lives in their country's service. After the first salvo, and while paying our respects to our liquid ammunition, Don Juan proceeded to tell us how the seven sailors came to be killed. Their wooden headboards stood in line in front of us."[17]

The British brig *Boxer* put into San Pedro Bay with some of her crew dead from an outbreak of disease aboard ship and her captain had their bodies interred on Deadman's Island.[18]

Alfred Robinson told of the death of Black Hawk, the last *male* Indian from San Nicolas Island, and of his burial on Deadman's Island.[19]

The feminine contingent of the island's ghostly crew was interred in 1858, the wife of Captain Parker of the *Laura Bevan*.[20]

15. Adams, Emma H., *To and Fro in Southern California*, (Cincinnati, 1887) 255
16. Corey, W. A., "The Island of the Dead," Los Angeles Sunday *Times*, August 28, 1898
17. Bell, Major Horace, *Reminiscences of a Ranger*, (Santa Barbara, 1927) 128-129
18. Kirkman, George Wycherley, "Lost Isles of San Pedro," Los Angeles *Times*, May 27, 1928
19. Robinson, Alfred, *Life in California*. New Edition (San Francisco, 1897) 248
20. Gleason, Duncan, *The Islands and Ports of California*, (New York, 1958) 115

Los Angeles Harbor 1850. From a daguerreotype taken by William Godfrey in 1850. Deadman's Island in upper left center. (*Courtesy, Historical Collection, Security-First National Bank, L.A.*)

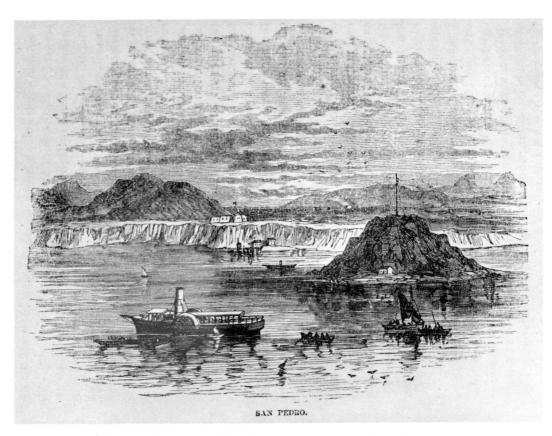

SAN PEDRO.

DEADMAN'S ISLAND, 1864. From a drawing by J. Ross Browne, to illustrate Harper's article, "Tour to Arizona." (*Property of E. G. Hager*)

"Deadman's Island as it appeared before demolition work started in 1929." (*Photos from the Hager Collection.*)

DEADMAN'S ISLAND

Livelier activity took place when a whaling company stationed on Deadman's Island reported twenty-five whales for the season of 1862.[21]

J. Ross Browne, in 1864, noticed: "The little island supposed to be the burial place of an unfortunate marine who came to an untimely end in that vicinity. A cross marks his grave and sea gulls and wild sea waves sing his lullaby."[22]

Another shipwreck took place on the 20th of December, 1879, when the *Adelaide Cooper* parted cables in a southeast gale, became unmanageable, took a sheer and went ashore on the inside of Deadman's Island, a total loss.[23]

The name, *El Morro*, continued to appear on various navigational charts and directories as late as 1886.

In 1887: "the importance of this land in connection with Deadman's Island as a site of future defensive works," was stressed in Senate Document Number 144, of the 55th Congress, entitled, *Military Reservation at or near San Pedro, Cal.*[24]

When the San Pedro *Times* on October 10, 1891, pleaded for the preservation of the island, conservationists applauded: "In the near future, owing to the new railroad interest heading this way, San Pedro will enter on a new era of prosperity. Visitors will flock here, as well as commerce, and no place will have more of a charm for the tourists, than to land on, and to examine, this old, historic island. It really would not be out of place to have a neat monument placed on top of the island in memory of the ones who were buried there in the years gone by, no doubt, United States soldiers. Let us urge this matter, and try to save what is left of the old island, ere it too, be washed away and lost in the depths of the sea."[25]

Local "Tom Sawyers," six in number, had an excursion of their own which brought about some unexpected results. When rummaging about on the island, they discovered a rough redwood coffin and managed to pry off the lid, found a skeleton therein and reported it to the authorities on their return to the mainland.[26] "Various civic and military forces took charge in exhuming the bodies for a more fitting and final place of rest. Four bodies were found intact, while a portion of a fifth was secured. The remains were evidently hastily

21. Hayes' Emigrant Notes (Los Angeles, Vol. V. *News* of December 20, 1861) Bancroft Library
22. Browne, J. Ross, "Tour Through Arizona," *Harper's Monthly*, 1864
23. Swaine, E. L., "A Deep Water Harbor for Southern California," *Proceedings of Engineers and Architects*, March 6, 1895
24. U.S. Sen. Ex. Docs. 55th Cong., Ses. 2, No. 144, February 18, 1898
25. San Pedro *Times*, October 10, 1891
26. San Pedro *Sun*, February 17, 1893; "The Island That Moved to Let the Ships Go By," *Westways*, Vol. 28 (July, 1936) 18-19

"Skeletons removed during final stages of demolition work on Deadman's Island."

interred, as little or no evidence of any casket or coffin were to be found. It is said that the government has taken charge of the removal of the remains, and is being seconded by some English society in Los Angeles."[27] The Presidio, United States Army, San Francisco has no record of the relocation of these dis-interred bodies.

Spades of eager conchologists and archaeologists searched for fossil shells in the Pliocene and Miocene strata of rocks. Mrs. M. Burton Williamson in her splendid article, *Isla de los Muertos*, stated that nearly three hundred species and varieties of fossil shells were collected on the island.[28]

The Redondo *Breeze* suggested that a statue honoring Admiral Dewey be placed on top of Deadman's Island.[29]

This interesting item appeared in the San Pedro *Daily Times*, August 29, 1903: "There visited Deadman's Island, off San Pedro harbor, yesterday, a woman who kept her secret well from those who were with her. Kept it from all save one, and he knew. Her mission on that lonely little isle was to look upon the burial place of her father, whose life of storm ended when the sailors buried him there."[30]

27. San Pedro *Times*, May 27, 1899
28. Williamson, Mrs. M. Burton, *opus cited.*, 69
29. Redondo *Breeze* (as reported in San Pedro *Times*, April 29, 1899)
30. San Pedro Daily *Times*, August 29, 1903

DEADMAN'S ISLAND

Promotion pamphlets of the early 1900's emphasized the necessity of utilizing the little island for "gun emplacements and other warlike purposes, to repel the Japanese invasion that the eastern newspapers have been telling us about."[31]

The monument idea appeared again when Charles Holder urged the erection of a suitable monument to Cabrillo, Deadman's Island to be carved into an appropriate base for such a heroic statue.[32]

Before the breakwater lighthouse was built in 1915, red lanterns were installed to warn ships away from hazards. A flickering light was placed at the end of the breakwater and on a make-shift beacon off Deadman's Island.[33]

Transfer of control of Deadman's Island took place in 1916 when the War Department relinquished control to the Treasury Department.[34]

After the United States entered World War I, the Navy laid a mine field in the entrance of the harbor. Three-inch guns were emplaced at the water's edge of Deadman's Island as protection for the mine field. Guarding the mine field became a high priority duty. The Twenty-First Company of the California National Guard was transferred from Fort MacArthur to Deadman's Island to man the battery, on August 17, 1917, and lived in tents erected on Reservation Point. The four guns were set on concrete platforms at the extreme southern tip of the island, just above the high-tide line. High winter tides undermined the emplacements and canted the guns, but not enough to affect the accuracy of their fire.[35]

Rum-runners of the 1920's appreciated the vantage-point Deadman's Island offered; its sides, pitted with numerous small caves, proved convenient for the storing of contraband liquids.[36]

The death knell for Deadman's Island sounded with the award of a contract to the San Francisco Bridge Company and the United Dredging Company of Los Angeles to demolish the island.[37]

The Southwest Museum obtained permission to station a scientist at Deadman's Island during the entire period of removal, so great was the interest in it as a unique repository of fossils. Charles Amsden was named to undertake the research.[38]

31. Star, Frederick, "Rattlesnake Island," *P. E. Magazine* (July, 1908) 43
32. Holder, Charles, *Channel Islands of California*, (Chicago, 1910) 296
33. San Pedro *Pilot*, January 2, 1915
34. Gleason, Duncan, *opus cited.*, 115
35. San Pedro Daily *News*, April 16, 1917
36. Los Angeles *Times*, February 5, 1928
37. San Pedro *Pilot*, February 28, 1928
38. Los Angeles *Times*, February 5, 1928

DEADMAN'S ISLAND

In spite of black powder and dredgers the little island held back its secrets and, when a blast tore away a large part of the westerly end of the island, skeletons of four human bodies came to light.[39]

Later, eleven other skeletons were revealed—unknowns without a clue to their identity. One skull was pierced with an ancient stone arrowhead, dating it back to primitive Indian days.[40]

The last heavy blast, before old Deadman's Island sank below the waves, uncovered three adjacent graves—two men and a woman. About the latter's head was a mass of red-gold hair and the men wore the over-fold boots characteristic of the Sixteenth Century. By one of them was the hilt of an ancient cutlass.[41]

On June 1, 1929, the last blast was fired, shattering the final remaining rocky ribs, and the waves of the ocean rolled over Deadman's Island.[42]

In its place is Reservation Point, a sixty-two acre peninsula, a quarantine station and the United States public health and immigration service.

The Annual Report of the Board of Los Angeles Harbor Commissioners reported: "Dredging work, including both new excavations and maintenance work, has been accomplished. Deadman's Island at the mouth of the Main Channel has been removed by the United States Government and a full one thousand foot channel will be provided at this location."[43]

Conjecture is still rife as to the true number that were buried on Deadman's Island. Guinn made the statement that eleven persons were buried there, ten men and a woman, namely: the lost sailor, the English sea captain, Black Hawk, six of the U. S. S. *Savannah's* crew, a passenger of a Panama steamer in 1851, and Mrs. Parker.[44]

It is reasonable to assume that many a nameless skeleton was hauled from an unmarked grave by the insatiable dredge and dumped with other residue into the sea. Countless tourists, conchologists, school children and treasure seekers all scoured the little island in their time. Who tallied *their* findings and who kept record of what *they* saw or disturbed?

Speculation keeps the memory of this strange little vanished island ever green and of never-ending interest. It will probably remain one of the unsolved mysteries locked in the depths of San Pedro Bay.

---

39. San Pedro *Pilot*, March 31, 1928
40. *Westways, opus cited*, 18-19
41. ————— *opus cited*, 18-19
42. San Pedro *News Pilot*, June 1, 1929
43. Los Angeles Harbor Department, *Annual* Report, July 1, 1927-June 30, 1928, 56
44. Guinn, J. M., "Lost Islands of San Pedro Bay," *Historical Society of Southern California*, V, pt. 1, (1900) 66

THE CAPTIVE WARS

By LYNN R. BAILEY

This revealing paper on the baffling problem of Indian slavery in the United States, which persisted even after the constitutional abolishment of slavery, is the result of extensive research on the part of its author. The material he presents is well documented, and its startling revelations are of shock proportions. The problems involved in this Country's management of its Indian relationship difficulties with the Navajo—those once "proud Lords of New Mexico"—are intelligently considered. The Navajo incident, as presented, makes for informative and fascinating reading.

IT WAS SEVEN O'CLOCK on the morning of August 15, 1846 when the "Army of the West" marched through the drowsy New Mexican village of Las Vegas and encamped a short distance beyond. The village populace was turned out and assembled in the plaza to hear the words of the conqueror of New Mexico. From atop one of the flat-roofed adobe buildings surrounding the square, Brigadier General Stephen Watts Kearny explained that he and his army had come to take possession of the country, not as an enemy, but as a protector; and in the following words made known to the people that his government was aware of at least one of the many difficulties which had plagued the area for generations:

> The Apaches and the Navajos come down from the mountains and carry off your sheep and your women whenever they please. My government will correct all this. They will keep off the Indians, protect you in your persons and property.[1]

The fulfillment of General Kearny's promise of protection was not to be as easy as it sounded. For nearly 250 years before the coming of the "Army of the West" intermittent war had existed between the New Mexicans and the Navajos, until reciprocal raid and reprisal had become a traditional endeavor. The source of these difficulties is not easy to determine, as both peoples contributed equally to keeping animosities alive. By the late 17th century the Navajos had adopted those Spanish traits which would put them on the road to plunder, and throw New Mexico into the abyss of war. The Diné,[2] as the Navajos call themselves, had adopted to their economy the horse raising and sheep grazing complex; and sought to increase their numerical strength by taking captives. Acquirement of these possessions transformed the Navajos from a part-time agricultural, food-collecting people to a tribe of raiders who reckoned their status and wealth in terms of the number of sheep and captives they possessed. Unable to draw the elusive Diné into decisive battles, the

---

1. George R. Gibson. *Journal of a Soldier Under Kearny and Doniphan, 1846-1847.* Ed. by Ralph P. Bieber. Glendale: Calif.: 1935, pp. 75-76.
2. Both the Navajos and their cousins, the Apaches, speaking essentially the same language (Athapascan), refer to themselves as Diné or Tineh, which means "The People."

THE CAPTIVE WARS

Spaniards contented themselves with partially defraying their livestock losses by also capturing women and children who would be placed upon the auction block and sold as menials to the ranchos and towns of New Mexico. The hostilities arising from the reciprocal slave raids set the stage for many of the problems which would confront military and civil authorities for the first two decades of United States occupation.

To fulfill his promise of protection for the Territory, General Kearny instructed his subordinate, the elected colonel of the First Regiment of Missouri Volunteers, Alexander W. Doniphan, to turn his attention to the Navajo menace. A rapid encircling movement of the tribe's domain was made, followed by a treaty on November 22, 1846 at *ojo del Oso* (Bear Springs). During the negotiations Doniphan gently rebuked the Diné for their constant raiding. He explained that, although the United States was at war with the Mexicans, he was still obligated to protect them. [3] This first treaty had little effect upon the Navajos and served only to form an acquaintance between the Americans and the Indians. As yet the Diné had no conception of the strength of the United States military; and because protection had been extended to the New Mexicans—for whom the Navajos held only enmity—the weakness of the former regime was associated with the newcomers. As a result, the Navajos continued their depredations, and other military expeditions followed in 1847 and 1848. [4]

The sustained hostilities from 1847-1849 had a profound effect upon the attitudes of the New Mexican people who were clamoring for the suppression of Navajo incursions. Plans were formulated, many for personal gain, ranging from total annihilation of the tribe to virtual enslavement of it. On every occasion New Mexican lawmakers pressed the army to undertake the task of subduing the Indians. But regiments were few and widely scattered in garrison duty, leaving New Mexico virtually unprotected. Frontier towns such as Abiquiu, Cubero, La Purgati, Cebolleta, and the pueblos of Jemez, Santo Domingo and Zuñi were struck at repeatedly by the Navajos. To elevate their beleaguered condition, the inhabitants of these and other towns frequently organized reprisal expeditions against the Indians. Although these forays were extremely hazardous, they were often very profitable, for as one early-day resident of Cebolleta recalled:

---

3. John T. Hughes. *Doniphan's Expedition: Containing an Account of the Conquest of New Mexico.* Cincinnati: 1847, pp. 71-72.

4. In the winter of 1846-47 Major W. H. T. Walker with a detachment of volunteers penetrated the Navajo country. One year later, Colonel Edward Newby conducted an unsuccessful campaign, terminating with a treaty which was never ratified. See A. B. Bender, "Frontier Defense in the Territory of New Mexico, 1846-1853," *New Mexico Historical Review*, Vol. IX, July 1934, pp. 252-53; also Frank D. Reeve, "The Government and the Navaho, 1846-1858," *ibid*, Vol. XIV, January 1939, pp. 82-115.

THE CAPTIVE WARS

> taking some [Navajo] man or woman captive . . . was one of the greatest rewards
> of a campaign, depending upon whether they were lucky with the captive whom
> they had risked their lives in taking. If the captives were of average age, or young
> and could be domesticated and taught, then their capture bore rich fruits.[5]

Regardless of how rewarding these volunteer excursions were, they invariably incited the Navajos to greater hostilities.

On July 22, 1849, James S. Calhoun[6] arrived in Santa Fe to assume the duties of Indian agent for New Mexico. He was directed by the Commissioner of Indian Affairs, William Medill, to gather data that would lead to an intelligent understanding of the Indian problems of the region. Calhoun plunged into the task of administering the affairs of peaceful tribes and suppressing hostile ones. Faced with halting Navajo hostilities, he sought council with headmen of the tribe, and went to work through a continual correspondence with the Commissioner of Indian Affairs and the Secretary of War to gain adequate protection for the New Mexican frontier. The new Indian agent sought the official establishment of a militia which could be on call at a moment's notice. However, Calhoun's movement for the organization of irregular companies would add the impetus to the Indian slave traffic which would cease only when the attention of the Nation had been focused upon it.

On July 19, 1851, Colonel Edwin V. Sumner[7] assumed command of the Ninth Military Department, a jurisdiction which included virtually all of the present-day states of Arizona and New Mexico. Sumner was instructed by the Secretary of War to cooperate with Calhoun—who by now was governor and Superintendent of Indian Affairs—in all matters dealing with the Indians. Despite this order, Sumner and Calhoun soon disagreed violently on points of major policy. Calhoun, on the day that he assumed governorship (March 3, 1851), issued a proclamation authorizing the raising of volunteer companies.[8]

---

5. C. C. Marino, "The Seboyetanos and the Navahos," *New Mexico Historical Review*, Vol. XXIX, January 1954, p. 11.

6. James S. Calhoun, the first territorial governor of New Mexico was a stanch whig, and professed a great admiration for General Zachary Taylor which gained for him a captaincy of a regiment of Georgia volunteers during the Mexican War. He served in this capacity from June until May, 1847, at which time he was commissioned a lieutenant colonel commanding a battalion of Georgia volunteers. With the opening of President Taylor's administration, Calhoun received the appointment of United States Indian Agent at Santa Fe; and on March 3, 1851 was inaugurated as governor, assuming the duties as Superintendent of Indian Affairs for the Territory. See Annie H. Abel (comp. & ed.), *Official Correspondence of James S. Calhoun while Indian Agent at Santa Fe and Superintendent of Indian Affairs in New Mexico*. Washington: 1915.

7. Although not a West Point graduate, Edwin V. Sumner was an eminent officer. He entered the service on March 3, 1818 as a second lieutenant of infantry, and served throughout the Black Hawk War. In 1833 he was transferred to the Second Dragoons, and began his service on the frontier with the rank of captain. Sumner served with General Scott throughout the Mexican War, and was commissioned lieutenant colonel of the First Dragoons. From 1851 until 1853, he was commander of the Ninth Military Department as well as serving a short term as civil governor of New Mexico. See R. E. Twitchell, *Leading Facts of New Mexican History*. Cedar Rapids: 1912, Vol. II, p. 286.

8. Abel, *op. cit.*, pp. 300-305.

But here the governor unwittingly furthered the cause of the slave-raiders. For the next five months "Calhoun's Volunteers" ranged the Navajo country, raking in a profitable harvest of captives and livestock.

The organizers of "Calhoun's Volunteers" hoped to expand their operations, and on July 20, 1851 the governor was presented with a petition prepared by the Territorial Legislature enumerating the great loss of property occasioned by Navajo forays. This document requested permission to raise additional volunteer companies, at no additional cost to the already strained territorial budget. According to this request the militia, armed with weapons furnished from regular army stores, would not receive their pay from territorial funds or from military appropriations, but instead would share equally "all the captives, and other spoils that may be taken."[9] When Sumner was presented with the petition, he clearly saw that here was one of the sources of the Indian troubles which had plagued New Mexico for generations. Volunteers had made habitual forays against the Navajos as freely as the Diné had against the settlements. Sumner felt that if hostilities were to be halted, private incursions had to be restrained and the Navajos put under military surveillance, both for their own protection as well as for that of the Anglo population of New Mexico.

Sumner's hands, however, were tied by the instructions from the War Department advising him to work in close accord with civil authority. Thus he could only accede to the request for arms—but with reservations. The weapons issued to the volunteers would be subject to recall by the commanding officer of the Ninth Military Department, and were never to be used in hostile forays into Indian country unless the militia was acting in conjunction with regular troops. Needless to say, these stipulations produced an unfavorable reaction among those who did not wish to be restricted in their raids against the Navajos.[10]

Not only were New Mexicans endeavoring to gain official sanction for their raids against the Navajos, but other Indian tribes as well. The pueblos of Zuñi and Jemez, both targets of Navajo aggressions, sought arms and assent from United States authorities. Even among the Navajos themselves certain individuals were seeking to gain from attacking their own brethren. A band of renegades, known to their tribesmen as *Dine-'ana'ih* (Enemy Navajos), who had long resided in the vicinity of Cebolleta, constantly allied themselves with the New Mexicans during the conduct of reprisal expeditions. This band and

9. *Ibid.*, pp. 386-87.
10. *Ibid.*, pp. 449-454.

THE CAPTIVE WARS

its leader, Antonio Sandoval,[11] had for a number of years maintained friendly relations with the frontier settlements of Cubero and Cebolleta; and had used this favored position to barter Navajo prisoners captured from more recalcitrant bands. It was because of his participation in the lucrative slave trade, and his outward demonstration of friendship toward the Navajos' sworn enemies, that Sandoval was held in disrepute by his own tribesmen.

Sandoval's role as slave-raider is high-lighted in many reports by military men and early-day travelers; and he was without a doubt the leading exponent of the trade in New Mexico. The Reverend Hiram Read, Baptist missionary, while visiting Cebolleta, described the chief's activities of March 11, 1851 in these terse words:

> A famous half-tamed Navajo [sic] Chief named Sandoval who resides in this vicinity, came into town today to sell some captives of his own nation which he has recently took prisoners. He sold one young man of 18 years of age for thirty (30) dollars.[12]

The great vigor with which Sandoval pursued his profession was pointed out in a letter by Governor Calhoun to Commissioner of Indian Affairs, Luke Lea, dated March 31, 1851:

> Sandoval, our Navajo friend near Cebolleta, returned about the 20th of the month from a visit to his brethren with eighteen captives, a quantity of stock and several scalps.[13]

Not only did reprisal expeditions pose a problem, but the wandering merchant frequently assumed the role of slave raider. Numerous traders still penetrated Indian country, and their clandestine operations were difficult to control and served only to agitate the natives. These individuals, who would sell their kith and kin, reaped enormous profits from the sale of the human commodity. The frontier towns of Abiquiu, Cebolleta and Cubero, were favorite rendezvous points for unscrupulous merchants, whose range was the whole extent of Navajoland, and even beyond.[14] These traders of human

---

11. Sandoval, known to his people as Hastin Késhgoli (Crooked Foot), was of the clan Tohedlíni or Crossed Waters People. He and his son acted as guides for Doniphan's expedition—the first United States military expedition into Navajoland, as well as subsequent ones. See Richard Van Valkenburgh, "Navajo Naataáni," *The Kiva*, Vol. XIII, No. 2, January 1948, p. 19.

12. Lansing P. Bloom (ed.), "The Rev. Hiram Read, Baptist Missionary to New Mexico," *New Mexico Historical Review*, Vol. XVII, April 1942, p. 133.

13. Calhoun to Luke Lea, March 31, 1851; *National Archives;* New Mexico Superintendency Papers, Record Group 75, Letters Received. Hereafter cited as NMSP, LR.

14. Mormon missionary, Daniel W. Jones, demonstrated the widespread activities of New Mexican traders during 1851 with the following account: "the people of New Mexico . . . were making annual trips, commencing with a few goods, trading on their way with either Navajos or Utes (generally with the Navajos) for horses, which they sold very cheap . . . These used-up horses were brought through and traded to the poorer Indians for children. This trading was continued into Lower [Southern] California, where the children . . . would be traded to the Mexican-Californians for other horses, goods or cash." Daniel W. Jones, *Forty Years Among the Indians*. Los Angeles: 1960, p. 47.

flesh were always anxious to keep hostilities alive between the United States and the Navajos, for then they would readily gain official sanction to assume the role of "volunteers"—their compensation being permission to keep and dispose of as they saw fit, all Navajo women and children which were captured during their campaigns.

By the end of May, 1852, Colonel Sumner could report that the Navajos had at least demonstrated a sincere desire to resume friendly relations. The relaxation of Navajo raids was due, no doubt, to the establishment of Fort Defiance in September of 1851.[15] For the next few years a precarious peace existed. But many incidents involving the taking of captives occurred between the Navajos and the New Mexicans which threatened to erupt into open warfare. One such incident took place on the night of May 3, 1853, as a sheep owner named Ramon Martín, his two sons, María and Librado, and four herders, were watching over their flock near Chamas. From out of the underbrush a volley of shots brought down Señor Martín, mortally wounded. María, upon seeing his father shot, ran for cover and hid until morning. From his place of concealment the boy saw four Navajos approach the sheep pen and round up his brother and the four other shepherds, as another Indian secured the horses. Each youth was then roped about the neck and led away for about a quarter of a mile to a watering place. Three of the captives were then set free and told in broken Spanish to return and inform their people that, when the Mexicans gave up a paint horse and a mule stolen from the Navajos, the animals would be returned to the owners and the two captive boys given up. With the delivery of these words, the Navajos rode off with Librado and the other boy.[16]

Informed of the murder of Martín and the kidnapping of the two boys, Governor William Carr Lane immediately saw the danger inherent in the explosive situation and ordered Donaciaro Vigil, Territorial Secretary and a man thoroughly familiar with the Navajos, to ascertain the identity of the murderers; and proclaim to the tribe that failure to give up the culprits and captives would be considered a justifiable cause of war.[17] In compliance with the Governor's orders, Vigil proceeded to the Navajo country and parleyed with Chiefs Armijo and Aguila Negra on May 17. Upon receipt of the Governor's ultimatum, the Navajos released the two boys and promised to

---

15. Departmental Order No. 29, September 18, 1851; *National Archives;* Fort Defiance Post Returns, Record Group 98.

16. John Griener to William C. Lane, (n.d.); NMSP, LR.

17. William C. Lane to Donaciaro Vigil, May 9, 1853; *ibid.*

THE CAPTIVE WARS

cooperate in the apprehension of the culprits.[18] Fortunately for New Mexico, the tensions eased and a period of watchful co-existence followed.

Not only were the Diné intimidated by a military garrison in their country, but they were held in check by the constant threat which the Army reiterated—that unless the Indians kept the peace "the Mexicans, the Pueblos, Sandoval's people and the Americans would be let loose upon them, their flocks seized, their men killed, their women and children taken prisoner." That the commanding officer of the new post in Navajoland, Captain Henry L. Kendrick, was an advocate of this peace-keeping method is exemplified in a letter to the Assistant Adjutant General of New Mexico, in which he stated:

> I feel constrained to say that the most efficient rod in terrorem to be held over these people is the fear of a permission being given to the Mexicans to make captives of Navajoes and to retain them, a permission at once wise and philanthropic and one which would at an early date settle the question.[19]

By 1857, however, Kendrick's "wise and philanthropic" solution to the Navajo problem was beginning to break down. War finally erupted early in 1858, due in large measure to the insidious activities of slave-raiders.

In February of that year the Indians were put in a belligerent mood by an attack by New Mexicans upon a peaceful band of Navajos near Albuquerque. The following month, Navajos were again attacked by another party of New Mexicans and Utes who set out from Abiquiu in pursuit of animals believed stolen by the Navajos. Instead of following the trail left by the thieves, the pursuers struck directly into Navajo country and attacked the first party of Indians seen. As usual the attackers redeemed their losses by taking captives who were sold upon the party's return to Abiquiu.[20] The real war, however, broke out at Fort Defiance and was precipitated indirectly by the usual cause—slaves. On July 12, 1858 a Negro slave belonging to the post commander, Major W. T. H. Brooks, was slain by a Navajo; and the return of the murderer was demanded of Chief Zarcillas Largos. Instead, the Indian suggested that traditional blood money be paid; but this would not satisfy Major Brooks, and the Navajos were given twenty days to produce the killer. The Diné attempted to deceive the Major by presenting the body of a Mexican slave. The Major denied that the corpse was that of the culprit, and this was an insult to Navajo integrity and a provocation for war.

---

18. Annie H. Abel (ed.), "Indian Affairs in New Mexico Under the Administration of William Carr Lane," *New Mexico Historical Review*, Vol. XVI, July 1941, p. 341.
19. Capt. H. L. Kendrick to Lt. S. D. Sturgis, June 11, 1853; *National Archives*, Records of the War Department, Department of New Mexico, Record Group 98, Letters Received. Hereafter cited as Department of New Mexico.
20. John Ward to Samuel M. Yost, April 9, 1858; *National Archives*, Records of the New Mexico Superintendency of Indian Affairs, Record Group 75, Letters Received from Agencies. Hereafter cited as RNMS.

THE CAPTIVE WARS

Hostilities began in August, and from then until December the Navajo country was scoured by military expeditions. Corn fields were burned, hogans demolished, and hostiles sent retreating for the safety of the more inaccessible areas of Navajoland. By Christmas the Indians had felt the full impact of the United States Army and sued for peace. A new treaty was proposed and, in the negotiations which followed, the return of captives were demanded of the Navajos by Department Commander, Colonel Benjamin L. E. Bonneville. As usual, the Indians failed to comply with the stipulations and the Government overlooked ratification. During the early months of 1859 depredations continued, and by fall had extended to the vicinity of the Rio San Juan in the country of the Utes. War parties from both tribes crossed and recrossed the ancient war trails leading from Navajoland northward into Ute country. Numerous women and children from both nations were carried into captivity and sold to New Mexican slave procurers.[21]

By January, 1860 the Mexican population of the Territory had become discontented over the lack of adequate military protection from Navajo incursions. Again the traditional reprisal expeditions were organized—many in league with Ute war parties—and the Navajo country was scoured for sheep, horses and slaves. Although the Indian Department in New Mexico had always taken a dim view of the slave trade, and saw it as a source of constant hostility, its hands were tied. Superintendent of Indian Affairs, James L. Collins, wrote to Commissioner Greenwood of the futility of trying to reclaim the captives:

> I have, so far as I could, prevented the purchase, but I find it impossible to do so entirely, and when once in the possession of the Mexicans it is next to impossible to recover them.[22]

Despite Collins' opposition to slave taking and the organization of volunteer expeditions, the evil continued. In mid-June a party of 300 men were organized by Ramon Baca of Cebolleta for the expressed purpose of invading the Navajo country. By the first week of July the group had penetrated the Chusca Mountains where they picked up the trail of a party of Navajos. Giving chase, the expedition drove the Indians through Washington Pass, northeast of Fort Defiance, and succeeded in capturing 2,000 sheep, fifty horses, and fourteen women and children.[23] Not all of the volunteer expeditions were as lucky as Baca's, however. Late in June a party of about

---

21. *Annual Report of the Commissioner of Indian Affairs, 1859.* Washington: 1859, p. 717.
22. J. L. Collins to A. B. Greenwood, January 8, 1860; RNMS.
23. (Santa Fe), *Weekly Gazette*, July 18, 1860, p. 2, col. 1-2.

THE CAPTIVE WARS

eighty New Mexicans was surprised by Navajos at Laguna Grande on the east side of Chusca. There were thirty killed and thirteen wounded, and the survivors were lucky to make their way back to Fort Defiance.[24]

Depredations continued until the outbreak of the Civil War, at which time Indian conditions in New Mexico grew worse. The Comanches and Kiowas on the east, Apaches to the south and west, and the Navajos in the north ran riot as posts were abandoned and officers and troops defected to the South. To this was added another menace: Texas Confederates under General Henry H. Sibley were marching up the Rio Grande late in 1861, driving the Union forces before them. During their brief occupation of the Territory the Texans came face-to-face with the Navajos, who made no distinction between soldiers in blue or grey. Sibley had been in the Territory but a short time when he formulized a plan to end the Indian problem—legal enslavement of all hostile tribes.[25] The Confederates, however, were never to realize their plans for the conquest of the desert Southwest, nor the enslavement of the Indians. From out of the west marched the California Column under the command of General James H. Carleton, and from the north came Colorado Volunteers led by Colonel John B. Slough, to crush the Texans at Glorieta Pass in February, 1862. The Civil War had come and gone in New Mexico, but here the slavery issue was not to be settled by the victory of Northern principles over Southern.

The system of peonage and Indian slavery was not affected by the Emancipation Proclamation, as both were never regarded as involuntary servitude. Peonage was recognized in the Territory by the "Law Regulating Contracts between Masters and Servants," passed by the legislative assembly in 1858 and 1859. This act provided that a peon receive a wage of five dollars a month, with which he was expected to provide for his family. Since he drew all his subsistence from his master, the peon's debts continually grew until a life of servitude invariably resulted.[26] Among New Mexicans no distinction was made between peonage and the enslavement of Indians. Both were considered as voluntary servitude in the statutes of the Territory and in the traditional way of thinking. But a distinction was very apparent, even to the most casual of observers. Peons were not bought and sold as chattel; but Indians, particularly Navajos and Apaches, were traded as if they were swine or sheep. Slave owning was not confined to the wealthier families, for any house-holder who could raise $150 could purchase a Navajo slave, and many

---

24. J. L. Collins to A. B. Greenwood, July 27, 1860; NMSP, LR.

25 *The War of the Rebellion: A Compilation of the Official Records of the Union & Confederate Armies.* Washington: 1883. Series I, Vol. IX, p. 512.

26. W W. H. Davis, *El Gringo: or New Mexico & Her People.* Santa Fe: 1938, p. 98.

had four or five. Estimates of Navajo slaves in the Territory varied from as few as 500 to as many as 6,000. It was claimed that in Santa Fe alone, 500 Navajos were held in bondage.[27] Many of the prominent and influential citizens of the Territory were the leading slave holders. Governors, federal officials and even Indian agents and Superintendents owned Navajo menials.

Although the New Mexicans are accredited with holding the greater number of slaves, the Indians also had their share. The Navajos took hundreds of captives from the New Mexicans and from various peripheral tribes. The treatment of these individuals, and their integration, was governed by the social structure of the Navajo. The number of clans composing the tribe varied from fifty to sixty according to interpretation,[28] including some which were considered alien or "slave clans" such as the Mexican, Ute, Zuñi, and Paiute.[29] Those originated as aliens came into the tribe, either as captives or by their own volition, and through inter-marriage and concubinage. As these groups grew in number new clans were formed.

The social organization of the Navajo did not encourage slavery as it was commonly regarded during the period of the Civil War. While many captives were reduced to servitude, for the most part they and their offspring were absorbed into the tribe within a few generations and thus lost their servile status.[30] The sex of a captive usually decided the issue between amalgamation or slavery. Females were often taken in marriage, and were assigned a proper clan affiliation as tribal members. Males, however, enjoyed no process of amalgamation; they were always slaves and suffered every indignity. Many were emasculated, some had their tongues removed to prevent them from talking if recaptured, and others had their ears cut off to mark their servile status.[31] The life of a slave could be taken at any time by his master, or he could be sold or traded at will. If his captor was well-to-do, he kept the prisoner;

27. Estimates of the number of Indians held in bondage are variable due to the fact that Indian slaves were easily amalgamated with the Mexican population. For estimates on numbers of Indian slaves held throughout the Territory, see *Condition of the Tribes, 1867*. Washington: 1867, pp. 332, 334. Also *Annual Report of the Commissioner of Indian Affairs, 1866*. Washington: 1866, p. 137.

28. The number of clans depend entirely upon interpretation by past Navajo scholars. Washington Matthews recorded 51; Berard Haile of the Franciscan Fathers listed 58; and Gladys Reichard, 64.

29. The presence of "slave clans" points to a life of marauding for the Navajos, whose specific aim was the taking of captives and other possessions. These clans, no doubt were swelled by the arrival of peoples, who, from time to time found sanctuary with the Navajos. It is generally accepted that many pueblo peoples found refuge with the Navajos following the rebellion of 1680 and the Spanish Reconquest that ensued. See Berard Haile, Ethnographic Notes, Box 5, folder marked "Family Relationships," in the *Haile Collection*, University of Arizona, Special Collections.

30. For years a distinction was thought to have existed between "real" and "slave" clans. But Reichard found that among 3,500 Navajos which she interviewed, not one claimed to have belonged to a slave clan. It may be assumed therefore, that both clan types now possess the same status. Gladys A. Reichard. *Social Life of the Navajo Indians*. New York: 1929, p. 15.

31. William R. Palmer, "Pahute Indian Government & Laws," *Utah Historical Quarterly*, April 1929, p. 40.

THE CAPTIVE WARS

otherwise he was traded to some *"rico"* of the tribe.

Incited by the raids of New Mexican irregulars, the Indian situation of the Territory was—by fall of 1862—entirely out of hand; and the military finally were compelled to take steps to curtail slave raiding. On September 9, General Orders No. 81 were issued from Department Headquarters at Santa Fe:

> ...Whenever the Commander of any post receives information that captives from any Indian tribe have been sold into slavery, he will cause them to be reclaimed, and to be kept at his post subject to the orders of the Superintendent of Indian Affairs, and will report the names of both sellers and purchasers in order that proceedings may be instituted against them.[32]

Because these privately sponsored expeditions did not discriminate between "friendly and the unfriendly Indians," additional orders were issued in early October directing post and district commanders to restrict *any* irregular forces which were not duly authorized by the commander of the Department.[33] The steps, however, were somewhat belated; for now the Navajos were beyond all restraint.

The Navajos and Mescalero Apaches realized that the attentions of the Army had been diverted to repelling the Confederate invasion, and they stepped up depredations. But the threat from Texas passed; and General James H. Carleton, veteran Indian fighter and organizer of the "California Column," was able to launch his plan for the pacification of the Indians. The New Mexican Volunteers, organized to repell the southern invasion, were put under the command of one of the Territory's leading citizens—Colonel Christopher Carson, who ruthlessly applied sword and torch to the Indian country. The roundup of the Mescaleros began in January of 1863, and the "Long Walk" of the Navajos followed six months later. Both terminated at a disease-ridden reservation upon the banks of the Pecos River in east-central New Mexico—known as Bosque Redondo.[34] Certain unscrupulous individuals realized that the roundup of the Navajos would end forever their slave trading activities and took this last opportunity to obtain a few more menials—with the blessings of the military, who officially sanctioned such conduct.

During the campaign, the Navajo country was alive with New Mexicans seeking women and children who would be ruthlessly snatched from groups of

---

32. A copy of General Orders No. 81, Department of New Mexico, Sept. 9, 1862, is found in *NMSP*, LR, 1864-65.

33. J. C. Shaw To Benjamin C. Cutler, Oct. 6, 1862; *NMSP*, LR, 1862.

34. The establishment of the Bosque Redondo Reservation was recommended by the Office of Indian Affairs on January 14, 1864, and laid before the President and approved by him on January 16, 1864, For many of the official reports and correspondence relative to Carleton's campaign against the Mescaleros and the Navajos, and the establishment of Bosque Redondo, see *Condition of the Tribes*, 1867, *op. cit.*

FORT DEFIANCE, 1855   (*Schoolcraft, Vol. IV.*)

NAVAJO PRISONERS AT BOSQUE REDONDO.   (*National Archives*)

THE CAPTIVE WARS

Indians making their way to Forts Wingate and Canby to surrender.[35] Companies of irregulars from Cubero, Cebolleta, and Abiquiu made frequent inroads upon the Navajos. One such company of volunteers was recruited by Ramón A. Baca of Cebolleta, and was highly successful in its forays, for "they took hundreds of prisoners, who, as was the custom . . . were sold as domestics all over the Territory, sometimes at very high prices."[36]

The Diné's old enemies from across the Rio San Juan also struck the helpless Navajos. Kit Carson reported large concentrations of Ute warriors ranging the country in search of captives,[37] and even employed them as scouts and guides. In true mountain man fashion, Carson wanted to reward his Ute allies for "their continued zeal and activity" in the Navajo campaigns by permitting them to retain women and children. The "Rope Thrower" was convinced that captives disposed of in this manner would be better off than at Bosque Redondo, as the Utes would sell them to Mexican families who would care for them; thus they would "cease to require any further attention on the part of the Government." He also advocated distributing the captive Navajos as servants to New Mexican families in order to break up "that collectiveness of interest as a tribe which they will retain if kept together" at Bosque Redondo.[38] These ideas were promptly altered when Carleton informed Carson on April 18, 1863, that:

> *all* prisoners which are captured by the troops or employes of your command will be sent to Santa Fe, by the first practicable opportunity after they are, from time to time, brought in as prisoners. *There must be no exception to this rule.*[39]

Carleton was not the only person concerned with the welfare of the Navajos, as well as other tribes. In Washington there was a growing suspicion that many Indian wars were provoked by the "aggressions of lawless white men;" that the number of Indians was growing steadily less, due to disease, and the "cruel treatment on the part of the whites—both by irresponsible persons and by government officials," and by the ever-increasing encroachment of the westward movement upon the domain of the Red Man. On March 3, 1865, a Joint Special Committee of the two Houses of Congress was appointed to inquire into these conditions. The work which this committee undertook was so immense—covering the problems of a continent—that the holding of regular hearings was impossible. Instead, a circulating letter was sent to

---

35. *Condition of the Tribes, 1867*, p. 336.
36. Nathan Bibo, "Reminiscence of Early Days in New Mexico," (Albuquerque) *Evening Herald*, June 11, 1922.
37. *Official Records, op. cit.*, Series I, Vol. XXVI, pp. 233-234.
38. *Ibid.*
39. *Condition of the Tribes, op. cit.*, p. 128.

regular Army officers, Indian agents, and superintendents, inquiring into their knowledge of Indian affairs. The Special Committee was split into three divisions, and its chairman—Senator James R. Doolittle (Wis.), Vice-President Lafayette S. Foster, and Representative Lewis W. Ross (Ill.) were assigned New Mexico, Utah, Colorado, Indian Territory, and the state of Kansas.[40] The report issued by Doolittle and his colleagues had severe repercussions in the Halls of Congress. It revealed for the first time the depth of the trouble caused by the slave trade, and threatened to split asunder the political foundations of the Territory of New Mexico.

The Doolittle Committee exposed the fact that New Mexicans for years had made slave raids into Navajo country, and that captives brought back from these raids were auctioned off as if they were livestock. To such an extent had this prevailed that thousands of women and children were held as servants in New Mexican homes. Previous to the Civil War, the price of these menials varied from $75 to $150; but, with the increased military concentration and the establishment of Bosque Redondo, a tremendous rise in price had occurred. According to Chief Justice Kirby Benedict, Navajo captives now were being auctioned off for $400 apiece.[41] On July 4, 1865, Judge Benedict presented his statement to the Doolittle Committee. His statement revealed that many of the people holding Indian slaves were the most respected citizens in Territorial affairs. The judge further pointed out that these individuals were alarmed at the increasing interest in the Indian slavery question, and were fearful of court action. Benedict pointed the finger of accusation at the family of Governor Henry Connelly and at the Superintendent of Indian Affairs— Felipe Delgado—and even Associate Justice Hubbell was accused of selling an Indian woman.[42] General Carleton's report to the Committee substantiated Benedict's claims, and added the detail that many leading citizens objected to the establishment of the Fort Sumner reservation because it would put a stop to the slave raids. They were fearful also, he said, that a cut in the military force would ensue, reducing the millions of dollars annually expended in the Territory.[43]

The legality of the system of peonage and Indian slavery was next analyzed. Summoning his legal knowledge, Justice Benedict stated that he knew "of no law in this territory by which property in Navajo or other Indian can be recognized in any person whatever, any more than property can be

---

40. *Ibid.*, pp. 3-4.
41. *Ibid.*, pp. 225-226.
42. *Ibid.*
43. *Ibid.*, p. 324.

THE CAPTIVE WARS

recognized in the freest white man or black man." In several court proceedings, the judge said, he had tried to uphold this conviction. In 1855, while holding district court in Valencia County, a *habeas corpus* case was brought before his bench by a wealthy woman. She claimed the possession and services of a Navajo girl, then twelve, whom she had held for seven years. Benedict judged the girl to be a free person. But such cases were few in New Mexico. Although the courts—at least those of Benedict's—were available to the Indian slave or peon, they were usually so intimidated by their masters and the conditions with which they lived, that few—if any—sought legal aid.[44]

After the Civil War, men of national prominence believed that the Emancipation Proclamation was all-embracing, including white, black, and red peoples. When the Doolittle Committee revealed that slavery was still very much in effect in New Mexico, the ship of state was violently rocked. "Free Soiler" and ardent reconstructionist, Senator Charles Sumner of Massachusetts, delivered from the floor of Congress a speech denouncing the evils of the system. In this speech he condemned General Carleton and Governor Henry Connelly for letting it persist. The New Mexican delegate to Congress, J. Francisco Chavez, climbed on the bandwagon. A slave owner himself, Chavez leveled allegations at Connelly and Carleton. A few people in the Territory rushed to the defense, and on February 2, 1867, Chavez's and Sumner's accusations were answered by an open letter in the *Santa Fe Gazette:*

44. *Ibid.*, p. 326.

NAVAJO CAMP SCENE AT BOSQUE REDONDO.   (*National Archives*)

THE CAPTIVE WARS

General Carleton and Governor Connelly and those who have cooperated with them in New Mexico, have uniformly and persistently done all they could have done to break up the trade in Indian captives, and if they have not done as much as you gentlemen of the east think . . . you ought to take into consideration the difficulties by which they were surrounded.

The *Gazette* next leveled an attack at Chavez. He was charged with retaining more peons and Indian slaves than any other householder in the Territory; and his mother's family was also accused of holding peons. Together, it was charged, the Chavez family exerted an almost insurmountable obstacle to overcoming the insidious practice.[45]

The evils of Indian slavery had at last been exposed, and in Washington the wheels of justice began to turn. On March 2, 1867, Congress passed an act to abolish and "forever prohibit the system of Peonage in the Territory of New Mexico and other parts of the United States." This inclusive act renounced all traditions, laws, and orders permitting bondage which had persisted since the days of the Spanish, and set severe penalties for violators. The new law, however, served only to draw people's attention to the evil; it liberated few if any slaves. In Santa Fé, on June 10, 1868, acting Governor Herman H. Heath proclaimed, via a circular, his recognition of the newly passed act and reiterated the penalties awaiting those persons still holding slaves and peons. Heath also requested the aid of all civil officers and "all true and loyal citizens" of the Territory in stamping out this "crime against mankind."[46] Still the people tenaciously held to their traditional system of slavery, and it was seen that more drastic measures would have to be resorted to if the goals of the Congressional and Territorial laws were to be reached.

The deciding measure was adopted on July 27, 1868, when Congress passed Joint Resolution No. 65. This resolution invested power in the hands of a man capable of bringing swift results—the commanding general of the United States Army. Lieutenant General William T. Sherman now was authorized to use the most efficient means at his disposal to reclaim from bondage the women and children of the Navajo tribe and return them to their reservation.[47]

The actions of Congress had a profound effect on the citizens of New Mexico. Thousands of Indians were held throughout the Territory, many by prominent families who would resist any Congressional attempt to liberate their "property." When the United States District Attorney was directed to

45. (Santa Fe) *Gazette*, February 2, 1867.
46. Proclamation abolishing involuntary servitude in New Mexico issued by Acting Governor Herman H. Heath, June 10, 1868; in Holliday Collection, Arizona Pioneers' Historical Society, Tucson, Arizona.
47. (Santa Fe) *New Mexican*, August 6, 1868.

THE CAPTIVE WARS

commence grand jury investigations, three hundred witnesses were subpoenaed from Taos, Santa Fe, and Rio Arriba Counties. The hearings were a fiasco. Those witnesses owning Indian slaves declined to testify; and grand jurors themselves owned Indians and were not sympathetic to the proceedings; and those personally affected by the hearings mustered their last energies to withstand the military and civil investigators. Finally, on August 6, the *Santa Fe New Mexican* published a "humanitarian plea" in answer to General Sherman and the court sessions:

> . . . The Navajos are a savage and barbarous people. These captives from this tribe have now for years lived among civilized people; have learned the language of the country, have become christianized—all being Catholics; and their habits have become those of the civilized race among whom they dwell, and one in fifty of them desire to leave their civilized life for a renewal of the barbarous and uncivilized life of their tribes. They prefer a life among our people to one among their own. They are free—they may hire to any person whom they may please to serve; but it is certain, that, constituted as they are most if not all of these who come under the classification of "Navajo captives," prefer to remain in homes where they have so long been domesticated, and where they possess the advantages not only of religion, but of civilized life . . . It becomes then a serious question of humanity, whether those Navajos who are now voluntarily living among our people . . . shall be forced back upon savage life against their will . . ., or whether, by voluntary action they shall remain as they are, the objects of care by the church, and civil protection by the Territory.[48]

General Sherman did not heed this plea; and from his St. Louis headquarters ordered Major General George W. Getty, commander of the District of New Mexico, to convey to the Navajos the intentions of the Army to comply with the recently passed laws "in justice to the women and children affected." Sherman further urged that should any of the tribe desire to search for relatives held in bondage, Getty would permit them and provide for it out of the funds which he held in trust for the Navajo people, and act as guardian for any women and children that may be returned and see that they reached their tribe safely.[49]

But the Navajos had little desire to search the settlements of New Mexico for their women and children. They had been hopelessly whipped into submission; their sheep and horses taken from them; as a tribe they had been hounded into capitulation and then herded to a wretched reservation on the banks of the Pecos. There, the Diné still suffered from slave-raiders. New Mexicans, Comanches and Kiowas made incursions against them. Now the

---

48. *Ibid.*
49. *Ibid.*, Sept. 26, 1868.

NAVAJO CAPTIVE—BOSQUE
REDONDO. (*Smithsonian Inst.*)

Navajos desired only to be returned to their homeland. Their women and children, still held in captivity among New Mexican families, would have to make their own way to freedom—which many did—or remain where they were and lose their identity as their blood gradually mingled with that of their captors.

The Diné were granted their desire at Fort Sumner on June 1, 1868, when Peace Commissioners William T. Sherman and Colonel Samuel F. Tappen signed the last treaty between the tribe and the United States government which granted their release and provided for the Diné's removal to a reservation set aside for them in their homeland.[50] At sunrise on June 15, 1868, the pitiful remnants of the once "Lords of New Mexico" started on the long trek back to their picturesque domain, where they have remained ever since in comparative harmony with the surrounding tribes and the White Men who still cast covetous glances at their scenic and rich lands.

50. William A. Keleher, Turmoil in New Mexico. Santa Fe: 1952, pp. 464-467.

NAVAJO BRAVE — BOSQUE
REDONDO. (*Smithsonian Inst.*)

NAVAJO BRAVE — BOSQUE
REDONDO. (*Smithsonian Inst.*)

NEW LIGHT ON AN OLD MURDER

By W. W. ROBINSON

We have yet to examine the writings of an author who, in our opinion, has Mr. Robinson's unique ability to express so much in so few words. The following article, reprinted—with permission—from Volume XV Number 1 (1963) of *Manuscripts*, is indicative of this fortunate quality in the writings of the Southland's distinguished author of California regional history. In this paper Mr. Robinson depicts an entirely new and serviceable approach to research procedure. We believe this to be the most helpful article of its kind that we have ever read.

RECENTLY I HAD OCCASION TO RUN DOWN, for publication, the details of a murder committed in 1851—111 years ago—in Cajon Pass. Cajon Pass was and is the connecting link between the grim Mojave Desert and the lush San Bernardino Valley in Southern California.

The scene of the murder of Irishman Patrick McSwiggen and Creek Indian Sam was then in Los Angeles County. Today it is in San Bernardino County. Accordingly, I sought out certain old criminal files in the office of the County Clerk of Los Angeles County. The proceedings were referred to as "the Lugo Case" or, more exactly, as "The People of the State of California versus Francisco Lugo, et al".

With some difficulty I found the papers in the case. They were in the old Hall of Records in Los Angeles and were in the unnumbered files of the Court of Sessions. This Court had been established in 1850 in each of the original California counties. In the Lugo Case were 171 handwritten pages, yellowing sheets, the ink badly spread, the writing often on both sides of the paper and hard to read. But what a treasure of colorful and factual detail they revealed!

The Lugo Case, it should be explained, had been mentioned briefly and confusingly in California county histories, like Thompson & West's and in early-day reminiscences. Always it was referred to as an important and sensational affair, but the details given were vague and contradictory. The only good account was one written by the attorney for the defense—fifty years after the events. His exciting story was published in 1926 in New Orleans in a book so rare I was determined to have it republished. Or, if that was not possible, to go to the original sources and write my own story of the killing and the extraordinary impact it had on the three thousand inhabitants of Los Angeles. When permission was not immediately forthcoming I began to dig into primary source material—official records—especially since bookseller Glen

NEW LIGHT ON AN OLD MURDER

Dawson was eager to publish the story of the Lugo Case in his "Famous California Trials" series. It was fortunate I did so, for what I found greatly supplemented what had been printed.

Out of my "find" of 171 handwritten pages came the vivid testimony of a procession of rancheros, vaqueros, and soldiers who were in the vicinity of the Cajon Pass at the time of the murder. The murder itself was an aftermath of a raid by a party of thirty or forty Ute Indians who swept down the Pass on horseback one moonlight night and drove off several hundred of the finest horses of José María Lugo, one of the owners of the huge Rancho San Bernardino, member of a famous Southern California family. Charged with the murder were his two young sons, both of whom participated in the pursuit of the Indians. They were the grandsons of Antonio María Lugo, wealthiest cattle and land owner in the southern part of the state, a man who symbolized the California ranchero and invariably rode, Spanish style, with sword attached to his saddle.

My first glance at the papers in the case was rewarding for I came upon the coroner's inquest, which probably had not been looked at for 111 years. From it I was able to make this excerpt for my story:

The white man's clothes had been drawn up over his head and his pockets were turned inside out. Further examination of the corpse showed the head and face much bruised, as from being dragged over the rocks. There was a bullet wound and clotted blood on the head, and the face was black. The livid mark on one leg could have been caused by a rope. A few yards away was a hat with a small bullet hole, and upon the tail of the wagon there were spots of blood. The body of the Indian, on the other side of the trail, also gave evidence of having been dragged.

How much more revealing these precise details than merely the historical comment that "Two men were murdered in Cajon Pass."

Among the papers was the climactic statement of the star witness for the prosecution, a page and a half of lively and incriminating description. Also there were oddities of testimony by other men, including the casual mention of swords and lances as weapons, in addition to rifles and pistols. One man avowed that the murdered Indian could not have been a Ute for he had eyebrows and eyelashes. In this case, too, were the sprawling signatures of many Los Angeles pioneers, lawyers and judges, as well as several bailbonds signed by X's.

I have no intention of telling here the story of the Lugo Case, or its outcome, or the fact that it involved street mobs bent on hangings, tense

NEW LIGHT ON AN OLD MURDER

feelings arising from race prejudice, a gang of bandits, savage Indian justice, a massacre, and an attempted assassination of the prosecutor. Enough to say that the examination of official records revealed a tremendous story and provided it with spice and broad color as well as factual background.

My favorite official records in California are those of the County Clerk's Office, filled with lawsuits and criminal proceedings—like the Lugo Case—and with the administration of estates; those of the County Recorder's Office, wherein is unfolded the exact land-ownership story; those of the United States Land Office, with its revelation of the first passing into private hands of public lands of the district; and the land-grant files of the United States District Court in San Francisco—its papers untouched by earthquake or fire—in which is the key to the story of each Spanish or Mexican rancho in California. (The last mentioned records of the United States District Court were transferred, under order of May 7, 1962, to the Bancroft Library at Berkeley, California.) There are other official records of city, county, state, and United States that on occasion need to be drawn upon. The County Surveyor may offer a surprise in his early-day maps, with their exact location of roads, lakes, and homes no longer in existence. The City Clerk may delight you with an ordinance revealing a way of life that has passed, such as one restricting the riding of horses at a speed greater than eight miles an hour, or the one forbidding persons under the age of eighteen from driving hacks, or the one establishing the boundaries of the local "redlight district." The Board of Supervisors has the material out of which a social history of a county may be partly compiled. Of course the state and national archives in California and Washington are in themselves vast fields for historical research.

The local historian who consults some of these easily available sources will be rewarded. Speaking personally, I find great satisfaction in the results of a close study of the minutes or proceedings of the city council (the *ayuntamiento*) of the Pueblo of Los Angeles during the Mexican period and their continuation into the early American period. I looked up every reference made to Indians of the area. Out of this study came a small book—*The Indians of Los Angeles: Study of the Liquidation of a People*— published in 1952. It told exactly what happened to the brown-skinned villagers of Yangna, the location of which was near the first plaza of Los Angeles. It was partly at variance with what had already been written by men who failed to consult original sources. It quoted the ordinance of 1850 which established the auction block by which Indian prisoners, arrested for drunkenness, were offered for private service to the highest bidder, a process that speeded the death of the simple Shoshoneans.

NEW LIGHT ON AN OLD MURDER

The same minutes or proceedings revealed the full story of Ord's Survey, which was the first mapping of Los Angeles' downtown area, made in 1849 to enable the townsmen to go into the real estate business. This story, vital to the account of the rise of a city that today is the third in size in the United States, appeared in the September-December, 1937, issue of the *Quarterly* of the Historical Society of Southern California, under the title of "Story of Ord's Survey, as Disclosed by the Los Angeles Archives." It began with the council's request to the Territorial Government for the services of a surveyor. It continued to the results of the first auction of lots—and beyond.

When doing the research for *Lawyers of Los Angeles*, published in 1959, I hoped to find the names of the first Los Angeles residents admitted to the bar under the judicial system installed by the first American legislature. Naturally I went to the office of County Clerk Harold J. Ostly, a friendly man interested in history. He allowed me to look over the volumes of the minutes of the District Court which he had in his own personal office for safekeeping. Presently I found that at the first session of this court, held June 5, 1850, four Angelenos were admitted to practice. A photostat of the record of this historic event was obtained for publication.

It was while looking through the volumes in County Clerk Ostly's office that I made an interesting discovery—typical of the discoveries that any researcher makes amid early-vintage official records. Ostly had stored on his shelves a variety of oddities that had found their way to him over the years, old books that no one ever called for or seemed to know about. He was thinking about their transfer to the new courthouse which was almost ready for occupation. At the bottom of one pile within a glass case were two small books, one with a red cover. They had been given Ostly some time before when the office of the Board of Supervisors was being treated to a housecleaning. A glance at them showed me what they were—in spite of the rather meaningless title of "List of Property Owners in Los Angeles County." They were the first assessment roll of the county, prepared in 1850, extremely valuable source material—and missing for half a century. The result? Ostly saw to it that the roll and other rarities in his office were deposited in the Los Angeles County Law Library under strict custodianship.

Many other illustrations might be given of the personal use of official records to establish facts important or interesting in local and regional history. To find substantial proof that Rancho San Pedro in Los Angeles County was California's first real rancho seemed worthwhile. To be the first person to uncover the story of Inglewood's, Culver City's, and Whittier's first settlers

COUNTY JUDGE AGUSTIN OLVERA

Justice of the Peace,
JONATHAN R. SCOTT

COUNTY ATTORNEY BENJAMIN HAYES,
who prosecuted the Lugos.

J. LANCASTER BRENT
who defended the Lugos.

NEW LIGHT ON AN OLD MURDER

gave me pleasure. To tell for the first time how Pershing Square in downtown Los Angeles got its start gave a thrill. To publish first the chain of title of Santa Catalina Island seemed a minor but pleasant achievement. To reveal new facets of San Fernando Valley's early history gave me a glow of satisfaction. To bring to light old wills drawn in the Spanish or Mexican period, like that of Don Bartolo Tapia which left Rancho Malibu and a collection of the images of saints to "my old woman," was a pleasure. All these are typical of the satisfactions the local historian draws from his digging into the public records of city, county, state, or federal governments.

In emphasizing the use of public and official records I have no wish to underestimate the importance of using all other sources whether written or not. Interviewing pioneers is important and, with the passing of the years after the interviews, will seem increasingly so. However, I defer that sometimes thrilling activity to the last, when undertaking a research and writing project. This is because the reminiscences of "old-timers" are so often unreliable. By putting the personal interview last, I am then able to ask the right questions and to evaluate the answers.

How the worker in local history uses the results of his discoveries in primary source material really determines their value. If he maintains a broad perspective and keeps the quality of his writing high, what he has to say about a small or even minute area becomes a part of the history of the state and the nation. Donald Culross Peattie in the late 1930's wrote the biography of a square mile of Illinois land in so effective a manner that it really summed up the story of America. His *A Prairie Grove*, published by Simon and Schuster, attracted the attention of the reading public of the entire country and is still being circulated and read.

The local historian, drawing upon official records for factual data and using them to the best of his ability, may not be a Peattie. He may honestly feel, however, that he has made a useful and perhaps exciting contribution to the community, the county, and the state.

"Little White Chieftain"

J.B.G. - '63

CLARENCE A. ELLSWORTH

"LITTLE WHITE CHIEFTAIN"

By IRON EYES CODY

No one is better qualified to write of the life and accomplishments of Clarence Ellsworth than Iron Eyes Cody, who was his close friend and next door neighbor. Their relationship resembled that of father and son. This intimate paper reveals a close personal insight into the life and character of our beloved fellow Westerner. A generous portion of the article is given over to a taped recital by Mr. Ellsworth of his life and experiences, with particular emphasis upon his interest in art and the gradual development of this exceptional talent.

I FIRST MET CLARENCE IN 1924, at Paramount Studios, known then as Famous Players Lasky, when I was working there as a bow-and-arrow expert and technical adviser on American Indians. Our mutual interests, like bow-and-arrow hunting, photography, Indians, and painting, brought us together; so much so, that we became life-time friends. We lived as neighbors; later, after the death of his mother, I gave him my next-door lot so he could build his home, and paint. This pleasure, plus our living next door, led to an intimacy that developed into a close family relationship.

Homer Boelter, close friend of Clarence Ellsworth, pays beautiful tribute to his memory in these words:

"To me, Clarence Ellsworth was one of the great Western artists. He was a sincere delineator of the American Indian, especially the Plains Indian. He continually strove to be accurate and realistic as well as sympathetic in all his work. He belonged to that group of painters, such as Remington, Russell, Farny, Schreyvogel and Smith, who devoted so much of their talent in preserving on canvas the most colorful period and people in American history.

"Clarence was a true individualist and never would he compromise his art even though it sometimes meant a meager existence. He would not over-dress a Crow Indian nor misplace an Oglalla Sioux in a Blackfoot environment, just to make a picture or even to satisfy a prospective customer. To some he appeared meek, even naive; but he could be stubborn and singleminded when it affected his art. There never was a more sensitive, generous or dedicated artist and friend than Clarence Ellsworth."

What better way to tell Clarence's story than through his own words, both written and tape recorded? I have rearranged his story in a more or less chronological order; and shall incorporate, from time to time, certain interesting events which he has omitted.

MY HOME ON THE PINE RIDGE RESERVATION

About his birth and early childhood, Clarence had this to say:

"I was prematurely born, September 23, 1885, at Holdrege, Phelps County, Nebraska. For two weeks I was kept wrapped in a wool blanket, annointed with whiskey, and kept in the oven of our cook stove. In those primitive times there were no incubators for babies.

"There was no hospital in that little town of Holdrege, which had sprung up almost over night shortly after the Burlington Railroad had been built. Many of the buildings of the town had been lifted up on rollers and transported from other sections of the country, as was my father's drug store.

"The store originally had been built at a little inland town called Sacramento, 10 miles from the new town of Holdrege. My father had partitioned off the front part of the building for his drug store, and he and my mother lived in two rooms in the rear.

"My grandmother and an older sister of my mother were in attendance at my birth; also an old doctor named Guild, who my mother always credited with saving my life. (The name Guild rhymes with wild.)

TWO SIOUX OLD TIMERS
Friends of Clarence

BLACKFOOT
Southwest Museum collection

"Two years later my mother gave birth to another boy, who was named *Clinton.* He died at the age of seven."

Clarence was of English descent. His mother's name was Lillie Miller, and she was born August 10, 1865 in Hope, Indiana. Her father's name was Christian Miller, and her mother's name was Carolina Petticord. Clarence's father's name was Lester V. Ellsworth, and he was born in Pennsylvania. Lester's father was J. F. Ellsworth and his mother was Naomi Waterman.

"My mother and father had a common interest in music. She played the piano and had a good voice and sang well. My father was a good violinist and they both were in great demand at the country dances and other gatherings. My earliest recollections are of a much larger home. My father, in addition to running the drug store with a partner whose first name I bear, also was appointed to the position of the clerk of the district court. As such, he had a stenographer on his staff. This young lady had a room and boarded at our house, as did two other ladies.

CHIEF RED CLOUD

WAITING FOR THE RIGHT TIME

"The house always seemed crowded with people, including my grandmother and an aunt or two on my mother's side and later my father's sister. He soon got rid of her because she would not help my mother do the work.

"My father was always very busy, because he was studying law, and he became the first to be admitted to the bar in Nebraska.

"I was always sickly; and at two years of age I weighed just 16 pounds. I used to cut out horses and dogs and cats and men from the wrapping paper that came from the grocer and butcher. I could wield a pencil well enough to amaze the guests.

"At five years of age, I saw my first Indians. It was at a Kickapoo medicine show that played in the Holdrege opera house. There were about a dozen Indians and they had marvelous headdresses, double trailers, and the women were well dressed. I think they had a lot of red paint on their faces. They had a little boy with them, named *Seven-up*, and he had clothes like the grown-ups.

BLACKFOOT
Southwest Museum collection

INDIAN BURIAL

"I went with my mother and grandmother, and I was thrilled beyond measure. I can see them yet, as plainly as if it were only yesterday, as they sat on the stage back of the 'doctor' while he extolled the virtues of the 'sagwa' he was selling. And when they danced, the women stood in one place, making a slight up-and-down movement, and the men danced in a circle—the little boy along with the rest. The impression on me was deep indeed. After I came home I showed my mother's boarders, and anyone else who would watch, all that I had learned from that program with its songs and dances.

"One day my father came home and said that *Seven-up* had been down on the street and a white boy started a fight with him. The little Indian licked the tar out of the other boy. This made a hit with me, although I was pretty small at the time. From then on I was much taken up with Indians. After the show left town, I made fringe on my clothes from an old shawl my mother had. I paraded around with that, as much as I could, like an Indian.

SIOUX GIRL
Pine Ridge

INDIAN HAZING HORSES

"When I was about 8 years old, we moved to a little town of possibly 150 people, called Holstein. It was a German settlement. Because I was sickly, I had not been sent to school; but now that I was 8 years of age, I started. My brother started at the same time. However, he passed away a year later.

"The schools in those days were far different than now. We had a big raw-boned profane man for a teacher, who sat up on the rostrum with his feet out the window, his back to the pupils, chewing tobacco and spitting frequently out the window. Some of the boys would flip wet paper wads from the end of a ruler at him, but he soon caught them. It seemed he could reach from the rostrum down halfway to the back of the room, grab a boy by the coat collar, yank him right out of his seat, and slam him up against the blackboard back of the teacher's desk. There before the whole school he would whale the daylights out of the kid with a strap or switch and toss him back into his seat.

"Some of the kids were tough and challenged him to make them cry. They took

SIOUX BOY

Pine Ridge

SIOUX GREETING THE SUN

terrible beatings. I got my share, some of them for things I did not do. Once I got a licking every day for more than a week. Then I played hookey for two weeks. It was in the winter time, and I stayed around the blacksmith shop near the forge where I would get warm if need be.

"In the summer, about this time, a traveling medicine show stopped in town for a couple of weeks and camped about a block from our home. Among them was an Indian named *Little Bird*, who acted as a roustabout for the company in the daytime; and at night, when the program was put on, he danced and sang.

"Naturally I hung around the camp continually. *Little Bird* took a fancy to me and we would take walks out into the country along the railroad tracks. He taught me how to make horsehair traps for birds and how to set snares for ground squirrels and rabbits. *Little Bird* told me many fascinating stories about his people and many interesting stories about animals. I became interested in nature and animals. And this was the beginning of a life-time interest in the American Indian.

BLACKFOOT
Southwest Museum collection

HALFBREEDS

"My folks moved about a great deal after that, my father always thinking he could do better some place else. We went back to Holdrege and I went to school. In the summer vacations I spent much time out in the country at my grandparents where I read a number of books, among them the Fosdick 'Frank' books. I got some of the thrilling literature, which today people call 'classics'.

"Another town we moved to was Grant, out in the western part of the state. I had a good time there, because I had a gun and the sandhills contained lots of rabbits and other game.

"From there we went to the extreme eastern part of the state, near Falls City. The town was Dawson. There was a creek there and I fished continually.

"I had learned something about photography at Grant; and when I moved to Dawson I got some better equipment and made a few dollars finishing photos for the townspeople.

GOING TO THE SUN DANCE
Pine Ridge

BLACKFOOT   BLACKFOOT

Southwest Museum collection

"I always loved Mark Twain's books; and when I lived in a little town called Mason City, Nebraska, not far from Broken Bow, I made good use of a little creek which ran through the middle of the town. It was called Mud Creek, and was about twenty or thirty yards wide. We often fished in it.

"I was about 10 years old, and I got some of the boxes that drugs came in from my father's drugstore, and I built a row boat. Some of the kids helped me, and we could sail about a mile or so. From then on I was always interested in that kind of thing.

"Later I painted houses, barns, store fronts, signs, window cards, and so on. I seemed to have abandoned photography for a time, as I had only a little 3¼ by 4¼ camera, and took few pictures.

"I had quit school, and I had heard that certain individuals traveled around the country painting signs on windows in various little towns, and that they made a good living at it. So I got some paints and brushes and made compartments in a cigar box to carry them in and, with a small satchel and a few clothes, I started out. I had four dollars.

THE SIGNAL

BLACKFOOT

THOMAS LONG PLUME

I stopped at the next station—my destination was Denver. I canvassed the stores and made two or three dollars; then went on to the next town the next day, as there was only one train a day.

"In a week or so I had arrived at a town in the northern part of the state where I had some cousins. I stopped there for a few days, then went out to the ranch of one of my cousins where I went to work driving 'staker team' in the hay fields.

"Somewhat later I found myself at the town of Rushville on the Northwestern. I took a stage over to Pine Ridge, South Dakota, the agency for the Oglallas, where I put up at the little hotel.

"At first I sketched the Indians secretly, as they objected to being portrayed. One day, however, a young man named *Charlie Brave* saw some of my drawings at the hotel. He requested me to make one of him, which he happily carried away with him. His friendship helped break the ice with the Indians. I was seventeen years old at this time, and I really got among the Sioux and started making sketches of the Indians on the reservation.

WHITE BUFFALO HUNT

SITTING BULL   RAIN-IN-THE-FACE

"In due time I arrived in Denver with a bundle of drawings under my arm. This was in the year 1903. I searched around until I found a cheap rooming house that needed its sign painted, and made arrangements with the proprietor for two dollars cash and the job of painting his sign for two weeks' rent.

"I then went to the Denver *Post* and showed them my sketches. They turned me down. One of the staff members, knowing I was a greenhorn, told me where to go to get a job drawing Santa Claus scenes. The money I received from this job, I can say, was the first money I ever received for an out-and-out drawing."

I would like to mention here that Clarence never took regular art lessons, only those given in the usual process of his school work. But he had an originality of his own, which came out naturally. He was called upon to show the other children in school how such things were done. He often said: "Art came to me naturally."

"Two weeks after I arrived in Denver I got a job with the *Rocky Mountain News* for five dollars a week. My very first assignment was to reconstruct the features of a

MEDICINE-MAN HUNTING THE BUFFALO COW

SILVER MOON CODY

Brother of Iron Eyes

CLARENCE'S SIOUX GIRL FRIEND

mangled face so it could be identified.

"It was here that I met William McCloud Raine, who was destined to become famous as a writer of western stories.

"Every week on the *News*, I got a five dollar gold piece in a little envelope. I became ill with pneumonia at the end of about five months and was sent home.

"I soon became fed up and I hit out for Omaha and got a job, first on the Omaha *Daily News*, then the Omaha *Bee*, and a little later with *Baker Brothers Engraving Company*.

"A pal and I shipped out of Omaha for a labor camp in Creston, Wyoming. We got off the train at Cheyenne and took off for Denver on another train. We got as far as Pueblo, Colorado.

"At Colorado Springs I set up a little stand in the Garden of the Gods and sketched portraits of people at twenty-five cents each. I ran out of funds at Pueblo, and went a couple of days without food. I sent home for some money and started for home. Shortly after my arrival my father passed away.

SIOUX FUNERAL

"We moved to my uncle's farm, ten miles from Fremont, Nebraska, where we lived in a sod house. Later my mother bought a little house in town for $300.00. I sketched window cards, painted signs, did a little painting and anything else I could to earn a few dollars.

"In 1908, my mother got word from some friends in Alberta, Canada, to come up there and live. So we went up there, and one of my aunts and her husband and little girl moved in with us.

"I found many fine examples of Indians to sketch during my spare time; but after nine months of this wilderness we returned to Fremont.

"In 1910 the restless spirit struck me again and I went back to Denver, got a job with the *Post*, sent for my mother, and settled down to being a newspaper man.

"When I first went to work on the Denver *Post*, the managing editor was Eugene Taylor. After him came Josiah Ward. (Ward had been city editor). The *Post* had quite a sizeable art staff, foremost among them being Wilbur Steele, Paul Gregg, Frank Finch (Doc Bird), Ralph Springer, James Lynch, Leo Giffons, Walter Foster, Kay Kind, Les Wallace and myself.

FRINGE OF THE HERD

"In that same year I submitted a painting in pastel to Johnnie McGuire, then owner and publisher of the sports magazine *Outdoor Life*. He accepted it and asked for more. Thereafter I made many covers for him.

"Somewhere along the line I found myself back in Fremont, where I made a dozen or so *Outdoor Life* covers. I also made drawings for Sandy Griswold's nature stories and Uncle Ross' stories.

"In a couple of years I accepted an offer to work on the *Rocky Mountain News*. I was there for seven years, but I never lost contact with my old friends on the *Post*.

"While I was in Denver, I met a Creek Indian girl whom I liked very much. Her name was Leah Summers. We didn't get very serious, and later she married a Cherokee. She had a friend named Minnie O'Neil, who was half Arapaho and half Irish. These girls, and another Indian girl named Tsianina—a Creek and still my good friend, my mother and I, used to go on picnics together. I took lots of photographs of these girls.

"During my vacations I made trips to the Pine Ridge Indian Reservation in South Dakota. It was here that I met a beautiful Sioux Indian girl whose name was Naota.

SIOUX BUFFALO SIGNAL

She was a daughter of a chief and we were very serious. I lived on the reservation for three summers to be close to her.

"I was taken in by her family, Indian way, and was named *'Little White Chieftain'*. I went through a ceremony and they made me a tipi to stay in when I spent my vacations there.

"I would paint and sketch the Indians, always giving the old timers a painting of themselves which they appreciated very much. I would play games with the young men.

"I tried to get Naota to come to Denver with me, and we would get married. She passed away before this could happen. She was the only girl I ever got real serious with. Her family was very close to me and I made many pictures of Naota and her folks."

Clarence painted many of the old time Sioux and corresponded with a great many of them until the time of his death. Their children and grandchildren would frequently visit him in his home, and talk of old times.

"One family with whom I spent a great deal of time at the Pine Ridge Reservation

CHEYENNE CAMP

was the Red Clouds. When Jack Red Cloud, son of the great Sioux Chief by that name, passed away on July 1, a boy came dashing up on a horse to the hotel where I was staying and told me that Jack's family and friends wanted some pictures taken of the deceased, which I did. Also, they asked me to take pictures of the burial later.

"On the morning of July 3, I attended the services at the church. Then I hastened out to the cemetery and took a few pictures. The minister objected strenuously, on the grounds it was disrespectful to the dead, and he told me to leave. He then informed the Indians, through an interpreter, that I was taking pictures to be exhibited in show windows in the East.

"This so enraged one of the Indian women present that she drew a knife and was prepared to stab the minister. Fortunately, one of the Indian police restrained her, and I continued taking pictures. I believe this policeman stopped the murder of the preacher. To show their contempt for the minister, the Indians turned their backs on him during the actual internment. It was their rebuke to him.

THE LAST BULLET

"Jack Red Cloud was a fine man and a splendid specimen of Indian. He was about 62 years of age and he went to his grave without realizing his ambition to be chief.

"He had applied for chieftainship upon two or three occasions, but had been turned down by the Oglalla council, composed of from twenty to one hundred of the leading Sioux full-bloods. Such applications are always debated by the council, and the verdict of the council is final.

"I have heard Jack Red Cloud sing, have seen him lead the dance, and I have heard him speak. His voice being deep and resonant, he possessed all the charm and power of Indian oratory.

"By inheritance he was entitled to be chief, his father having been one of the greatest of all Indian chiefs. But this fact wasn't sufficient to gain him his ambition.

"One year I went up to the Red Lake Chippewa Reservation in Northern Minnesota and I camped with the Indians. I tried to photograph some wild deer with a flashlight rigged up with a mechanism on my camera. I had an Indian take me out to where there

THE LONE PRAIRIE

were deer tracks. I couldn't see them, but he showed them to me. I set my camera up on the trail, fixed a thread with a flashlight, covered the flashlight with a piece of tin foil so it wouldn't get wet, and left it for several days; but no deer came along and I didn't get any pictures."

Clarence's interest in photography led him to invent a flashlight and camera shutter synchronizer. On November 1, 1915, he filed with the Commissioner of Patents a drawing and several pages of minutely detailed descriptive directions on the use of his invention. The object of his invention was to provide mechanical means for releasing or operating the shutter of the camera simultaneously with the flash of light. Two years later, on March 27, 1917, he was granted Patent No. 1220325 on his invention. He assigned one half of his right, title and interest in this improvement to Harry C. Rubincam of Denver, Colorado.

"While working on the newspaper in Denver, I got an idea of going down the river in the eastern part of Oklahoma. I knew an artist named Paul Gregg and he was from Oklahoma. He used to tell me stories about the Neosho and Grand Rivers. I had a little

APACHE INDIANS

money saved up, so one year I said to him—'Paul, I am going down there, build a boat and go down one of these rivers, just for a vacation.'

"I took the train and went to Chetopa, Kansas. This is in the southeastern corner of Kansas, about 3 or 4 miles from the Oklahoma border. I built a flat bottom boat, with the help of a blacksmith. He told me I should pour tar or pitch in the cracks. The boards ran crosswise and it was a scow-shaped object, heavy as lead. So I got an old tea kettle, boiled up some pitch, and with the blacksmith's help we fixed it so it would hold water. He charged me nine dollars.

"I put my things in it and laboriously tugged it down to the shallow and rocky river, dragging it along until I found water deep enough to float it. I had my trunk of photographic stuff, grub, clothes, bedding and paints on board. I went for about 10 miles until I came to open water. I went ashore then and pitched my tent on the bank, worn out from my labors.

'Several days later I met a fisherman who wanted to trade me his rowboat for my

IMMIGRANTS IN CANADA

craft. We traded even. It was much lighter than the one I had, and I made a deal with him to haul me to another creek.

"Happily I loaded my new boat and went to sleep peacefully. About the middle of the night I felt my boat floating down the stream. The water had risen and swept it out into midstream. I let it drift all night, stopping once to make tea. The next morning I arrived at Miama, Oklahoma, where I had a letter of introduction to an Indian in that city. My total distance was 135 miles.

"A week later I was in Kansas. I sold my boat and went back home by train. This was only the beginning of many more river trips. Two years later I made another trip down this river.

"In 1915 I came to California for a vacation. I visited the San Francisco Fair, and then I came on to Los Angeles where I spent a week with friends. I then went on to San Diego to visit more friends.

"In 1919, tiring of newspaper work where I had done layouts and cartoons, I had an

SCOUT AND WAGON TRAIN

offer from a friend of mine who was sure I could get more money in the movies.

"My first job was with Famous Players Lasky Studio, where I worked for 7 years in the art title department making mat paintings and decorative art titles. It was at this same studio that I met Iron Eyes Cody, a young Cherokee Indian, who was working with Tim McCoy on the *Covered Wagon*. I formed a life-time friendship with him.

"It was during this time I made a row boat trip of 400-miles through Dakota with a young cameraman from the studio. We went to Oral, South Dakota, and we built two rowboats. We went down the Cheyenne River in South Dakota, through Cheyenne and Missouri—a very crooked river, down as far as Pierre. It took us 4 weeks to make this trip.

"Once I took a three months' leave and visited my friends again on the Pine Ridge Reservation; and one year I visited Taos, New Mexico.

"My next job was with Universal Studios; then I went back to Paramount; then on to R.K.O. I worked in the art departments making decorative art titles and glass matt scenes.

A MURAL — THE TRAPPERS

"Tiring of studio work, I tried making bows and arrows. In this venture I was successful, often getting fifty dollars for a single bow. Iron Eyes and his brother, Joe Silvermoon Cody, would work along beside me in my shop, helping in this undertaking.

"We all joined an archery club called the 'Griffith Park Club'. We went in the park and helped clear the land of weeds and rocks, smoothing it off so we could have a nice meeting place. We helped plant the grass, and then put in benches and tables. Later, a group of us would go out there and shoot. Of course, in the earlier days we used to go out there and shoot rabbits and squirrels, until we were stopped by the park police.

"In 1928 I went back to Fremont, thinking I would stay there permanently; but my mother could not stand the climate. So I came back to Hollywood, and have made my home here ever since.

"My mother's serious illness forced me to stay home, so I could care for her. It was now that I had more time on my hands and, having saved quite a bit of money, I could really devote full time to my painting.

ATTACK ON THE STAGECOACH

"I expect I have painted over a thousand pictures during my life time. I have illustrated many books and made lots of magazine illustrations in pen and ink and in water colors. I made several paintings that were reproduced as prints; then sometimes they were reproduced in color for magazines and book covers and jackets.

"I had prints made to sell separately—one called the 'Rendezvous'; another the 'Indian Tracker', owned by Homer Boelter; another the 'Pipe of Prayer', posed for by Iron Eyes, who posed for a great many of my paintings; and still another called the 'Scouts of the U. S. Army', owned by Iron Eyes.

"I made about 40 paintings of Blackfoot Indians for the late Walter McClintock, and these are in the Southwest Museum. A mural I made hangs in my friend Dan V. Stephens' bank in Fremont, Nebraska. Many of my other paintings hang in banks, museums and private collections throughout the country. I did a jacket for Ernie Sutton's book called 'Life Worth Living'; also I made some 'Western Horseman' covers.

"I have made a lot of color and pen and ink sketches for 'The Westerners', a club

HUNTERS OF ELK

I belong to. Speaking about 'The Westerners', it is a club dear to my heart, and the only organization I truly have an interest in. My good friend, the late Mr. Homer Britzman, organized the Los Angeles Corral of 'The Westerners'. I joined as a charter member, later inducing my friend Iron Eyes to join.

"For Britzman, I expect I have made twenty-two or more paintings for his 'Rio Grande Booklets'; and I also did a cover for his 'Way to the West', and illustrated many of his other books. I illustrated my own booklet published by the Southwest Museum called 'Bows and Arrows'; also one for Iron Eyes called 'How Indians Sign Talk in Pictures'. I illustrated 'Cottonwood Yarns', a book by Dan V. Stephens; and Dr. M. R. Harrington's 'Dickon Among the Lenape Indian'; also The Westerners' 'Brand Book'; and many other books.

"I did a lot of illustrations of maps for Colonel Tim McCoy for his television show; and for Yewas (Mrs. Iron Eyes), illustrating her legends which she told on television; and anything else that Iron Eyes needed to illustrate his show on K.T.L.A. (Channel 5).

ELK

"Mr. Otha D. Wearin, one of my best friends, has a nice collection of my paintings. Sometimes, during the summer, I would go back to Hastings, Iowa, and stay a couple of months at his place.

"After the death of my mother in 1944, Iron Eyes, my good friend, gave me the empty lot next door to him; and here, in 1947, I built my home from a design I had made, complete with dark room.

"I did illustrations and paintings for various people. During one summer a man paid a visit to Mrs. Iron Eyes, while I was away in Iowa and Iron Eyes was in Mexico. He had seen some of my work in 'The Brand Book' in libraries he had visited. He liked it and wanted to stop by and see me. Mrs. Iron Eyes showed him the paintings they had hanging in their home and which they had bought from me over a period of some 30 years, and he wanted to buy some of theirs. She told him they were not for sale; so, as soon as he could, he wrote and asked me to paint for him. He said he would take everything I could paint.

THE ROPER

BAREBACK RIDER

"This man's name was Donald Dow and he was from Fort Worth, Texas; a young man, I assume. He takes all the work I can turn out."

This ends the taped and written story of our good friend Clarence Arthur Ellsworth.

The last year of his life was a hard one. Struggling for breath, it was only by the greatest effort that he finished a portrait of his namesake, Arthur, our youngest boy, as a gift for his birthday Nov. 22, 1960. This was his last completed painting. One large painting he had been working on for a long time, "The Custer Battle," was left unfinished. It is one of our most cherished possessions.

Clarence finished out his life with us, his adopted family. Our home was as his own, for he carried our front door key and would come in whenever he pleased. He always shared holidays and other festivities with us; and in his later years he ate his evening meal with us and then would retire to the front room to watch television.

LOS ANGELES CORRAL

JOHN SITTING BULL   JACK RED CLOUD

(Sculpture)

When he could no longer drive his car, my wife would take him shopping or for a drive in the park where he loved to watch the children play. He was as our own father, or adopted "Uncle." He knew that we would care for him until the end and take care of his final wishes.

He passed away peacefully as the result of bronchial asthma, after a prolonged illness, hospitalization, and final care at his home. On February 17, 1961, he was sitting in his favorite rocking chair, in which he sat to do all his painting and which was now placed in front of his fireplace. He was waiting for my wife to come in and fix his breakfast, after she had taken the children to school.

His last wishes were to have no fuss made over his passing, no flowers, no service; and he expressed his desire for cremation. We abided by his decision.

His good friend and fellow-Westerner, Homer H. Boelter, who made colored prints of some of his finest pictures, came to visit the day he died. He was of the greatest help to us in arranging the funeral. Westerners Col. Charles Benton, Tim McCoy, attorney Paul Mason—a corresponding member of 'The Westerners', and his friend Dr. H. G.

GROUP OF SCULPTURE

Bieler of Capistrano Beach, all helped us in carrying out Clarence's final wishes.

We could not possibly let our good *"Little White Chieftain"* pass without proper memorial to his name. On February 22, 1961, some forty Westerners, Indian friends, neighbors and children, all stood and paid proper tribute to his name. I am sure he was pleased when Chief Chris Willowbird arose and gave a moving Indian prayer.

The following day he was cremated and his remains placed in a niche in the Chapel of the Pines, not far from where his mother's remains repose.

It is difficult to close this story of a great artist, whose biography was carried in "Who's Who in American Art," 1959-61, for I am sure there are many facets of his life that we have not recorded.

He was a man that many could envy, for he lived his life as he wished. He was a gentleman at all times, gentle with children, generous to a fault with friends, always giving more than he received. He was a dedicated man, devoted to the American Indian. He depicted on canvas the spirit of the American Indian, leaving a pictorial record behind for future generations.

Clarence with his painting
THE LEADERS

Despite his wish for no services, he was a spiritual man in many ways, although not showing it outwardly. Our family always says grace before eating and, unknown to us, he must have said this prayer which we later found scribbled on a scrap of paper:

"Prayer at meals: Heavenly Father, we thank thee
                      for thy care, the food we eat—
                      the clothes we wear.
            Be with us everywhere.   Amen."

His firm belief was that he would return someday and that his great talent would not be wasted.

His final words to us were his usual ones, those he always spoke when leaving our home: "Well, goodnight. I'll see you tomorrow."

THE END

TO ARIZONA BY SEA 1850-1877

By JOHN HASKELL KEMBLE

Dr. Kemble, author and recognized authority on Maritime History, presents this penetrant study of water transportation from the Pacific Coast to the Arizona Territory prior to the coming of the railroad. This sea route traffic, opening in 1855, was operated mainly with sailing vessels until 1871 and with regular steamers thereafter. The article discusses not only the water route from San Francisco to the Colorado, but also the general outlines of steam boating up and down the river itself.

WATER TRANSPORTATION PLAYED A MAJOR ROLE not only in bringing goods and people to the Pacific Coast but also in distributing them once they were in the region. The stagecoach, the freight wagon, and the pack mule were important parts of the transportation system in the West; but not until the advent of the railroad, and still later of the automobile and the motor truck, was water transportation superseded where it could be used at all. For goods which were bulky or which could not pay high shipping charges there was no really feasible alternative to sea and river shipment. It simply did not pay to send mining machinery or ores by land except under the most unusual circumstances.

Thus, almost from the onset of the California Gold Rush, San Francisco became the center of a network of water routes by which the men and goods that came through the Golden Gate from distant ports could be distributed. Only a little later, when the Pacific Coast began to produce goods for export, these were generally gathered at San Francisco Bay for shipment to the eastern United States, Europe, or the Far East. The system of local water services included the steamboats which plied San Francisco Bay and the Sacramento and San Joaquin Rivers, sailing vessels and steamers which went up the coast to the Columbia River and to Puget Sound as well as south to San Pedro and San Diego, and local sail and steam coasters which brought lumber to San Francisco from the Redwood Coast and farm produce from a number of minor ports as far south as San Luis Obispo. Supporting these water connections with San Francisco, and growing independently as the Pacific Coast gained in economic stature and diversity, were the steamboat lines of the Columbia, the Willamette, the Snake, and the steamers which plied Puget Sound. At a greater distance, British Columbia and the coast of Alaska looked toward San Francisco as an entrepot for commerce, and their economic connections were largely with her by sea. Overcoming considerable natural obstacles, these water communications extended into the interior of the Southwest and touched Arizona by way of the Colorado River.

Arizona Territory had no seacoast. At first glance, it would seem that it had no geographic basis for the development of water transportation. The difficulties of land transport to and from Arizona were such, however, that the rather dubious potentialities of the Colorado River were exploited to the utmost, and Arizona became an economic tributary to San Francisco by means of the ocean voyage around Cape San Lucas, the tip of Baja California, north to the head of the Gulf of California, and thence up the Colorado River. The disadvantages of the route were underlined by the fact that it was abandoned as soon as the rails of the Southern Pacific reached Yuma in 1877.

Although the problems of land communications with Arizona brought about the development of the water route, the needs for any connections with the outside world were marginal. During the long period when the region was a part of the borderlands of New Spain, there were only peripheral mission centers, and these had their economic connections to the south. The overland trail from Sonora to the Alta California missions was open briefly between 1776 and 1781, but an uprising of the Yuma Indians was accepted as a basis for its abandonment. At the time of the acquisition of Arizona by the United States in 1848, its white population was only a few hundred. The Gold Rush to California brought thousands of Argonauts through this region on their way to the mines, and at the beginning of 1850 the first commercial ferry was established across the Colorado River at the mouth of the Gila.

The warlike and formidable Apache, whose country lay mainly below the Gila, were not brought under United States jurisdiction until the Gadsden Purchase of 1853; but their presence in the area was a deterrent to the development of a white population in the region. Miners began to locate claims along the Colorado in 1849 although it was five or six years later before serious mining activity developed. Meanwhile, troubles between the Yuma Indians and white interlopers led to the establishment of a military post, first named Camp Independence, near the junction of the Colorado and the Gila in 1850. This developed into Fort Yuma, an establishment on the California side of the Colorado River which was the first permanent military post in the area. A town was laid out across from it in 1854, known successively as Colorado City, Arizona City, and Yuma; but its real growth did not begin until about 1864. The 'sixties were characterized by the mining "rushes" common to other parts of the West in the same period. In general the mining camps grew up

TO ARIZONA BY SEA – 1850-1877

along the Colorado and in the country to the east, up the Gila and to the southeast to Tucson, and up the Bill Williams Fork toward Wickenburg and Prescott. The mines, particularly in the 'sixties and after when silver and copper as well as gold were sought, required machinery and fuel as well as men and provisions, and the bulkier materials could only be imported economically by water. By the same token, the unrefined or only partly refined, ores were shipped to San Francisco for final processing. Until the railroad had reached Arizona, it was patently impossible to carry such comparatively low revenue commodities except by water.

The penetration of Arizona by miners and other settlers increased the problem of supervising the Indians. Especially in the southern portion of the area, the Apache were a constant menace throughout the years from 1853 until well into the 'eighties. A series of military posts were established in the southern part of Arizona from the Colorado eastward, and farther north Fort Mohave on the Colorado and Fort Defiance were both located prior to 1860. During the Civil War, when military operations in Arizona were carried on by Union forces from California in opposition to a Confederate invasion from Texas, troops generally moved overland from the Los Angeles area to Arizona but supplies went by sea. Often, however, troops going to and from posts in the territory went by the water route, and supplies for the posts were brought by this means.

During the years that the mining and military activities in Arizona, as well as its mercantile life, were largely dependent on its marine communications with the outside world, the territory grew significantly in population. In 1860, the region which became the Territory of Arizona two years later had a settled population of some 6500. The Census of 1870 showed a population of 9658, and ten years later it had jumped to 40,440. Probably the majority of these people came into Arizona by land routes; but, prior to 1877, when the territory gained a rail connection with California, they or their jobs were mainly supported by the water communications of the territory.

The water gateway to Arizona was the mouth of the Colorado River at the head of the long Gulf of California. Spaniards had penetrated here as early as 1539, but the river itself was inhospitable and there was nothing along its shores to attract them. Jesuit missionaries, Father Kino in 1701-2 and Father Consag in 1746, explored the Colorado Delta. At the time of the acquisition of Arizona by the United States, however, the best description of the mouth of the river and the only drawing of it which could qualify as a chart were the work of Lieutenant R. W. H. Hardy of the Royal Navy, who visited the head

TO ARIZONA BY SEA – 1850-1877

of the Gulf of California in 1826 on a pearl fishing expedition in the schooner *Bruja* out of Guaymas. He described the shallow and shifting channel of the river, its low-lying banks, and the tidal bore which developed as the tide came up from the gulf and struggled with the current of the river. Despite these visits which were recorded in some detail, as well as others which must have occurred but with no accounts surviving, the lower Colorado remained one of the lesser-known parts of the West at the time of the American occupation of Arizona.

The beginning of the use of the Colorado as a means of supporting activities in Arizona dates from the establishment of the military post at the mouth of the Gila River. In October 1850, Colonel Joseph Hooker, then assistant adjutant general of the Third Division, U. S. Army, with headquarters at Sonoma, ordered Lieutenant George H. Derby of the Topographical Engineers to proceed to the mouth of the Colorado with a view to establishing this as a route of supply for the post to be located at the mouth of the Gila. Derby sailed from San Francisco on 1 November in the topsail schooner *Invincible* which was in the service of the War Department on the Pacific Coast as a transport. She was commanded by Captain Alfred H. Wilcox who was to be a leading figure in the sea trade to the Colorado as long as it lasted. *Invincible* called at San Diego and took aboard 10,000 rations for the troops on the Colorado, and then proceeded to her destination by the way of Cape San Lucas, Guaymas, and Angeles Bay. *Invincible* came in sight of the river on 23 December. On Christmas Day, Derby began his survey of the lower river as the schooner beat her way up its shallow channel against the swift current. The schooner was able to proceed only about thirty miles up the river, and thence Derby continued up the river in a pulling boat. On 13 January he made contact with Major Heintzelman, commander of the garrison, who returned to the schooner with Derby. Before the end of the month he had sent a party down the river by land to take the provisions. Her cargo landed, *Invincible* proceeded down the river on 29 January, called again at Guaymas and San Jose del Cabo, and was back in San Francisco on 6 March 1851. The feasibility of using the route for transporting supplies to Arizona had been demonstrated. Likewise, the impossibility of reaching the post at the mouth of the Gila in an ocean-going sailing vessel was made clear. Other means would have to be taken to make use of the river once it was reached. Derby, in his report, pointed out that a steamboat, drawing two and a half to three feet of water and preferably a stern-wheeler with a powerful engine, would be able to connect ocean-going vessels at the mouth of the river with the fort.

The dependence of the post at Yuma upon provisioning by sea was

TO ARIZONA BY SEA – 1850-1877

dramatically illustrated when, in June 1851, Major Heintzelman was forced to withdraw most of his force to San Diego because of lack of supplies. The last of the garrison departed in December. Army supervision of the Indians at the ferry across the Colorado was needed, however, and more careful plans were laid than before to insure the support of the garrison. In 1851 George Alonzo Johnson, together with some other former Colorado ferrymen, obtained a contract from the War Department to supply Fort Yuma. The schooner *Sierra Nevada*, chartered by the Army, was provided to carry the expedition to the mouth of the river. Commanded by Captain Wilcox, she sailed from San Francisco in October 1851, spent two months at San Diego loading provisions and preparing for the expedition and sailed thence for the Colorado on 24 January 1852. *Sierra Nevada* reached the mouth of the Colorado on 17 February, and succeeded in ascending the river about thirty miles. Captain Johnson had brought the frames and planking for two flatboats from San Francisco with a view to putting them together and carrying the cargo in them up to the fort if *Sierra Nevada* could not make it that far. It required nine days to assemble the two flatboats. Each was 50 feet long, 18 feet wide, and 3 feet deep. They were loaded with provisions for the fort, and set off to be poled up the river. One boat was swamped on the first trip, and both the boat and her cargo lost. Meanwhile Major Heintzelman had reoccupied the fort on 28 February 1852 and was anxiously awaiting the arrival of supplies. When they finally came, the rate of delivery was so slow that provisions were used up about as rapidly as the contractors could deliver them.

It was clear that not only were ocean-going vessels unable to reach Yuma; it was impracticable to use man-powered flatboats on the river. A new contract was awarded for the supply of the fort, this time to Captain James Turnbull. It was to extend from July 1852 until the end of the year, and provided for payment at the rate of $120 a ton for the first cargo delivered at Yuma, and $50 a ton for goods arriving subsequently during the year. The schooner *Capacity* cleared San Francisco on 1 August with stores aboard and with the components for a small steamer to be used on the river. At the mouth of the Colorado the parts of the steamer were unloaded, put together, and christened *Uncle Sam*. It was a slow process, and she did not appear at Fort Yuma until 3 December. She was really only an undecked, side-wheel steam launch of 40 tons register, 65 feet long, 16 feet wide, and with a depth of 3 feet 6 inches. Woefully underpowered by her 20 horsepower locomotive engine, her first voyage from the mouth of the river to Yuma took 14 days, due to strandings, the time required to cut wood for her furnace along the river bank, and her

RIVER STEAMER *COLORADO* of 1862 in the Colorado Steam Navigation Company's dry dock at Port Isabel.

TO ARIZONA BY SEA – 1850-1877

inadequate engine. She brought only 35 tons of stores; and although later she was making a round trip from Yuma to the river mouth every 12 days, the schooner *Capacity* still spent over seven months at the mouth of the river before she was unloaded.

Uncle Sam was far from a success. Captain Turnbull returned to San Francisco to obtain a better engine and arrived back at the Colorado in May 1853. The little steamer, however, while moored near Fort Yuma awaiting her new engine, filled and sank on 12 June, probably due to being holed by a snag or a floating tree trunk. After two days of efforts to raise her, she broke her moorings and disappeared. Captain Turnbull went once more to San Francisco with the intention of obtaining another steamer for the river; but this plan did not materialize, and he abandoned his Colorado enterprise.

Turnbull's withdrawal created another opening for Captain Johnson and his associates. In 1853 he, together with Benjamin M. Hartshorne and Captain Wilcox, organized the firm of George A. Johnson & Co. These men were to dominate trade to and on the Colorado for the next quarter century. It is notable that the business never seemed to attract any large capital, but remained in the hands of men who were primarily its day-to-day operators. Captain Johnson brought the steamer *General Jessup* in pieces from San Francisco to the mouth of the Colorado in the brig *General Viel*, and had her completed and ready for service in January 1854. She was a 49-ton side-wheeler, 104 feet long, and with a 70 horsepower engine. Her cargo capacity was only 40 tons, and it took her over two months to carry the freight brought by one ocean-going vessel up to Fort Yuma.

In 1855, Johnson & Co. added a second steamer to the river trade. This was *Colorado*, shipped out from San Francisco knocked-down and assembled on the river. She was larger than *General Jessup*, being 140 feet long, and she was propelled by a stern-wheel rather than side-wheels. This proved to be more satisfactory for navigating the shallow waters of the Colorado. The subsequent commercial steamers on the river were all stern-wheelers.

The sea route to Arizona was thus really opened in 1855 and it continued in constant use until 1877. Between San Francisco and the mouth of the Colorado traffic was carried principally in sailing vessels until 1871 and by regular steamers thereafter. Of scme 217 sailing craft listed as clearing San Francisco for the Colorado River between 1855 and 1872, over one hundred were schooners, 98 were brigs, and 17 were barks. Thus the great majority were small vessels averaging perhaps 200 tons register. From 1855 until 1863 the number of sailings for the Colorado was never more than eleven in one year,

TO ARIZONA BY SEA – 1850-1877

even as low as five in three of the years. The number jumped from eleven to nineteen between 1863 and 1864, and never fell below twelve thereafter until 1872. The top year was 1866, with twenty-four sailings.

In the first years of the trade, most of the sailing vessels in the service from San Francisco to the mouth of the Colorado were under charter to the War Department and carried supplies for the garrisons at Fort Yuma and elsewhere in Arizona. With the expansion of mining, and the growth of civilian population, more commercial vessels entered the trade. The War Department began to engage the freight space it needed in the ships which happened to be sailing for the Colorado, rather than chartering the whole vessel.

The voyage from San Francisco to and from the mouth of the Colorado was not easy. Although the distance was about 1900 miles on a direct course, ships depending wholly on sail could seldom accomplish this minimal route. There were generally favorable winds from San Francisco down the coast to Cape San Lucas, the tip of Baja California, but the Gulf of California was subject to variable winds and calms, and its increasing narrowness toward the northern end was an inhibiting factor. On the return voyage the prevailing winds along the Pacific Coast forced a vessel to get well out to sea, before heading toward the Golden Gate, in order to avoid the tedious beating up the coast in the face of almost constant adverse winds. Sailing time of two or three weeks southbound, and of a month or more in the other direction, could be expected. A vessel was seldom able to make more than three round trips a year.

Coastwise steamers were in regular service along the Pacific shore from 1849 onward, and they increased in numbers with each passing year and the growth in population. The advantages of steamships in the trade to the Colorado were recognized early in the history of the business. Wind conditions which hindered the schooners and brigs would have much less effect on steamers, and regularly scheduled voyages would be possible. Time would be saved in the delivery of goods to Arizona if the ocean and river vessels could be better coordinated. Steamers were slow in making their appearance in the trade from San Francisco, however, because of the small cargoes and consequent low revenue from the business. At the beginning, steamers made only special voyages to the Colorado with Army troops and supplies, and not until 1871 was there sufficient business to warrant a regular line of steamers. Even then they called at Mexican ports on their way to and from the Colorado in order to add to their revenues.

The first ocean steamer to come to the mouth of the Colorado was *Uncle Sam*, this time a 1453-ton ocean-going side-wheeler. In 1859 she was chartered

TO ARIZONA BY SEA – 1850-1877

by the War Department for a voyage to the Colorado with the troops and supplies destined for the new Fort Mohave, 300 miles above Yuma. She anchored in the gulf some twenty miles below the mouth of the river on 27 February, and discharged her passengers and cargo into the river steamers, *Colorado* and *General Jessup*, thus demonstrating the feasibility of a large vessel approaching close enough to the shallow bar of the river to transfer men and goods into the flatbottomed, non-seagoing river boats. Later in 1859, a smaller coastwise steamer, *Santa Cruz*, made a voyage to the Colorado. During the Civil War the Pacific Mail steamer *Panama* was dispatched to the mouth of the river, and cargo destined for Arizona was also shipped to Guaymas in the Panama-bound steamer, *Republic*, to be transshipped thence to the Colorado in a local coasting schooner.

In 1866, the Pacific Mail steamer *Oregon* made two trips to the Colorado, and the screw steamer *Continental* sailed from San Francisco for the river with three hundred soldiers aboard on 23 October 1866. After she was at sea it was discovered that the rations had been left behind, and she had to return to port and delay her final departure by two days.

The time was approaching when a regular steamship line from San Francisco to the Colorado would have enough business to be a paying venture. In 1866 the Johnson group, which had been the principal operators of steamboats on the river since 1854, reorganized as the Colorado Steam Navigation Co. Five years later they purchased the wooden, propeller-driven steamer *Newbern*, and dispatched her on its first voyage from San Francisco to the Colorado on 2 July 1871. She was a vessel of 943 tons gross register, 375 nominal horsepower, and 198 feet long, and with a beam of 29 feet. Built at Brooklyn, New York, in 1862, *Newbern* had been an Army transport during the Civil War, and had served the Quartermaster Corps between San Francisco and Alaska. She was now scheduled to make a round voyage each month from San Francisco to the mouth of the Colorado with calls at San José del Cabo, and Guaymas. Passenger fares were $75 first class and $45 steerage. In operation, *Newbern* was not quite fast enough to make a sailing every 30 days, since her time on the voyage alone averaged 15 days in each direction. The new service gave speed and regularity to Arizona's connections with the outside world such as had been unknown before, and by 1872 it was reported that *Newbern* was being offered more cargo than she could carry.

In order to meet the demand for more space, the Colorado Steam Navigation Co. added another ocean steamer to its line in 1873. This was *Montana*, a screw steamer of 1004 tons and about the same dimensions as *Newbern*.

STEAMER *NEWBERN* at anchor.

(*National Archives*)

TO ARIZONA BY SEA – 1850-1877

She had been built in Bath, Maine in 1865, and was acquired from the Pacific Mail Steamship Co. When *Montana* entered the trade to the Colorado in November 1873, it was possible for the line to offer approximately two sailings a month in each direction. The new steamer was dogged by bad luck, however. In December 1874 she went ashore on the Mexican coast, and missed a trip as a result. Then, on the night of 14 December 1876, just after leaving the wharf at Guaymas for the Colorado, she was found to be on fire. The ship was run ashore on Cape Haro where she and her cargo became a total loss, although passengers and crew got off safely. To replace *Montana*, the company put on the screw steamer *Idaho*, a sister ship. She made her first sailing from San Francisco in January 1877, and completed only two trips before the line to the mouth of the Colorado was suspended.

The steamers on the ocean route to Arizona were comparatively small, even for their day; and, since they had no competition, it is understandable that they were not operated in "spit-and-polish" fashion. They provided reliable transportation with accommodations and food which were not out of keeping with the standards of living in the remoter sections of the West. Frances Bishop, a school teacher who went to Arizona in 1872, wrote that the steamer *Newbern* from San Francisco provided by far the easiest and most agreeable means of reaching Arizona from the world. The accommodations were "pretty good," and there was usually interesting company aboard since all military and government officials travelled in her.[1]

When Martha Summerhayes, an Army bride fresh from New England, reminisced about a voyage in *Newbern* in 1874 from a vantage point of thirty-five years later, she could think of little that was good to say of the ship. She was seasick from San Francisco to Cape San Lucas, thought that hoisting cattle aboard by their horns at the cape shockingly cruel, and found the Gulf of California insufferably hot. In part she wrote as follows:

> "The heat of the staterooms compelled us all to sleep on deck, so our mattresses were brought up by the soldiers at night, and spread about. The situation, however, was so novel and altogether ludicrous, and our fear of rats which ran about on deck so great, that sleep was well-nigh out of the question.

> "Before dawn, we fled to our staterooms, but by sunrise we were glad to dress and escape from their suffocating heat and go on deck again. Black coffee and hard-tack were sent up, and this sustained us until the nine o'clock breakfast, which was elaborate, but not good. There was no milk, of course, except the heavily sweetened sort, which I could not use: it was the old-time condensed or

---

1. Frances V. Bishop to editor, *Jefferson County Journal*, Adams, New York, n.d., *Annual Publications of the Historical Society of Southern California*, Vol, XIV, part 3, p. 373.

SCHOONER *ISABEL* discharging cargo into a barge and a river steamer
at Port Isabel.

*(Reproduced from a photograph in Charles G. Johnson, HISTORY
OF THE TERRITORY OF ARIZONA, (San Francisco 1868)
by permission of the Huntington Library, San Marino.)*

TO ARIZONA BY SEA – 1850-1877

canned milk; the meats were beyond everything, except the poor, tough, fresh beef we had seen hoisted aboard over the side at Cape San Lucas. The butter, poor at the best, began to pour like oil . . . The ice supply decreased alarmingly, the meats turned green, and when the steward went down into the refrigerator, which was somewhere below the quarter-deck, to get provisions for the day, every woman held a bottle of salts to her nose, and the officers fled to the forward part of the ship. The odor which accended from that refrigerator was indescribable . . . [2]

The ocean steamers anchored at the mouth of the river, and their passengers and cargo were transfered to river steamboats and to barges which the steamboats towed. The river steamers found shelter from the frequently boisterous winds of the gulf in a slough which penetrated the flat delta land for some twenty-five miles. About eight or ten miles up the slough, the Colorado Steam Navigation Co. diked in a fifteen acre section of marsh land and built a dry dock, machine shop, carpenter shop, and other works necessary for the maintenance of the river steamers. This was Port Isabel, and here a number of the later river steamers were put together after being shipped knocked-down from San Francisco.

The trip up the Colorado from the mouth to Yuma was through flat desert country. The banks of the river were seldom more than six feet high, and were covered with a fringe of willows, cottonwoods, and high weeds. The river channel, which was seldom over five feet deep, was constantly changing as the great load of silt which the Colorado carried down from the interior was deposited as it approached the sea. Steamboats had to tie up at the bank each night since the channel might alter radically from one day to the next. Wood, which was the fuel of the river steamers, was cut and piled at various points along the bank by the Indians. With good luck, the hundred-plus miles of winding river between Port Isabel and Yuma could be negotiated in two days; but sometimes, in seasons of low water, it took much longer.

The shallow-draft stern-wheeler was the characteristic type of vessel on the Colorado. A half-dozen of these were built by the Colorado Steam Navigation Co. after 1856. They were small, had only the plainest of passenger quarters, and were very humble sisters of the splendid steamers of the same basic type which were plying the Sacramento, the San Joaquin, and the Columbia at the same period. [3]

---

2. Martha Summerhayes, *Vanished Arizona: recollections of my Army life* (Chicago, 1939), pp. 30-31.
3. The later steamers of the Colorado Steam Navigation Co. were:
   Cocopah [I], 140 ft. long, entered service 1859.   *Cocopah* [II], 145.7 ft. long, entered service 1865.
   Mohave [I], 133 ft. long, entered service 1863.   *Gila*, 149.47 ft. long, entered service 1873.
   Colorado [II], 127 ft. long, entered service 1865.   *Mohave* [II], 149.5 ft. long, entered service 1875.

RIVER STEAMER *GILA* (1872) alongside the levee at Yuma, Arizona.

(Detail from a photo by Carelton E. Watkins in "Arizona and views adjacent to the Southern Pacific R.R. (San Francisco,

TO ARIZONA BY SEA – 1850-1877

There was only one brief period when the Colorado Steam Navigation Co. had competition on the river. In 1864 Captain Thomas E. Trueworthy brought the 47-ton steamer *Esmeralda* to the river, and the same year the Philadelphia Mining Co. put *Nina Tilden*, a vessel of about the same size, into service. These interests merged to form the Pacific and Colorado Steam Navigation Co. in 1865. The company had difficulties, however; was reorganized as the Arizona Navigation Co., and sold its boats to the Colorado Steam Navigation Co. in 1867.

After 1856, steamers began to penetrate the river above Yuma as military posts and mining activities were pushed farther up the river. Captain Johnson took *General Jessup* up as far as Las Vegas Wash in early 1858, and later the same year Lieutenant Joseph C. Ives took the iron-hulled steamer *Explorer* as far as the Black Canyon. There were a few trips made as far up the river as Callville, 433 miles above Yuma; but La Paz, Ehrenberg, Aubrey, or Camp Mohave were commoner destinations. The upriver trade reflected mining and military activities of the region in the places which it served. Beyond Yuma the Colorado flowed through more rugged country, but the shallow channel of the river was as unpredictable as below. Groundings were frequent, and sandstorms presented another hazard to river navigation.

The transportation of passengers and cargo was, of course, the reason for the operation of the steamers. By common standards, demands for this service were not heavy; but it was vital to the existence of the population of Arizona. In 1875, 4500 tons of cargo were brought up the river to Yuma. Southbound there were 1000 tons of mineral ores, 60 tons of wool, 60 tons of general merchandise, 6170 hides, and 1440 pelts. Freight rates varied, but were generally high. In 1864, the rate from San Francisco to the mouth of the river was $20 per ton. On the river it ranged from $25 per ton, from the mouth to the Yuma region, to $75 per ton to La Paz.

The tracks of the Southern Pacific reached Yuma from Los Angeles in April 1877, and train service began early the next month. Passengers and goods could now come to Arizona by rail. *Newbern* left San Francisco on her last voyage to the Colorado on 16 May. The river steamboats continued to operate above Yuma, and did not disappear entirely until the 20th century. They were now feeders for the Southern Pacific, and later for the Santa Fe, at the Needles crossing. In 1877 the Colorado Steam Navigation Co. sold out to the Southern Pacific which thereafter ran the river steamers. In 1879 Captain John Bermingham, the general agent in San Francisco for what was now styled the California and Mexican Steamship Line which was running *Newbern* to Cape San Lucas, La Paz, Mazatlan, and Guaymas, wrote to Captain Wilcox who was president of the company and lived in San Diego:

> "The river business is used up. All Prescott freight now goes to Maricopa on R.R. The people of Ehrenberg are taking the windows and doors from their houses and starting for the interior. There is little or nothing doing at Williams Fork or Mohave. The river business is virtually done. We got out of that business just in time."[4]

Thus the appearance of the railroad began the reorientation of Arizona's transportation system. Rails replaced the sea as the principal means of access to the territory for goods. The development of highways and the coming of automobiles and trucks in the twentieth century completed the change. Arizona did not cease to be an economic tributary of San Francisco in an important degree, but the connections were no longer maritime.

---

4. John Bermingham to Alfred H. Wilcox, San Francisco, 3 May 1879, ms., Honnold Library, Claremont, California.

BIBLIOGRAPHY

ANONYMOUS, *History of Arizona Territory showing its resources and advantages . . .* , San Francisco, 1864.

BANCROFT, HUBERT HOWE, *History of Arizona and New Mexico, 1530-1888*, vol. XVII of *The Works of Hubert Howe Bancroft*, San Francisco, 1889.

BARTLETT, JOHN RUSSELL, *Personal narrative of explorations & incidents in Texas, New Mexico, California, Sonora, and Chihuahua . . .* , 2 vols., London, 1854.

BEATTIE, G. W., "Diary of a ferryman and trader at Fort Yuma, 1855-1857," *Annual Publications of the Historical Society of Southern California*, vol. XIV, part I (1928), pp. 89-128; part II (1929), pp. 213-242.

BELL, WILLIAM A., *New tracks in North America. A journal of travel and adventure whilst engaged in the survey for a Southern railroad to the Pacific Ocean during 1867-8*, 2 vols., London, 1869.

BERMINGHAM, JOHN, Letters to Alfred A. Wilcox, 1877-1879, ms., Honnold Library, Claremont, California.

BERTON, FRANCIS, *A voyage on the Colorado—1878*, tr. and ed. by Charles N. Rudkin, Los Angeles, 1953.

DERBY, GEORGE H., *Reconnaissance of the Gulf of California and the Colorado River, 1850-1*, Washington, 1852.

HARDY, R. W. H., *Travels in the interior of Mexico in 1825, 1826, 1827, and 1828*, 2 vols., London, 1829.

HODGE, HIRAM C., *Arizona as it is*, New York, 1877.

IMRAY, JAMES F., *Sailing directions for the West Coast of North America between Panama and Queen Charlotte, Islands*, 2nd ed., London, 1868.

JOHNSON, CHARLES GRANVILLE, *The Territory of Arizona . . .* , San Francisco, 1869.

JOHNSON, GEORGE A., "The Steamer General Jessup," *Quarterly of the Society of California Pioneers*, vol. IX (1932), pp. 108-113.

LEAVITT, FRANCIS HALE, "Steam navigation on the Colorado River," *California Historical Society Quarterly*, vol. XXII, No. 1 (March 1943), pp. 1-25; no. 2 (June 1943), pp. 151-174.

McCLINTOCK, JAMES H., *Mormon settlement in Arizona*, Phoenix, 1921.

MILLS, HAZEL EMERY, "The Arizona fleet," *The American Neptune*, vol. I, no. 3 (July 1941), pp. 255-274.

MOWRY, SYLVESTER, *Arizona and Sonora: the geography, history, and resources of the silver region of North America*, 3rd ed., New York, 1864.

ROLFE, FRANK (ed.), "Trip to Arizona," *Annual Publications of the Historical Society of Southern California*, vol. XIV, part 3 (1930), pp. 373-374.

SUMMERHAYES, MARTHA, *Vanished Arizona: recollections of Army life*, ed. by Milo Milton Quaife, Chicago, 1939.

SYKES, GODFREY, *The Colorado Delta*, New York, 1937.

U. S. WAR DEPARTMENT, *The War of the Rebellion: a compilation of the official records of the Union and Confederate Armies*, Series I—vol. L, parts I and II, Washington, 1897.

WOODWARD, ARTHUR, *Feud on the Colorado*, Los Angeles, 1955.

WYLLYS, RUFUS KAY, *Arizona: the history of a frontier state*, Phoenix, 1950.

JUAN FLORES AND THE MANILLAS

By DON MEADOWS

Not only is this article by historian Don Meadows one of compelling interest; it is flavorably seasoned with essential facets of early California history. Much has been written into it that has not, heretofore, been reduced to writing. Portions of the factual material contained represent data available only to the author. Without his revelation of them, they would unquestionably have been lost to students of the baroque Flores incident. We regard Mr. Meadows' authentic paper as an important historical accounting.

JUAN FLORES, TWENTY-THREE YEARS OLD, was a handsome, lithe, daring and unscrupulous native of Santa Barbara. With strong feelings about the American occupation of California he took it upon himself to avenge the Yankee invasion by agitation, theft and murder. In Los Angeles the Hardy brothers had a freight line that carried supplies from the "Queen of the Cow Country" to the surrounding territories. The corral in which they kept their stock and wagons was located on property southeast of the plaza owned by William Wolfskill. In May 1855 Juan Flores, who had been loitering around the pueblo for several months, spotted a good team of draft horses in the Hardy corral and, with two companions, stole the animals and headed for Mexico. The horses were plodders and not bred for speed, so the thieves were quickly overtaken and placed under arrest. Judge Myron Norton of the Court of Sessions sentenced the culprits to ten years in the penitentiary at San Quentin.

Naturally the fare and restraint of prison life did not meet with the approval of Juan Flores. Two months after his arrival at San Quentin he attempted an escape, but was unsuccessful. For more than a year he waited for another opportunity, and in October 1856 the big moment arrived. A brig was tied up at the penitentiary docks taking on a load of prison-made bricks. A hundred or more prisoners were loading the vessel when Flores and a fellow convict named Red Horse called for a break. Leading a gang of chain-shackled convicts to the brig the captain and crew were overpowered, the moorings were cast off, and the vessel was headed into San Francisco bay. From the prison, guards opened fire and killed many of the convicts. A six-pound field piece located on a promontory above the prison raked the ship with canister and mowed down more of the escaping prisoners. Heavier shot was fired at

JUAN FLORES AND THE MANILLAS

the brig but, with wind and tide in their favor, a small number of the convicts escaped to the Contra Costa shore. Among those who got away were Juan Flores and a hardened criminal named Pancho Daniel.

Fifteen or twenty convicts, led by Flores and Daniel, sneaked south through the Coast Range toward Los Angeles. At San Luis Obispo they made contact with Andres Fontes, an ex-convict who had been sent to prison by Sheriff James R. Barton of Los Angeles County. Fontes had sworn that he would kill Barton when he got out of San Quentin, and with the arrival of Flores and Daniel his mission became a possibility. He joined the gang on the promise that they would help him do away with the hated Sheriff.

As the desperados moved southward they developed a loose organization. They posed as patriots who were against American rule and, as such, were able to gain sympathy and help from a small part of the Californians who remembered the old days of Mexican authority. Pancho Daniel, the oldest and most conservative member of the gang, was looked upon as the head man; but Juan Flores, much younger and more daring, was the actual leader. The gang called themselves Manillas (Handcuffs, or Manacles), as an echo of their stay at San Quentin. For night-time recognition they adopted a series of questions and answers to prove their identity. The challenge was "Quien Viva?" (Where do you live?). The answer was "Isla!" (Island, probably because they thought the penitentiary was not part of the mainland.) "Que gente?" (What kind?) was the next question. "Manillas" (Manacles) was the proper answer; and the one challenged was recognized. A few weeks later, when some of them were captured and hung, the *Los Angeles Star* published a partial list of their names. They were Juan Catabo, alias Juan Sanripa, alias Juan Silvas; Francisco, alias Guerro Ardillero; Jose Santos; Diego Navarra; Pedro Lopez; Juan Valenzuela; Jesus Espinosa; and Encarnacion Berryessa.

Nearing Los Angeles the Manillas temporarily broke up their organization to keep from being conspicuous. Some who were strangers in the town mixed with the Angelenos and found sympathetic ears. By the middle of January 1857 the gang, some twenty-five or thirty strong, united at the old mission town of San Juan Capistrano.

On Sunday, January 18, 1857, Garnet Hardy, the youngest of the Hardy brothers, left Los Angeles with a four-horse team and a wagon load of merchandise destined for San Juan. It was late Tuesday afternoon when he reached the mission and drew up in front of the ruined church. Juan Forster, an Englishman who had married into the Pico family, was the owner of the mission buildings. He and his large family occupied that part of the mission

JUAN FLORES AND THE MANILLAS

that is now used as a gift shop and museum in the restored structure. As Hardy talked to Forster he noticed that a group of armed men were looking over his team and wagon. There was mutual surprise when Hardy recognized one of the men as Juan Flores, and Flores was more greatly surprised when he saw Garnet Hardy and two of the horses that had caused his trip to the penitentiary. Hardy explained the situation to Forster, and the owner of the mission had the teamster bring his team and wagon inside the mission walls. The Manillas wandered away with unconcern. That night Hardy sent a message to his brother in Los Angeles telling him about Flores and his gang.

San Juan Capistrano in 1857 was a sleepy Mexican village where Spanish was the dominant language. The town was divided into distinct social classes. Down along Trabuco creek peons and half-breed Indians lived in brush and adobe shacks. Along the west side of the wide pueblo plaza, extending southward from the mission, were the homes of the aristocracy. The families of Yorba, Avila, Valenzuela and Garcia had large adobe town houses where they lived when not on their ranchos in the surrounding territory. The east side of the plaza was lined by a row of small buildings occupied by stores, residences, grog shops, small trades and business houses. The Camino Real or Royal Road from Los Angeles swept into the northeast corner of the plaza between the ruined stone church and a large mission garden that was surrounded by a low adobe wall. At the south end of the village the Camino Real passed an orchard planted by the Franciscan Padres, and then swung to the southeast to cross San Juan creek. Eastward from the mission buildings, and north of the garden wall, a dusty road led into San Juan canyon. San Juan Capistrano was the largest town between Los Angeles and San Diego. The Manillas were camped on the San Juan canyon road just east of the mission.

The arrival of Garnet Hardy was disturbing to the Manillas. Flores knew he had been recognized, so he posted guards on all the roads from town to keep his presence from being reported to American authorities; but his safeguard was too late, for Hardy's message was already on its way. Los Angeles was sixty miles from San Juan and the bandits felt there was time to enjoy life before opposition could develop. At the far end of the eastern row of buildings was the home of a half-breed Indian girl named Chola Martina. Juan Flores had been in San Juan but a few hours before an amorous alliance had formed between him and the girl. The other bandits had also been successful in finding companions.

On Wednesday, January 21, the Manillas were restless. Their luck had held since leaving prison walls, but it was certain that a hunt was on for their

JUAN FLORES AND THE MANILLAS

re-capture. In the middle of the morning six of them called at the store of Miguel Kraszewski, a Polish Jew who had a place of business opposite the big house of Don Juan Avila. They asked if the merchant had a pistol for sale. Kraszewski had two, one in poor condition and one that he used for target practice. Juan Catabo took the good pistol and said he would buy it after he obtained a holster. Leaving the store he went to the home of Chola Martina where Tomas Burruel had a shoemaker shop. While Catabo was gone the other bandits amused themselves by shooting at a bull's head that lay in the pueblo plaza. With the bandits was a seventeen-year old youngster named Antonio Maria Varelas, nick-named Chino, or Curley, who had joined the Manillas in Los Angeles from a desire for adventure. He was the nephew of Juan Avila who owned the big house on the west side of the plaza. Kraszewski knew the boy and, while the other Manillas were shooting in the plaza, Chino came into the store and asked for something to eat. He was given some bread, wine and olives, and while he ate he told Kraszewski that his companions were going to the Cave Couts rancho of Guajome to work as vaqueros. Soon Catabo joined the group outside and rode off with them without paying for the pistol. Chino Varelas followed. Realizing that he was not to be paid for the gun, Kraszewski borrowed a horse standing outside his store and rode after the bandits. As he passed a neighboring house its occupant, named Monono, called—"Don Miguel, don't go, for they will kill you." Catching up with Chino Varelas he led the boy on horseback back to the store, where he demanded payment for the gun. Chino denied that he knew anything about the transaction and, when an opportunity arrived, broke away and headed toward the Manillas' hangout. In a matter of minutes all the Manillas were galloping toward the store, each bandit with a gun in his hand.

Next to Kraszewski's store was a grog shop where fifteen or twenty paisanos were playing viente-uno. Someone outside the shop shouted that the Manillas were coming, and in a moment the shop was cleared of players who streamed into the plaza to see what would happen. Kraszewski ran into the grog shop, hoping to find protection. Only one person, Librado Silvas, remained in the building; and with his help the front door of the building was closed and locked. There was a side door to the building that could not be secured. Kraszewski in his reminiscence says:

> "I heard the bandits outside inquiring after me and making a great noise; Chino
> Varelas in great excitement kicking at the front door and using threatening
> language. Silvas and I kept quiet inside the building, holding the side door
> closed with our hands. Silvas was right in front of me with both palms on the

JUAN FLORES AND THE MANILLAS

door. When I opened the door a little, Juan Catabo, who was on horseback, saw me and fired his, or my, pistol. By shutting the door quickly with my hand the shot passed through the door and through Silvas' wrist between the bones. Fortunately the wound was not serious and in about two weeks he was well again. Varelas kept up his violent motions and words in front, wanting to get into the shop. One of the residents of San Juan, named Pedro Verdugo, said to Varelas, who was asking for me, 'He is not inside, he is gone away.' All the protection I had when the door was broken away was a small counter about six feet long. The front part of it had only a piece of common sheeting. I sat down behind the counter with a big Spanish basket covering me. I looked upon myself as lost but did not lose my presence of mind, and intended if they rushed into the room, I would slide out through the cloth and out into the street. By the persuasion of Pedro Verdugo they didn't go in, but the chief of them, Juan Flores, said, 'Let's go into the store.' They did, and plundered it."

Loading a horse with loot the bandits left town by way of the San Juan canyon road. Two miles from the mission they stopped at the ranch of Tomas Forster and took another horse, then went down into the willows along the creek and camped.

The mission town was excited. Some of the people blamed Kraszewski for causing the trouble, saying that if he had not gone after Varelas nothing would have happened. Another storekeeper in the village, named Henry Charles, laughed at Kraszewski's misfortune, little realizing that he would be among the next that would suffer from the Manillas. Another message was sent to Los Angeles for help. There was a feeling in town that some of the paisanos knew a lot about the Manillas and their intentions. The aristocracy closed the doors and windows of their homes and loaded all the guns they possessed. Juan Forster, the most respected man in town, opened his home in the mission to any who wished to enter.

Days in January are short. Twilight had settled over the mission village when Don Juan Forster served dinner to his assembled guests. Kraszewski, Henry Charles, some of the Avila family, and other prominent citizens in town were taking advantage of his hospitality. The meal was ending when Monono, who had warned Kraszewski of danger that morning, came to the mission with terrifying news. George Pfleugardt, another merchant, had been murdered.

George Pfleugardt, a German, had a mercantile business just off the plaza a short distance south of the Kraszewski store. He was well liked by everyone in town and he felt no anxiety about his safety. His store was well stocked with fire arms. In addition to his regular business he loaned money on articles left for security, and usually there was considerable money in the

JUAN FLORES AND THE MANILLAS

establishment. Chola Martina had borrowed ten dollars from Pfleugardt, leaving a robosa—or shawl—as security. Pfleugardt's store consisted of two rooms: one he maintained as a bar; the other, opening on a side street, was his general store. The old mission fruit orchard was about two hundred yards southwest of his place of business.

It was almost dark when Chola Martina came into the Pfleugardt bar and asked to redeem her robosa. She gave the merchant ten dollars in silver and he went into his store room to get the shawl. There were no windows in the store so he opened the door on the side street to allow a bit of light to enter. While the merchant was getting the shawl the half-breed girl walked to the open door and lit a cigarette. As she stood in the doorway three men ran out of the orchard and entered the store. One of them thrust the girl to one side, while the other two began shooting at the merchant. He had no chance to defend himself. Before the smoke of gunfire had cleared, other bandits ran from the orchard and entered the building. Dragging the body of the dead merchant to one side they began helping themselves to food, liquor and merchandise. The bar was swept clean and for an hour the bandits ate and drank without paying any attention to the corpse in the room.

The bandits had been carousing for some time before knowledge of their activities reached Don Forster. He armed the men in the mission and went out to investigate. Henry Charles, who had laughed at Kraszewski, crawled under a bed for protection. The town was in an uproar. Shots were being fired at anyone whom the bandits did not recognize. Forster wanted to attack the Manillas but his family and friends objected. In the darkness the risk was too great. In the mission buildings preparations were made for defense. From the back streets and river bottom a noisy rabble gathered in the plaza. The Manillas were in revolt against law and order, and their actions appealed to the Indians and mixed-breeds.

The work of the Manillas was well planned. After the Pfleugardt store had been sacked of food, liquor, money and provisions the bandits moved up the street to the store of Henry Charles and it, too, was ransacked. Once again the Kraszewski store was entered and thoroughly searched for money. What the bandits did not want in the stores was thrown into the street where it was carried off by the mob. In his big house on the west side of the plaza Manuel Garcia, known locally as Portuguese Mike, had a small store of selected goods. Flores took some of his men to the Garcia store and demanded admission. Garcia gave the key to his store to the bandit chief and some of the contents were taken, but nothing else was disturbed. The bandits had stolen several

CASA de TOMAS BURRUEL in 1933. Home
of Chola Martina.   (*Photo by Don Meadows*)

CHOLA MARTINA in 1907.
(*From Terry Stephenson*)

JUAN FLORES AND THE MANILLAS

horses in San Juan valley and these were brought into the plaza and loaded with loot. About an hour before midnight the Manillas had completed their ghastly work. With loaded horses, and with a few parting shots at the home of Juan Forster, the bandits left San Juan. Juan Flores with about twenty men rode off to the north along the Camino Real; a similar group under Pancho Daniel turned off at the mission and set out through San Juan canyon. It was well past midnight before any kind of order returned to the pueblo.

While Juan Flores and the Manillas were terrorizing the town of San Juan, Sheriff Barton of Los Angeles County with a posse of five men was camped on the north bank of the Santiago creek, twenty-three miles away. Garnet Hardy's letter to his brother had reached the county seat late Wednesday night and was turned over to the Sheriff on Thursday morning. Barton assembled and deputized a small posse consisting of Constable William H. Little, Charles K. Baker, Frank H. Alexander, Charles F. Daly, and Alfred Hardy. An unnamed Frenchman, who was not armed, joined the group on his way to San Diego. Thursday afternoon the seven men left Los Angeles and arrived at the Santiago creek after dark. They made their camp about where Flower Street, Santa Ana, crosses the creek today.

At sunrise on Friday, January 23, 1857, Sheriff Barton and his posse rode to the hacienda of Refugio, owned by Don Jose Sepulveda. The large adobe home was located on present-day Artesia street, just south of First street, in Santa Ana. Don Jose was famous for his hospitality and Barton knew that he and his men would be welcome for breakfast. When the officers entered Refugio they left their guns on the wide veranda. Unknown to Don Jose there were Flores sympathizers around his home. There is a belief, unsubstantiated, that while the guns were left unguarded they were tampered with. It is certain, however, that some unknown person rode away from Refugio and warned the bandits that Sheriff Barton was on his way to the mission town.

There were three roads, or trails, that led across the wide San Joaquin ranch toward mission San Juan Capistrano. One, called the upper road, followed along the foothills of the Santa Ana mountains; the second, the one most traveled, was the Camino Real which is followed today by the Santa Ana Freeway. The third was called the lower road. It was little more than a wide trail that could be traveled only on horseback. It meandered southeast from Refugio, crossed the Swamp of the Frogs, and reached the base of the San Joaquin hills near the southern end of Central Avenue, Irvine. After crossing the Sanjon del Alisal, now called San Diego creek, it followed the south bank of the Sanjon to the Arroyo de las Palos Verdes, where it forked. The right-

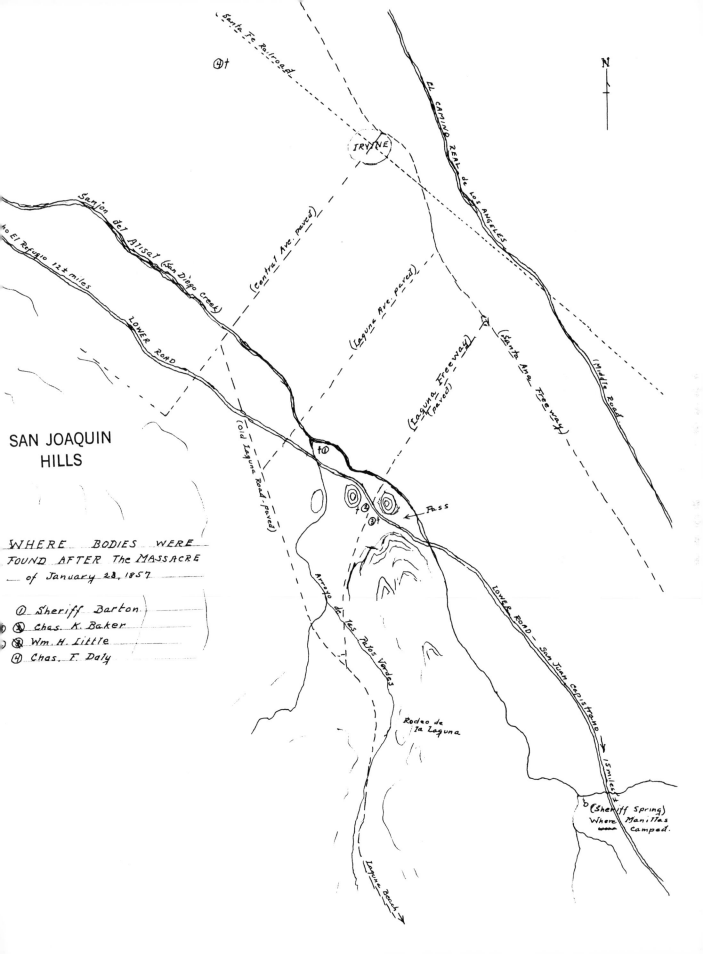

N

④ t

Santa Fe Railroad

IRVINE

EL CAMINO REAL de LOS ANGELES

Sanjon del Alisal (San Diego Creek)

ho El Refugio 12± miles

(Central Ave. paved)

(Laguna Ave. paved)

LOWER ROAD

(Santa Ana Freeway)

(Middle Road)

(Laguna Freeway (paved))

SAN JOAQUIN
HILLS

(Old Laguna Road-paved)

t①

②③
①④

Pass

WHERE BODIES WERE
FOUND AFTER The MASSACRE
— of January 23, 1857

① Sheriff Barton
⊗ Chas. K. Baker
⊗ Wm. H. Little
④ Chas. T. Daly

Arroyo de los Palos Verdes

Lower Road — San Juan Capistrano

Rodeo de
la Laguna

15 miles

b (Sheriff Spring)
Where Manillas
were Camped.

Laguna Beach

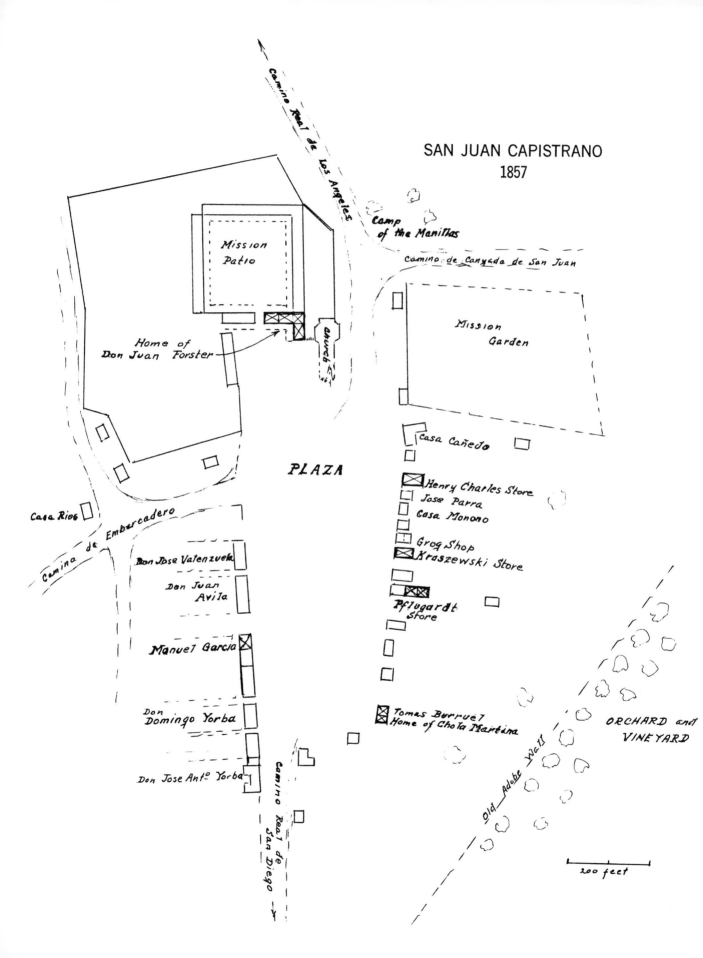

SAN JUAN CAPISTRANO
1857

Camino Real de Los Angeles

Camp of the Manilhas

Camino de Canyada de San Juan

Mission Patio

Mission Garden

Home of Don Juan Forster

Church

PLAZA

Casa Cañedo

Henry Charles Store

Jose Parra

Casa Monono

Grog Shop

Kraszewski Store

Pflugardt Store

Casa Rios

Camino de Embarcadero

Don Jose Valenzuela

Don Juan Avila

Manuel Garcia

Don Domingo Yorba

Don Jose Antº Yorba

Camino Real de San Diego

Tomas Burruel
Home of Chola Martina

Old Adobe Wall

ORCHARD and VINEYARD

200 feet

JUAN FLORES AND THE MANILLAS

hand branch led up the arroyo past the Rodeo de la Laguna and crossed the hills into the head of Laguna Canyon. The left branch continued over rolling country and went through a low pass in a spur of the hills. The lower road was the shortest way between Refugio and San Juan.

When Barton and his men left Refugio, their host—Don Jose—urged the Sheriff to take a larger posse, for the Flores gang was dangerous and could not be handled by six men. Barton took the suggestion lightly and said he could handle the situation.

It was mid-morning when the posse drew near the gap in the San Joaquin hills. The seven men were riding closely together when a lone horseman was noticed loping across the plain near the middle road. Little and Baker suggested that it might be a good idea if they rode ahead to learn where the stranger was going. They were about four hundred yards ahead of the Sheriff, and close to the pass, when fifteen or twenty men with drawn guns galloped from the hill on the right. Quick shots were exchanged; but, out-numbered, the officers were thrown from their horses and killed. Barton and his three deputies started to the rescue. The bandits rushed forward and closed in on the Sheriff. None of the officers' bullets seemed to have any effect. The Frenchman took off into the hills and was not molested. One bandit rode close to Barton and shouted—"God damn you, I've got you now!" It was Andres Fontes. At close range he shot Barton through the heart. Hardy, Alexander and Daly turned their mounts and began a retreat. Bullets whined about them but they escaped being hit. Daly was riding a mule and fell behind. Three miles from the first shooting the bandits reached him, and he was killed. Hardy and Alexander managed to keep ahead of the Manillas. The pursuit continued almost to Refugio before the bandits gave up the chase. At Refugio the two officers stopped for a drink, reported what had happened, and with fresh mounts galloped on toward Los Angeles. At Los Nietos they separated, Hardy following the Camino Real into the city, Alexander turning north through the San Gabriel river gap to El Monte.

On their field of victory the Manillas checked over the bodies of their victims. Robbing them of their valuables and desecrating the officers, the Manillas moved back to the spring where they had spent the night. Today the campsite is called Sheriff Spring. Loading their pack horses the bandits crossed the San Joaquin plain and entered the Santa Ana mountains through Aliso canyon.

When Hardy and Alexander reached Los Angeles and El Monte the towns were thrown into great excitement. All night long preparations were made to go after the bandits. Early Saturday morning forty men on horseback left for

Pass through a spur of the San Joaquin Hills through which the Lower Road to San Juan passed in 1857. Baker and Little were murdered near this point. (*Photo by Don Meadows, April 1963*)

Long Shot of the Pass and hills where Sheriff Barton was killed in January 1857.
(*Photo taken by Don Meadows, April 1963*)

FLORES PEAK, from which the bandits escaped when cornered by Andres Pico, 1857

(Photo taken by Don Meadows, April 1963)

Terry E. Stephenson and Wm. McPherson under the branch from which the bandits Ardillero and Catabo were hung in January 1857.

From Terry Stephenson (*Photo taken July 1930*)

JUAN FLORES AND THE MANILLAS

San Juan. Later in the day another party on horseback and in carriages set out with a wagon holding four coffins to bring back the bodies of the murdered men. The *Los Angeles Star* reported:

"The bodies of Barton and Baker were found within about ten feet of the lower road to San Juan, on the ranch of San Joaquin, on the near side of the small hills to the right of Arroyo de los Palos Verdes—on the Sanjon del Alisal (San Diego creek) about fifteen miles this side of the Mission San Juan Capistrano. Barton's body was lying on the right hand side of the road with the head toward the road, and about 300 yards this side of Baker, who was lying on the right hand side of the road. Little's body was lying about 100 yards from Baker, at about right angles with the road. (The Laguna Beach Freeway passes across the place where Little and Baker were killed.) The body of C. F. Daly, the blacksmith, was found about three miles from the road, as if he had started to go to the middle Santa Ana road. Little's horse was found within ten steps of the body of Barton, shot through the heart on the off side. The pockets of all were rifled of their contents, the robbers becoming possessed of three gold watches and chains, valuable diamond pins and other jewelry. Barton's papers, all torn in small pieces, were collected and brought in. Little's horse had the saddle on, Barton's boots were taken, his hat was near his body; the hats of Little and Baker were missing. Barton's body had three wounds in the region of the heart, the left arm was broken, and a shot in the right eye. Little was shot in the right eye, head and body. Baker was shot in back of head, also in the right eye and cheek. Daly was shot in the mouth and body, the face burned with powder. All the bodies had evidently been fired upon after death."

Andres Pico, who had fought Americans at the battle of San Pasqual and was an ardent Californian, stood for law and order. A natural born leader, he was placed in command of the operations to hunt down the bandits. He was methodical. All day Sunday he gathered men, horses and supplies for a rough campaign. On Monday morning he set out from Los Angeles with nineteen Californians armed with lances. At the rancho of his brother, Pio Pico, he obtained twenty-five more men; but, not having sufficient arms for that number, selected thirty-five and started for San Juan. At Refugio he recruited five others, and at San Juan was joined by the posse which had left the city when news of the tragedy had arrived. Altogether Pico had a company of fifty-one Californians. On Tuesday morning a party of twenty-six Americans under the leadership of Dr. Gentry left El Monte for the mission town, and there they placed themselves under the orders of Don Andres. The ex-Mexican General planned his campaign with care. Groups of armed men were placed on all the roads and trails that led away from the mission. Forty-three Indian scouts under command of Captain Manuelito were sent into the mountains

JUAN FLORES AND THE MANILLAS

to locate the bandits, and at San Juan a large group of rangers was kept ready to move if the Manillas were located.

In Los Angeles another company of twenty-seven riders was organized under the leadership of James Thompson. They were joined by a complement of soldiers sent to Los Angeles from Fort Tejon. Thompson and the soldiers watched all the roads and passes in the north that might be taken by Flores or Pancho Daniel if they escaped detection in the south.

Late Wednesday afternoon an Indian scout came into San Juan with the information that the bandits had been located in the upper Santiago canyon of the Santa Ana mountains. Since the moon would set early, and operations would be difficult in the dark, Pico waited until morning to start in pursuit. Later at night another Indian arrived with the news that he had talked to Chino Varelas; and the young man, disillusioned by the bloody activities of the Manillas, wanted to surrender.

As soon as it was daylight Pico led his men out of San Juan and part way up Trabuco canyon. Crossing over rolling hills they dropped into Aliso canyon. Travel was slow, for the brush was heavy and the advance was kept as inconspicuous as possible to guard against detection by the Manillas. An express was sent into the upper Trabuco to tell Dr. Gentry, stationed there, to meet the Californians in Aliso canyon. By sundown the rangers were in camp waiting the arrival of Dr. Gentry.

Early Friday morning, January 30, exactly a week after the death of Sheriff Barton, Dr. Gentry's men joined up with Don Andres; and the combined parties, numbering 119 men, moved up the trail (now covered by pavement) that led from the head of Aliso canyon into the Santiago. The bandits were camped on a flat in the canyon that is now covered by a dude ranch and an olive grove. Flores had been expecting pursuit, and from a high point of rocks looking down into Aliso canyon he spotted the rangers below and quickly joined his ruffians. They abandoned their camp and moved higher into Santiago canyon.

The sun was high when Pico got his men into the Santiago and had them deployed for the attack. The canyon was choked with sycamore and alder trees and the slopes were covered with cactus, sage and manzanita. The rangers were organized into three groups: one under Dr. Gentry covered the northern slope of the canyon, another under Mr. Copewood worked through the canyon bottom, and Andres Pico kept to the south and was ready to help the other groups if necessary.

Flores realized that the canyon would be a trap. A half mile above where

JUAN FLORES AND THE MANILLAS

the Manillas had camped, the Santiago narrowed into a deep gorge; then, after a few hundred yards, was joined on the left by a fair-sized canyon, now called Harding because a bee-man of that name once lived there. Between Harding canyon and the Santiago a narrow, brushy ridge led toward the higher mountains. Here was a means of escape. Keeping some of his men in the rear to hold up the advancing rangers, Flores turned up the ridge. It was a fatal mistake. Gentry's men, some on foot and some on horseback, worked their way into Harding canyon. Pico stayed with the Santiago, and Copewood moved up the ridge after the bandits. Progress was slow, for the brush and terrain were rugged. Shots were exchanged whenever a target was visible. Oddly enough, no one on either side was struck by a bullet. The range between the fighters was too great. Some of the bandits abandoned their horses and crawled through the chaparral. Chino Varelas hid in the brush and surrendered to a family friend, Don Tomas Sanchez. Flores, Jesus Espinosa and Leonardo Lopez on horseback led the bandits along the ridge. Suddenly they were faced with a new danger. The ridge broke off into an escarpment several hundred feet high. Copewood's men were drawing near. Bullets were singing around the Manillas. Faced with death on all sides, the bandits dropped their guns and surrendered; all but Flores, Espinosa and Lopez. They hesitated at the edge of the precipice and looked down. There was a small ledge about fifty feet below. Flores dismounted and sent his horse over the edge. It rolled into the depths of Santiago canyon. With no more hesitation the three men slid over the brink and tumbled down the face of the cliff. Brush and nubbins of rock broke their fall. Flores' gun discharged and a bullet passed through his right arm. At the foot of the escarpment the heavy chaparral began again, and the three men crawled into the brush. High above them their cohorts were taken into custody. Juan Catabo, afraid to make the desperate leap with Flores, surrendered to Mr. Copewood. Down the ridge in Harding canyon Francisco Ardillero was captured by Dr. Gentry. Deep twilight filled the canyons when all the prisoners were assembed and placed under heavy guard. Only one of the rangers was injured. Jose Antonio Serrano, mayor-domo of the Pio Pico rancho, received a broken thigh when his horse slipped on the mountain side. From Chino Varelas, Pico learned that Pancho Daniel and others had left San Juan by an eastern trail and were not with Flores.

Many years later the great Polish actress, Madame Helena Modjeska, built a home in upper Santiago canyon. Just north of her homesite, across the canyon, is the high rocky bluff over which the bandits jumped. Appropriately, it is called Flores Peak.

JUAN FLORES AND THE MANILLAS

As soon as it was daylight on Saturday morning, Dr. Gentry and a chosen group of rangers took up the trail of Flores and the escaped bandits. The rest of the posse went into camp for a rest after their week of strenuous work. The trail of Flores led over the ridge between the Santiago and Silverado (then called Madera) canyons, then down the Silverado toward the flatland beyond the foothills. All day long Dr. Gentry and his posse kept on the trail, but at nightfall the bandits had not been found. At sunrise they were again on the trail, and soon discovered that the fleeing bandits had turned north in an effort to reach the Santa Ana canyon. About noon three men were seen on a high ridge, and the rangers spread out to make a capture. Many shots were exchanged, and the bandits sought shelter in a rocky cave. Surrounded, they were forced to give up.

Northeast from the road that approaches Irvine Park, and far across the wide valley of Santiago Creek, a conspicuous nubbin of rock stands clear against the horizon. Locally it is known as Robbers Roost, and according to a vague tradition it was the place where robbers were captured many years ago. There may be an association between the square-topped butte and Juan Flores. At least, it is close to the place where Juan Flores was captured, and there is a cave on its western face.

When Flores, Espinosa and Lopez were secured they were taken to the old Yorba settlement of Santa Ana, now called Olive. There they were placed under guard in an adobe building, and a messenger was sent to Pico telling him that all of the bandits were now in custody. Pico broke camp, and with his prisoners moved down the Santiago, headed for Los Angeles. An overnight camp was made at the mouth of Limestone canyon on a spot that now is covered by the water of Irvine Lake. On Monday morning Pico left the main party and, with a few companions and two of the prisoners—Catabo and Ardillero, started a short cut through the hills toward the Sepulveda home where he wanted the two prisoners identified as escaped convicts. He had gone only a short distance up Precitas canyon (now followed by the paved Santiago Canyon Road) when a horseman arrived with exasperating news. During the night Flores and his two companions at old Santa Ana had slipped their bonds and were free again. In a rage Pico declared that two of the bandits would not escape, and looked about for a suitable tree where Catabo and Ardillero could be hung. There were no large trees in Precitas canyon, but about a quarter of a mile up a tributary valley was a group of sycamores. Here his prisoners were strung up. (A year later, after coyotes had dug up the bodies from a shallow grave, they were re-buried by the old '49'er, Judge Joseph E. Pleasants.

JUAN FLORES AND THE MANILLAS

In 1920 he pointed out the spot. The trees are still visible in the little valley on the right of the Santiago Canyon road, about 2/10 of a mile before Irvine Lake is reached when going into the Santa Ana mountains.) When the executed bandits were buried, Andres Pico hurried on to old Santa Ana, again to direct the capture of the slippery bandit chief.

Through northern Los Angeles County James Thompson and the Tejon soldiers had all the roads and passes under surveillance. On February 7 the *Los Angeles Star* published the following:

> "On Tuesday last (Feb. 3) Juan Flores came to the Simi (Santa Susana) Pass in search of water. Two soldiers who had been placed on watch behind a rock quickly stepped up behind him, and with their guns leveled and cocked ordered him to stop, which he immediately did, and dismounted. At this time he was without arms, had not even a pocket knife, was mounted on a very poor horse, and had only a little dried beef on his saddle behind him. He was questioned as to who he was, where he was going, and where he had come from, etc. In reply he stated that his name was Juan Gonzales Sanchez, that he belonged to, and had come from San Fernando mission, that he was out hunting for horses and he was going no further. He was conducted to camp where he was recognized by Don Pancho Johnson, one of the guard, as Juan Flores, the noted robber and murderer. He was of course secured. (Flores was turned over to Captain Thompson.) Flores stated to Mr. Thompson that he, Espinosa and Lopez had escaped from the guard at Santa Ana on Sunday night, that they had then separated and he had not seen them since. He said he had stolen a horse, saddle and bridle at Santa Ana, or near there, and had reached San Fernando, where he caught the horse that he was riding when captured. He requested Mr. Thompson to bring him into town so that he might have the benefit of a clergyman, make confession, and write to his mother, and then he was ready for his fate."

On Thursday afternoon Thompson and Flores arrived in Los Angeles in a buggy. During the journey Flores maintained a spirit of coolness and self possession, but when the city was reached and he saw a great crowd assembled he begged Thompson to stay with him until he was safely lodged in jail. There he was placed with the others that had been arrested.

Again, the *Los Angeles Star:*

> "On Saturday last, (Feb. 14) the people of this city, and a large number from the towns of the county, assembled together for the purpose of determining what should be done with Flores and the other prisoners then in jail. After a good deal of talking a vote was taken, and it was resolved, without a dissenting voice, that Flores should be executed forthwith. It was resolved to hand the other prisoners over to the authorities, their crimes being only attempts at

JUAN FLORES AND THE MANILLAS

murder, burglaries, and horse stealing. When the meeting adjourned, the people marched to the jail and took possession of Flores. He had been expecting this visit. In a short time he was led out and was received by Capt. Twist's company who guarded him to the place of execution. These were followed by Capt. Farget's company, the whole escorted by a large company of mounted Californians and Americans. The Rev. Father Raho and Rev. Vicente Llover were in attendance, and accompanied the prisoner to his last scene. The prisoner walked with firmness and seemed composed as any one in the crowd. The distance from the jail to the hill on which the scaffold was erected is about a quarter of a mile. The prisoner was dressed in white pants, light vest and black merino sack coat. There was nothing in his appearance to indicate the formidable bandit which he had proved himself to be.

"On arrival at the place of execution the prisoner was led to the foot of the gallows, still accompanied by his spiritual guides. His arms were then tied to his body, and thus pinioned, he firmly ascended the drop. He expressed a wish to address the people, who instantly became silent. His remarks were interpreted, and were merely to the effect that he was now ready to die, that he had committed many crimes, that he died without having ill-will against any man, and hoped that no one would bear ill-will against him. Observing some persons among the crowd whom he had known he called one or two toward him and gave some final directions leaving his body to them. He then handed a white handkerchief to one of the attendants and wished his face to be covered with it, which was done. His legs were then bound and the rope adjusted around his neck, during which he continued in conversation with those in his immediate vicinity. The attendants took farewell of him, left the drop, and immediately after the plank was drawn from under him, and the body of Flores swung in the air. The fall was too short, and the unfortunate wretch struggled in agony for a considerable time. After a protracted struggle, very painful to behold, the limbs became quiet and finally stiff in death. Thus ended the brief but stormy life of the bandit captain, Juan Flores."

Justice in the old days was rapid and direct. Espinosa and Lopez were captured and hung without ceremony. Some of the prisoners lodged in jail were quietly removed and executed. Others stood trial and were sent to the penitentiary. Chino Varelas, because of his youth and family connections, was set free. A year later Pancho Daniel was captured in San Jose and returned to Los Angeles where the people gave him the same attention they had given Juan Flores. Many bad men and ruthless gangs infested southern California during the days of early American rule, but none of them was as notorious as Juan Flores and the Manillas.

JUAN FLORES AND THE MANILLAS

BIBLIOGRAPHY

There are many accounts of this affair, most of which have been written from hearsay and garbled information. This account is based on source material recorded by persons who were present during the episode or who received information directly from those who were involved. Two gentlemen, both long gone, personally contributed toward building this version. The friendship and association with Judge Joseph E. Pleasants and Terry Elmo Stephenson will always be cherished.

BANCROFT, H. H. . . . . . Popular Tribunals, Vol. I

BELL, HORACE . . . . . Reminiscences of a Ranger. 1881

CLELAND, ROBERT G. . . . . The Cattle on a Thousand Hills. 1941

HAMILTON, DWIGHT . . . . (Early maps of San Juan Capistrano and Orange County.)

HAYES, BENJAMIN . . . . . Pioneer Notes. 1929

KRASZEWSKI, MIGUEL . . . . "Acts of the Manillas" from a manuscript in the Bancroft Library, published by the Orange County Historical Society, Vol. 3, 1939

Los Angeles Star . . . . . File in the Huntington Library.

NEWMARK, HARRIS . . . . . Sixty Years in Southern California. 1930

PLEASANTS, J. E. . . . . . "The Killing of Sheriff Barton" in Armor's History of Orange County. 1911.

STEPHENSON, TERRY E. . . . Caminos Viejos. 1930
Shadows of Old Saddleback. 1931

WARNER, J. J. . . . . . . Illustrated History of Los Angeles County. 1889.

YORBA, ALFONSO (Bruce Conde) . Unpublished notes on San Juan Capistrano.

THE TEMECULA MASSACRE

By HORACE PARKER

Who ever heard of the *Temecula Massacre?* Our well-informed author tells us it was the "bloodiest battle of the Mexican War in California." The *Temecula Massacre* arose as an aftermath of the *Pauma Massacre* which, in turn, had its inception in the *Battle of San Pascual.* The historic significance of these three inter-related events supplies the nucleus of this study. Dr. Parker, author and historian, is unquestionably our most knowledgeable source on the Anza-Borrego country; and he is intimately familiar with the region round about Temecula.

FEW CALIFORNIA HISTORIANS ARE AWARE that the bloodiest battle of the Mexican War in California was the Temecula Massacre. This climactic engagement between the Californians and the Indians took place in Southern California during January, 1847, just a few days prior to—or perhaps even after—the Cahuenga Capitulation on January 13, 1847 which terminated the Southern California Revolt.

It is of interest because more lives were probably lost in this single engagement than the sum total of all the casualties of the Mexican War in California. The massacre also demonstrates how a series of seemingly unrelated events can eventually weave themselves into a common web of destiny. Furthermore, there was a confusing clash of many nationalities and loyalties in the Southern California Revolt, with the Indian's role now largely forgotten or neglected.

The seeds of the Temecula Massacre were sown in Los Angeles by Commodore Stockton and Captain Archibald Gillespie late in September, 1846. According to Dr. John Walton Caughey, "Stockton had erred in the tone of his proclamation," and Gillespie, left with an inadequate garrison, "unwisely issued tactless regulations." As one of the participants, José del Carmen Lugo, states in his reminiscences, "A few days later the Americans began making prisoners of certain Californians and others who had given information that tended to be unfavorable to the United States." Lugo estimates that about twenty Californians had been taken prisoner when—in a moment of *bravado*—a group of youthful Californians, probably with a skinful of *vino*, attacked Gillespie and the garrison. The Californians were poorly armed; and when the Americans returned their fire the youths beat a precipitous retreat. Gillespie retaliated for the attack by initiating additional controls and curfews on the Angeleños.

THE TEMECULA MASSACRE

Idle gossip and threats of an uprising by boastful Californians in San Bernardino reached the ears of B. D. Wilson, who was on a hunting trip with friends in the nearby mountains. Wilson, who had never renounced his American citizenship, was actually returning from scouting the movements of the Mexican General Castro through Warner's Pass for the Americans. He hastened back to lend assistance to the beleagured American garrison in Los Angeles. After the scouting expedition and the hunting *pasear*, Wilson and his party were short of ammunition and stopped at Wilson's home on the Jurupa to replenish it.

According to Lugo's account, Wilson sent word that he was going to take Lugo prisoner. Lugo also stated that he knew of no reason why Wilson should make this threat against him. Angered by Wilson's challenge, José del Carmen Lugo ". . . returned home and prepared myself with men and arms to go to meet Wilson." With about twenty-one men he proceeded to Wilson's home, only to find that Don Benito had left for the Rancho Chino. Lugo started in pursuit.

On the way he overtook some Indians and disarmed them of bows and arrows, which he used to arm his own men. Lugo sent a scouting party of five men ahead who encountered an American ". . . carrying a rifle of eighteen shots . . ." The American with his marvelous rifle made good his escape.

While reconnoitering the Chino house Lugo met, in a willow thicket, a Mexican officer sent by General Flores in Los Angeles who ordered Lugo to join him with his force. As Lugo said, "Until this moment all I had done had been the result of threats made by Señor Wilson, but now I was taking orders from a recognized military authority." Lugo, in turn, sent word to General Flores for help inasmuch as he estimated there were about fifty well-armed men in the Chino adobe. According to Lugo, if the Americans in the ranch house had made a sortie, ". . . they would have finished us since we had no more than four or five guns and a few pistols—plus one or two lances and a few Indian arrows."

Reinforcements arrived from Los Angeles and the Californians attacked. Lugo made a daring ride on horseback and succeeded in firing the thatched roof of the adobe, which caused the defenders to surrender. Lugo said, "In the affair at Chino we took forty or fifty prisoners, *and a great many firearms and ammunition.*"

The versions of the Battle of Chino are nearly as numerous as the participants. One second-hand account, as told by Benjamin Butler Harris in his journal of 1849, reaches the rank of a Texas tall tale:

"I learned from him [Isaac Williams] that during the Mexican War about

THE TEMECULA MASSACRE

five hundred cavalrymen had surrounded his place [the Chino adobe] and demanded his surrender. Entrenching in his home with ten men, he kept them at bay for several days until, at length, they sent a flaming arrow into his grass roof and his house burning overhead, he surrendered. Repenting the deed, his captors aided in extinguishing the fire and arresting further damage."

This unexpected victory, plus the supply of firearms and ammunition, encouraged the Californians; and the Southern California Revolt burst into full bloom.

After the so-called Battle of Chino, Gillespie surrendered in Los Angeles and he and his men were allowed to make their way to San Pedro unharmed on condition that they embark immediately and leave the City of the Angels. Before Gillespie and his men sailed, however, reinforcements arrived from San Francisco. In the eyes of the Californians Gillespie broke his parole by returning with the reinforcements in an attempt to recapture Los Angeles.

Once again the Californians were victorious at the Battle of the Old Woman's Gun (Battle of Dominguez Rancho) on October 8, 1846. The next day the invaders were forced to drop back to San Pedro. Lugo apparently took no part in these engagements although the morale and captured material obtained at Chino no doubt assisted the Californians' successful stand.

In the meantime the merchants of Los Angeles had contributed loans of money for the defense of Alta California. These funds had been turned over to a Mexican official named Segura. It was intimated that the Mexican General Flores had arranged with Segura to flee the country with the borrowed loot. Don Diego Sepulveda heard of Segura's flight and, enlisting Lugo's help, the two men with a small force started in pursuit. On their arrival at Temecula they heard that the Indians in San Bernardino had risen and were threatening the ranchos. Lugo left Sepulveda to pursue Segura while he returned to "... placate the rebellious Indians ...," which he did.

Lugo started again in pursuit of Segura. Arriving at Warner's rancho he learned that Sepulveda had turned back and that one of his men had been killed. Segura had passed through the area eight days earlier.

Lugo continued on to Santa Ysabel where he encountered some Sonorans, with a herd of horses, fleeing to Sonora. He stopped them "... by right of the general order I had, as that seemed to be in the best interest of the country." The entire party camped at Santa Ysabel where the local Indian *Capitan* Mateo warned Lugo that the Indians from Pauma, Temecula, and the Agua Caliente (Warner's Hot Springs) were going to attack during the night. "Within three or four hours Captain José Alipaz came from the presidio at San Diego with eleven men and joined me." They spent an alert but uneventful night.

THE TEMECULA MASSACRE

The next day "...when we reached Pauma I took leave of Alipaz, charging him to watch the Sonorans closely. The reason for this attitude towards them was that they were conveying stolen horses, and also I had orders to allow no one to leave California." Lugo then returned to Los Angeles via Pala and Temecula.

About a week later, *mas y menos*, Lugo learned that the Indians had killed some Californians on the Warner's rancho. Unfortunately, his reminiscences omit dates and known events which occurred at this critical time. The killing of the Californians at the Agua Caliente on the Warner's ranch is now known as the Pauma Massacre. It seems to have been a frontier rule that when only whites were involved in a conflict it was called a *battle;* but when Indians were involved it became a *massacre*. Historians think the Pauma Massacre took place a day or two after the Battle of San Pascual which started on December 6, 1846, and ended with Kearny's rescue on December 11. Judge Hayes' expresses it in euphonious Spanish terms: "The day (of the Pauma Massacre) is remembered only as between *dia de la virgen* (December 8) and that of *Guadalupe* (December 12)."

According to Hudson's account of the Pauma Massacre there were eleven men killed by the Indians at the Agua Caliente. There were no survivors. The Californians were encamped at the adobe on the Pauma Rancho. In spite of numerous warnings they posted no guards and opened the door of the adobe at the request of usually friendly local Indians. The Indians fell upon them and carried the eleven men to the Agua Caliente. With encouragement from William Marshall, the bloody merchant of the Agua Caliente, the Indians tortured, killed and mutilated the unfortunate *Californianos* "in a manner too horrible to describe."

Why these men were at Pauma has never been fully explained. The most plausible story is that, after the Battle of San Pascual, the California Rangers broke up into small groups and disappeared into the countryside. This may have been one of those groups. There is a breath of coincidence inasmuch as this was about the time Lugo had left eleven men under Captain José Alipaz at Pauma to guard the *caballada;* and we know eleven Californians were killed at the Agua Caliente. There was an Alipaz listed among the victims, but apparently it was not José. Additional research may, however, show this to have been the same group, which would explain their reason for being at Pauma.

It is also a mystery why the usually friendly Indians of Rincon and Pauma should suddenly turn on the Californians. We do know that Kearny talked to the Indians at the Agua Caliente on December 2nd and 3rd, prior to the

THE TEMECULA MASSACRE

Battle of San Pascual. We do not know exactly what he said, but what he said or left unsaid may have triggered the uprising. We do know that at this same time Lt. Davidson and Kit Carson made a raid on a herd of horses and mules at Aguanga belonging to General Flores. This, and the Battle of San Pascual itself, could have been an exciting factor among the Indians. Sgt. Nathaniel V. Jones, of Cooke's Mormon Battalion which followed Kearny into California, states in his diary, "The Indians, a few days before we came to Warner's, had taken eleven Spaniards and killed them in cold blood, the Spaniards had killed some forty of the Indians for it. They (the Indians) probably thought that we (the Americans) were their friends and (the Indians) would kill off the Spaniards." And again, the Indians may have revolted to revenge themselves on the Californians and Mexicans for past wrongs, actual or imagined. In spite of insipid stories to the contrary, the Southern California Indian had been exploited, sometimes cruelly exploited, by the Spaniard, Padre, Mexican and whites in general. The Indian no doubt felt that a change, any change, was better than the status quo; and the Americans were a means of accomplishing it.

These were exciting and bloody times around the skirts of Palomar Mountain. Loyalties were vacillating. We find, for example, Lugo pursuing Segura, a cohort of the Mexican General Flores, while at the same time enforcing the general orders of Flores against fleeing Sonorans and Mexicans. Even though California was a Mexican province, the native Californian of Spanish ancestry and tradition did not consider himself a Mexican; if they could not be Spaniards, then at least they were Californians and not Mexicans. Lugo indicated this rift quite strongly when he said, "The Mexicans said that we, the Californians, would not amount to anything in an emergency, because we would not trouble ourselves enough. My promptitude in carrying out the orders that the *podido* of a Flores gave me at all times gives them the lie. I call him this because he was an intriguer and a thief who kept us (the Californians) undergoing fatigues while he sat in Los Angeles with the Americans."

Strange little whisperings and rumors have come out of the Southern California brush country through the years as regards the Indian and his conduct at the Battle of San Pascual. One of these is to the effect that the Indians, who were no doubt excited and interested spectators at the battle, were instrumental in forcing the Californians to break off the engagement under threats of allying themselves actively with the defeated Americans. The Indian guide who accompanied Beale and Carson under cover of darkness, and actually preceded the two Americans into San Diego and obtained rein-

SITE OF THE TEMECULA MASSACRE—at this point, where the old road to San Jacinto emerged into the Long Valley, Lugo's Californians and Indian allies turned and gave battle to the pursuing Luiseño Indians. The ambush of fifteen Californians and fifty Indians was probably behind the low hill in the center right of the picture. This spot is now known to Vail Company employees as the Adobe Windmill.

SANTA GERTRUDES—or Adobe Spring, famed camping spot along the old road between Temecula and San Jacinto.

THE TEMECULA MASSACRE

forcements, was undoubtedly a local Indian well-acquainted with the terrain. In fact, Dan Tortuga, former Indian Justice of the Peace on the Pichanga Indian Reservation near Temecula and in later years the town shoemaker, was a rumored descendant of this forgotten San Pascual Indian guide.

After killing the Californians at the Agua Caliente, many of the still excited Indians made their way to Temecula to celebrate their deeds with both participants and non-participants. Manuelito Cota, one of the ringleaders of the Pauma Massacre, was in Temecula and survived the Temecula Massacre. Another of the leaders, and one whom the Californians always regretted had escaped death in the Temecula Massacre, was Pablo Apis.

It is well at this point to wipe clean the escutcheon of Pablo Apis insofar as the black deeds at the Agua Caliente are concerned. Pablo Apis, or Hapish, was the respected and well-known chief of the Temeculas, friendly to the whites and owner of the Little Temecula grant. He may have participated in the Battle of San Pascual on the side of the Californians; but during the Pauma Massacre he was protecting the Californians at Pala from the Indians. For many years I have been puzzled by Pablo Apis protecting the whites at Pala and at the same time being accused of participating in the Pauma Massacre. Hudson, in his account of the massacre, says: "The principal chief of the Paumas was Manuelito, then a young man, whose home was at Pauma, but who sometimes lived at the Agua Caliente. With him was associated Pablo Apis."

A short, unpublished note by Judge Hayes in the Bancroft Library solved the mystery.

> "PABLO APIS—It is not altogether a *scandal*, that makes him (that is, Pablo Junior) a *Machado*, on the parental side son of Don Manuel Machado, the same who was owner of the rancho Rosario, in La Frontera, of Baja California. Machado's children always called Pablo their "hermano." The mother, Cosilda Coyotes de Apis, for a considerable length of time has lived at the Rincon, on the Pauma rancho with Francisco, a brother of the General Olegario."

This is good proof that Pablo Apis Senior may have suffered in the annals of history for the misdeeds of his stepson, Pablo Apis Junior.

General Flores ordered Lugo to gather a force of men and put down the rebellion of those Indians responsible for the Pauma Massacre. Lugo left Los Angeles with fifteen well-armed men, no doubt armed from the booty of the Battle of Chino. He enlisted additional men along the way until he had a small force of twenty-two. They set up camp at the Santa Gertrudes Spring (later known as Adobe Spring) on the present Borel ranch in the Auld-Alamo country between Murrieta Hot Springs and Winchester. He sent eight men

THE TEMECULA MASSACRE

and a Mexican officer to reconnoiter the country around Temecula and Aguanga where the guilty Indians were thought to be located.

After contacting the Indians the Mexican officer Rojas and his men beat a hasty retreat with four or five Indians in pursuit on horseback. Rojas and his troop were terror stricken at the thought of the large Indian contingent and suggested "... that it was undesirable for us to remain so near so hostile a force." Rojas stated that the Indians numbered at least a thousand fighting men. This was probably an exaggeration.

Lugo sent a messenger to Los Angeles for reinforcements; but, during the interim, he heard that Ramon Carrillo was at San Luis Rey with ten men. He sent word to Carrillo to join him, which he did. Still dubious about attacking such a large and hostile Indian force, Lugo decided to enlist the help of Juan Antonio, Chief of the Cahuilla Indians, who was loyal to Lugo and lived with his people near Jurupa. There Lugo contacted Juan Antonio, who agreed to assist the Californians on their errand of revenge. The following is Lugo's account of the Temecula Massacre.

"We (Lugo, Juan Antonio and his warriors) went together to Temecula, carrying two pieces of white cloth to use as a special signal to Juan Antonio's Indians. We reached Santa Gertrudis and rejoined Ramon Carrillo and his force. We notified our people that we were leaving immediately, to fight the hostile Indians at daybreak. We started at eleven o'clock at night. It was daylight when we came to the enemy. We arranged our plan of attack. There were high hills and rather deep canyons, but not extensive. In one of the canyons from which we could reach the enemy, I placed an ambuscade of fifty Indians and fifteen white men, with strict orders not to show themselves until the last of the Indian enemies passed.

"I stationed myself in the mouth of the canyon with some men, and Carrillo went to trick the enemy by calling their attention and leading them to follow him. As soon as they saw him they rose and went after him. He passed them (remained in front), fired at them and retreated slowly and in an orderly manner until he came to where I was. The Indians followed him eagerly. *My men who had rifles and other good arms,* of whom I had placed five on the ridges or high places in the canyon, were told to fire only at the fighters because they were the chiefs and came in the middle of the main body.

"We lured them on about a league until they passed the ambuscade. Then the men rushed out from the ambush upon them from the back at the same time that we fought them from in front.

"We made a great slaughter, and falling upon them from the rear killed many of them. Before reaching Aguanga in their flight, eighteen or twenty of them turned back and gave up their arms. They were made prisoners and placed in charge of Chief Juan Antonio, who told me to care for my men and he would care for the prisoners.

THE TEMECULA MASSACRE

"On reaching Aguanga we amused ourselves killing some three Indians who continued fighting. After terminating the affair, *in which perhaps a hundred Indians perished*, we went back to Juan Antonio and found that he had killed all the prisoners. I reproached him for these acts of cruelty, and he answered me very cooly, that he had gone to hunt and fight and kill Indians who kill him; that he was sure that if they caught him they would not have spared his life but would have burned him alive.

"The booty collected amounted to no more than a few sarapes, arrows, lances, and other trifles, all of which I gave to Juan Antonio and his people.

"We betook ourselves to the camp where we had to await the arrival of the aid we had asked, to a little house between Temecula and Santa Gertrudis (probably what is now known as the Agua Media). There I had my wounded men treated, six in number. We had no deaths. One horse perished.

"I had a small beef brought to feed the men. Shortly afterward the aid (from Los Angeles) under the command of my friend Diego Sepulveda, and consisting of twenty-five men, arrived. He informed me that owing to the bad condition of the horses he had to make short trips, and this delayed him.

"I took some of his men to act as lookouts at the four points of the compass, for we were not sure that the hostile Indians would not return and attack us.

"Daybreak came without anything occurring. The outposts were redoubled, and we decided to return to Aguanga where we had left the Indians in order to rest our animals.

"On arriving there we saw only a few Indians—old ones, blind, lame, and so on, of both sexes. At the rancheria we found seeds, chickens, ollas, and so forth, which our own Indians collected. (The main rancheria of the Aguanga Indians was at the spring in back of the present Aguanga store on the road to Cahuilla. This is a distance of twenty miles, *mas y menos*, from where the main fight took place. There must have been a rancheria, at this time, nearer the head of Nigger Canyon, perhaps in the area where the present bridge crosses the Temecula Creek). Our people occupied themselves in registering everything, cooking, eating, and so on, on the hillside. I lay down to sleep after giving my horse an allowance of barley.

"I slept for some time when the men came arguing that we should go forward. I did not agree, because I neither wished nor felt able to do so. One of the soldiers who came with the aiding party, named Carlos Dominguez—son of the Mariano Dominguez whom the Indians had killed in the valley of San Jose [Warner's ranch]—begged permission to advance, and that he be given an escort of twenty men, in order to avenge the murder of his father. The Californians that were killed numbered three—men who had gone there because they did not wish to have any part in the war against the United States. (Here is an excellent example of how clouded the events surrounding the Southern California Revolt have become. Lugo, even though thirty years had passed since the Temecula Massacre when he dictated his reminiscences, was still not sure of the number of men killed at the Agua Caliente, who they were, or even the circumstances surrounding the Pauma Massacre.)

THE TEMECULA MASSACRE

"I answered that I could not accommodate him in that manner, and he promised that he would not go more than one or two miles forward. He wished to discover whether there were Indians on the road since there was another Indian settlement farther on known as El Negro. He promised that if he encountered any Indians he would let me know. Upon this, I put twenty men at disposal of Carlos Dominguez, and they started out at once. About two o'clock in the afternoon that same day they returned saying that they had seen none but dead Indians on the road they traveled.

"We left Aguanga for Santa Gertrudis, spent the night there, and then pushed on toward San Bernardino . . ."

Judge Hayes, in his notes in the Bancroft Library, mentions the Temecula Massacre on a number of occasions. In one instance he says,

". . . it might commemorate the bloody battle that took place near Ahuanga, in January, 1847, between the Cahuillas under their famed chief, Juan Antonio, and the insurrectionary San Luiseños, commanded by Manuelito Cota and *young Pablo Apis*. This was a sequel to the massacre of Pauma, in the month of December previous. The Cahuillas really were led by a Californian, Don José del Carmen Lugo, of Los Angeles, and placed themselves in an ambuscade. Don Ramon Carrillo, at the head of a strong party of native Californians, attacked the Indians of Apis. These retreating without thought fell into the hands of the Cahuillas who showed no mercy; *great numbers were slain.*"

Bancroft dismisses the massacre with a short footnote:

"The evidence is still conflicting; but the S. Luiseños under the chiefs Manuelito Cota and Pablo Apis seem to have been the victims of an ambush and bloody fight near Ahuanga, the Cahuillas under Juan Antonio aiding the Californians under José del Carmen Lugo and Ramon Carrillo."

As a small boy growing up in Temecula I heard various garbled tales of "the big battle." It wasn't until years later, after I had become acquainted with the historical works of George William Beattie and Helen Pruitt Beattie of San Bernardino, that the pieces of the puzzle began falling into place. By this time most of the old Indian bridges with the past had died. Fortunately, Antonio Ashman—one of the most intelligent and respected Indians of Temecula—remembered many of the details of the Temecula Massacre as told him by the *viejos*. His version parallels and substantiates the Lugo account. A few years ago we retraced and reinacted the Temecula Massacre over the original terrain. With the exception of Mr. Ashman and myself, I doubt if anyone living knows the exact site of the massacre.

While doing this "on the spot" research I decided, also, to look over the Santa Gertrudes Spring (Adobe Spring) to see if Lugo and his Californians had left any trace. Alex Borel of Murrieta, who owns the spring, is an old schoolmate of mine and was most happy to cooperate. On some high, boulder-covered

THE TEMECULA MASSACRE

promontories overlooking the spring, Alex showed me a number of man-made, rock-wall enclosures. They are similar in appearance to the old rock-wall fortifications used by Kearny's dragoons atop Mule Hill on the San Pascual Battlefield. There is no doubt these rock walls are old and man-made, and they could well have been fortifications erected by Lugo and his men prior to the Temecula Massacre; or they may be old antelope blinds constructed by the Indians, or perhaps even the remains of Indian *kish* sites.

While encamped at the Santa Gertrudes, and after the Mexican officer Rojas had reported a thousand Indian warriors assembled, Lugo had sent a messenger to General Flores in Los Angeles for reinforcements. During the messenger's absence Lugo heard that Ramon Carrillo was at San Luis Rey with ten men and he sent word for Carrillo to join him.

Mr. Ashman tells an interesting story which perhaps accounts for Lugo knowing Carrillo was at San Luis Rey. According to an old Temecula Indian, when he was a young man he worked on the Santa Margarita Rancho. One day he was given an excellent horse and a message which he was to deliver to some Californians encamped near Temecula. He was also given explicit directions as to which trail to follow to find the Californians and he was not to deviate from it. He followed orders and found the *Californianos*.

After resting overnight he was given a return message and once again admonished not to make any side trips. The young man was a Temecula and, with a top horse, he could make good time; so, in spite of the warnings to the contrary, he decided to make a side trip and visit his home at the Temecula Indian village. When he arrived he found the village deserted. Searching through the *rancheria* he heard some low moanings in one of the adobes. Entering it he found an old, infirm Indian woman almost dead from thirst and hunger. He asked her where the people had gone but she was too weak to speak. The young man brought her some water from the creek and mixed her a gruel of seed flour that he found in the house. Regaining strength, but still too weak to talk, she pointed toward the Nigger Canyon which forms the the northeastern portal into the Temecula Valley. With this news, frightened by the still unexplained deserted village, and with no time to investigate, he continued on to the Santa Margarita.

This must have been Lugo's messenger to Carrillo. It would also indicate that the Indians, forewarned by the Mexican officer Rojas' reconnoiterings, had sought shelter in the rugged Nigger Canyon.

According to Mr. Ashman's account, the Indians were well concealed and would have been safe within the defiles of the canyon. The Californians, or

NIGGER CANYON—as it looks down stream from Vail Dam. This is where the Temecula Indians hid prior to the massacre. Through this canyon at various seasons, passed the old Gila or Southern Emigrant Trail.

ANTONIO ASHMAN—respected Temecula Indian and one of the last living bridges with participants in the Temecula Massacre and their descendants. It was Mr. Ashman who knew the exact site of where the massacre began.

(All photos by Horace Parker)

THE TEMECULA MASSACRE

Mexicans as he called them, rode into the canyon and began taunting and hurling insults at the Indians. Seeing such a small force, enraged at the insults and still excited after the Pauma Massacre, the Indians left their places of concealment and charged. The Californians retreated and, being well mounted, rode tantalizingly just out of range of the Indians' arrows. With the exception of probably a half dozen old guns the Indians were armed primarily with bows and arrows, crude lances, clubs and knives. Under normal conditions the Californians would have been as poorly armed and no match for the more numerous Indians. However, the superior American arms captured by Lugo at the Battle of Chino soon turned the tide of battle.

According to the Indian accounts of the battle, Manuelito Cota implored his poorly armed and undisciplined warriors not to leave the shelter of Nigger Canyon. Even though he was suspicious of a trap, Cota was forced forward by the excited and enraged Indians. The Indian warriors poured out of Nigger Canyon on foot and horseback pursuing the Californians up a smaller side canyon to the west through which the Old Road to San Jacinto traverses. For over three miles they pursued the Californians, until they reached a point where this side canyon enters the Long Valley which roughly parallels the Temecula Valley to the west. Here, behind a low hill on their right, was Lugo's ambuscade of fifteen "... men who had rifles and other good arms ...," and Juan Antonio's fifty Indian warriors whom Lugo had obtained at Jurupa. When the last of the Indians had passed into the Long Valley the trap was sprung.

The Californians stopped their retreat, held their ground and began to fight. The Indians paused. At almost the same instant the fifteen well-armed men began firing on the Indians' rear. In consternation and fear the Indians turned to flee, only to find all their exits of escape blocked by the deadly fire of the Californians.

At this point, with the Temeculas caught in this desperate situation, Juan Antonio and his warriors charged. Mistaking Antonio and his Cahuillas for allies the Temeculas rallied briefly; and, no doubt calling to acquaintances among the Cahuillas, envisioned a glorious victory. To their utter amazement and dismay the Cahuilla Indians began killing Temeculas. This turn of events resulted in an individual rout with every man fleeing for his life.

The well-mounted Californians slaughtered the fleeing Indians with lances and firearms. Juan Antonio and his warriors spread out on foot and killed the wounded, the stragglers, and those who endeavored to hide. This slaughter raged for hours, driving the remnants of the Temeculas and their allies up through the Nigger Canyon to a point in the Aguanga country, somewhere

THE TEMECULA MASSACRE

between where the highway bridge crosses the Temecula Creek and the Aguanga store. It is hard to pinpoint the exact spot of the *rancheria* because there are a number of old village sites all along the Temecula Creek and the springs bordering it. Undoubtedly it was only sheer exhaustion on the part of the Californians that eventually stopped the slaughter.

The number killed will never be known exactly. Judge Hayes in his notes made just a few years later states, "... great numbers were slain ..." Colonel Cooke mentions the number as thirty-eight. Sgt. Jones mentions forty. Lugo calls it "... a great slaughter ..." and "... perhaps a hundred Indians perished ...". Mr. Ashman snorted at the number of thirty-eight killed and stated the *viejos* claimed that the bones of the unburied dead could be found for years all the way through the Nigger Canyon and into the Aguanga country. So, once again using the old Californian term, we may assume that a hundred Indians, *mas y menos*, were slain during the Temecula Massacre.

Antonio Ashman related two interesting stories of the battle. One was told him by an old Indian survivor, who had concealed himself among the low bushes in one of the many gullies along the route of the massacre. Peering out he observed his brother pursued by some mounted Californians. The brother on foot was soon overtaken by the mounted men and, as he watched, the Californians drove their lances into the cringing body of the defeated man.

The *viejo* told Mr. Ashman he still had his bow and arrows and his first impulse was to run to the assistance of his doomed brother. As he grasped his bow there flashed before his eyes a mental picture of his children and the question of what would become of them if he were killed. So, closing his eyes to shut out the scene before him, he sank back into his place of concealment and survived the massacre.

Another story is told about Manuelito Cota, who was apparently one of the few mounted Indians. His horse was killed. On the horse was a saddle and bridle he valued highly. It is rumored that the equipment was silver-mounted. In any event he didn't want this prize to fall into the hands of the Californians or the Cahuilla Indians. Removing the saddle and bridle in the heat of the battle he was fortunate enough to catch a riderless horse, exchange saddles, and escape death at the Temecula Massacre.

There is an old saying among the Temecula Indians: "Never trust a Cahuilla." The Temeculas and their allies were not only thoroughly cowed and beaten, they were also humiliated and angered. They felt the Cahuillas had betrayed them. The years have softened and mellowed this betrayal between the Cahuillas and the Temeculas. Antonio Ashman stated simply

THE TEMECULA MASSACRE

that there were probably two reasons for Juan Antonio's treachery. The Cahuillas had been bribed with whiskey and goods and they had also suffered a defeat in battle years before with the Temeculas.

Before the coming of the Spaniards, the Indian clans around Palomar Mountain had well-defined territorial lands. Food was always a problem and the boundaries of the clans' lands were zealously guarded. One time the Cahuillas invaded the lands of the Temeculas by way of Palomar Mountain and in the vicinity of Pichanga and the Pala Grade. They were identified by a young Indian woman who was a Cahuilla married to a Temecula man. The Cahuillas kept themselves well-concealed, penetrating along the south foothills of Wolf Valley near the present home of Erle Stanley Gardner. The Temeculas knew they were there, but didn't know precisely where, and couldn't flush them out.

Using a bit of primitive strategy the Temecula warriors concealed themselves under cover of darkness in the general area of where they thought the Cahuillas were hiding. At daybreak they sent out a number of young Indian girls, ostensibly to gather seeds and acorns. The sight of this tender, feminine pulchritude was irresistible to the hidden Cahuilla warriors. With a whoop they gathered up the brush chicks, but not before they had exposed their places of concealment. The Temeculas attacked and routed the Cahuillas.

Forty years ago along the base of the hills, in little clearings in the brush and along the trails, the kids would pick up scores of arrowheads. At one time I had a collection of thirty or more perfect points found on the old battle site.

On January 23, 1847, Colonel St. George Cooke, leader of the Mormon Battalion, talked to "Bauptista," one of the Cahuilla chiefs, and found that "A somewhat independent band of his nation lately defeated and slew thirty-eight of the San Luis tribe who were pursuing the Californians." Cooke reprimanded Bautista and warned him to remain loyal to the Americans.

By this time Colonel Cooke had decided to go to the assistance of the American garrison at Los Angeles. This meant taking the road to the Pueblo via Aguanga, Temecula, Laguna Grande (Elsinore). Antonio Garra, who had served as interpreter for Cooke at Warner's, asked to accompany him to Temecula in order that the soldiers might protect the Temeculas while they buried their dead. "Antonio then accompanied me with ten Indians; he is guide until I get into the Valley of Temecula."

Cooke entered the Temecula Valley on January 25, 1847. As Standage, a member of the Mormon Battalion, says, "...a line of horsemen stretched across the valley which were taken to be Spaniards but after proved to be

THE TEMECULA MASSACRE

Indians who thought we were Spaniards and were prepared to attack them." In spite of their humiliating defeat, the Temecula Indians were apparently still ready to fight if pressed.

On the morning of January 26, Standage noted, "This morning the Indians were burying their dead. The Mexicans or Spaniards and them had had a battle previous to our arrival."

Once again, in a musing tone, Judge Hayes writes — "The battle of Temecula — *they made a new grave yard*, to bury their relations slain in this battle by the Cahuillas, under Juan Antonio."

Little did Cooke, the Mormon Battalion, Judge Hayes and the Temecula Indians realize that the victims buried in this new *camposanto* would be immortalized in Helen Hunt Jackson's novel *Ramona*. Twenty years later, on June 15, 1867, a priest wrote to Bishop Amat about the graveyard in Temecula, ". . . they have fenced the cemetery which will be five or six hundred feet square, with a wall of adobe, well boarded door and all arranged nicely. I would wish that your Excellency would grant me the authority to bless it, if you would judge it opportune. They have many and great desires to have it blessed, and I believe that it is suitable because it is in reality worthy of it. . ."

When Mrs. Jackson's novel appeared in 1884 she described the cemetery faithfully:

"It was surrounded by a low adobe wall, with one small gate of wooden paling.
As they reached it Alessandro exclaimed, 'The thieves have taken the gate!'
'What would they have wanted with that?' said Ramona.
'To burn,' he said doggedly. 'It was wood; but it was very little. They might have left the graves safe from wild beasts and cattle!' "

And just as Alessandro predicted in fiction, today cattle graze over the forgotten graves in Old Temecula where rest the victims of the bloodiest battle of the Mexican War in California—the Temecula Massacre.

AUTHOR'S POSTSCRIPT—*Temeku* is an Indian locative name changed by the early Spaniards to the more euphonious Temecula. Many times it is difficult to translate word meanings exactly from one language to another. This is true of *Temeku*. After consulting a number of Indian informants, the literal translation of *Temeku* is, "That place where the sun breaks through the white mist."

Temeku or Temecula, is among the oldest place names in the Southwest. Actually, since the 1880's the name Temecula has served two towns. Old Temecula was at the site of the Wolf Store, on the Little Temecula Rancho, and now headquarters for the Vail Company ranch. New Temecula was established at its present site after the completion of the California Southern Railroad through the Temecula Canyon in 1882. The two towns, with a single name and six miles apart, have been confusing to later historians.

THE TEMECULA MASSACRE

BIBLIOGRAPHY

AMES, GEORGE WALCOTT, JR.: *A DOCTOR COMES TO CALIFORNIA—The Diary of John S. Griffin M.D.;* 1943; California Historical Society; San Francisco.

ASHMAN, ANTONE: *Temecula Indian, interviews with in 1956.*

BANCROFT, HUBERT HOWE: Vol. XXII, *History of California*, Vol. V, 1846-1848; 1886, San Francisco.

BEATTIE, GEORGE WILLIAM and HELEN PRUITT: *HERITAGE OF THE VALLEY—San Bernardino's First Century;* 1951; Biobooks; Oakland, California.

BEATTIE, HELEN PRUITT: *VIDA DE UN RANCHERO* by Don José del Carmen Lugo as told to Thomas Savage 1877. 1961; Quarterly San Bernardino Museum Ass'n; Vol VIII, No. 2.

BIEBER, DR, RALPH P.: *Exploring Southwest Trails 1846-54.* 1938. Arthur H. Clark Co., Glendale, Calif.

CALVIN, ROSS: *Lieutenant Emory Reports.* 1951; Univ. of New Mexico Press, Albuquerque.

CARTER, KATE B. and STEELE, CLARA B: *THE MORMON BATTALION.* 1956; Daughters of Utah Pioneers, Utah Printing Co.

CAUGHEY, JOHN WALTON: *California.* 1946; Prentice-Hall, Inc.; New York, N.Y.

GOLDER, FRANK ALFRED: *The March of the Mormon Battalion.* 1928; The Century Co.; New York, N.Y.

HARRIS, BENJAMIN BUTLER (Ed. by Richard H. Dillon): *THE GILA TRAIL. The Texas Argonauts and the California Gold Rush.* 1960; Norman, Oklahoma; Univ. of Oklahoma Press.

HAYES, JUDGE BENJAMIN: *HAYES' EMIGRANT NOTES.* By permission of the Director, The Bancroft Library.

HUDSON, MILLARD F.: *The Pauma Massacre.* 1906. Historical Society of Southern California; Vol 7.

JACKSON, HELEN HUNT: *Ramona.* 1884, Boston.

PARKER, HORACE: *The Brush Country Journal.* Aug. 5, 1956 to Dec. 2, 1956, Riverside Press-Enterprise.

PEET, MARY ROCKWOOD: *San Pasqual a Crack in the Hills.* 1949, Highland Press; Culver City, Calif.

ROBERTS, BRIGHAM H.: *The Mormon Battalion; Its History and Achievements.* 1919, Deseret News; Salt Lake City, Utah.

TYLER, DANIEL: *A Concise History of the Mormon Battalion in the Mexican War.* 1881, Salt Lake City, Utah.

WOLCOTT, MARJORIE TISDALE: *Pioneer Notes from the Diaries of Judge Benjamin Hayes.* 1929; Privately Printed; Los Angeles, Calif.

WOODWARD, ARTHUR: *Lances at San Pascual.* 1948; California Historical Society; San Francisco, Calif.

QUEEN LILIUOKALANI

On the throne of Hawaii, 1891-1893.
This was taken when she was queen.

LILIUOKALANI
THE ISLAND QUEEN

By EARLE R. FORREST

Author of several notable books relating to Indian customs and culture, Earle Forrest here turns his attention to a colorful episode in Hawaiian history—the funeral of Queen Liliuokalani. In this article Mr. Forrest includes a letter, written from Honolulu on the occasion of the funeral, by the Honorable Henry W. Temple. We have not elsewhere read a more revealing description of this event than that given in Mr. Temple's eye witness account; nor do we know of one that more vividly reflects Hawaiian customs and traditions.

A LOW MOAN THAT SWELLED INTO A LOUD DEATH WAIL, echoing from cliff to cliff, was carried by the night winds from island to island. It was the grief stricken chant of "aloha oe" sobbed by a people in mourning for their beloved Liliuokalani. Although she had not been their queen for a quarter of a century she was still their own Liliuokalani, "bringing fresh remembrance of the past." Their old queen, last of a long line of native rulers, was dead.

Born September 2, 1838, near the site of the Queen's Hospital, at the base of the Punch-Bowl, Liliuokalani was one of ten children of Kapaakea and his wife, Keohokalole. For six generations her ancestors of the Kamehameha dynasty had ruled over Hawaii. Following the ancient custom of exchanging children, she was given away in her infancy to another chieftain by whom she was adopted under the name of Lydia Kamakaeha. At the age of four she was sent to the Royal School, founded and conducted by Mr. and Mrs. Amos C. Cooke for children of the royal family and high chieftains, where she learned English and was taught the Christian religion. Although she joined the Episcopal denomination, throughout her life she clung to many of the rites of her own ancient Hawaiian faith.

In 1862 she married John O. Dominis, son of an American sea captain, with whom she lived happily for nearly thirty years. Her husband was a man of high standing, who became a member of the House of Nobles and Governor of the Island of Oahu.

When her brother, David Kalakaua, ascended the throne of Hawaii in 1874, he had no children and proclaimed Liliuokalani as his heir apparent. On two occasions during his absence she was regent; first when he toured the world, and again when he went to California in a vain effort to restore his health. He was a very sick man when he returned to Honolulu from his world tour, and he was advised to seek the climate of California. As the guest of Rear Admiral Brown he left on the cruiser *Charleston;* but he was too late,

LILIUOKALANI–THE ISLAND QUEEN

and on January 20, 1891, David Kalakaua, the last King of Hawaii, died in San Francisco. Cable communication had not been established between California and the Islands at that time, and the Hawaiians did not learn of the death of their sovereign until the *Charleston* steamed into the harbor of Honolulu with his body.

Liliuokalani succeeded her brother as imperial ruler on January 20, 1891; but her reign was brief, stormy, and tragic. Seven months after she ascended the throne her husband died. When she became queen he was made Lieutenant General of the Kingdom with the rank of His Royal Highness, Prince Consort. She had relied much upon his judgment, and had he lived the revolution may never have occurred.

Her trouble began when she attempted to carry out the policies of her brother. Under the old constitution certain restrictions had been placed upon the Crown, which Kalakaua had fought unsuccessfully to abolish; and as soon as she became queen, Liliuokalani renewed the battle. In secret she had a new constitution drawn up which removed these restrictions, and the guaranties of the independence of the Supreme Court were eliminated. But perhaps the one article that did more to bring on the revolution than anything else was the provision which permitted only native Hawaiians to vote.

Although Liliuokalani did not realize it, the handwriting was already on the wall for ancient Hawaii. The old order would soon pass. The members of the cabinet not only refused to sign this constitution, but they took their cause to the people and appealed to the leading citizens for support. Then came the revolution, perhaps the first bloodless revolution in all history. Excitement in Honolulu reached a high pitch, and only a spark was needed to start a bloody civil war. At a public meeting the business men appointed a Committee of Safety. This was followed by a mass meeting on January 16, 1893, at which the appointment of the committee was ratified; and the next day a provisional government was organized with Sanford B. Dole as President.

Two days before the mass meeting the United States cruiser *Boston* arrived from Hilo. Just why the war vessel happened to steam into the harbor at this opportune time has never been definitely established; but it is a fair guess that United States Minister J. L. Stevens, in view of the trouble that was brewing, in some way managed to get a message through to her captain. At any rate the cruiser was there, and at Stevens' request a force of Marines was landed after the mass meeting was over on the evening of the sixteenth. Stevens later explained that he took this action to protect American lives, and guard property in case of mob violence.

LILIUOKALANI–THE ISLAND QUEEN

The provisional government was to exist until union with the United States and until a treaty of annexation was drawn up. However, as soon as he took office, President Cleveland withdrew the treaty from the Senate on the grounds that Minister Stevens, backed by the Marines, had improperly aided the revolution. Perhaps the President was right; perhaps Stevens, who was on the ground, was right; for without those Marines there might well have been rioting and bloodshed. The feeling of the American people and the press was that the President was wrong, and cartoonists pictured him with Queen Lil as his sweetheart.

After a conference with her ministry, Queen Liliuokalani decided to surrender her authority to prevent civil war; and so Hawaii's revolution came to an end without loss of life. The Republic of Hawaii was established on July 4, 1893, with Sanford B. Dole as the duly elected President.

The old year of 1894 went out on the night of December 31st to the tune of rifle fire in the hills around Honolulu instead of the traditional "Auld Lang Syne," when officials of the Republic discovered a royalist plot to bring back the monarchy and restore the Queen to the throne. The royalist forces were routed, probably without bloodshed as no casualties were reported, and the leaders captured. Charged with participating in the plot, Liliuokalani was arrested on January 16, 1895, on evidence alleged to have been discovered in her home. Eight days later she surrendered all claim to the throne of Hawaii, and appealed to the officials of the Republic for clemency for all who had taken part in the conspiracy. As evidence of her good intentions she wrote and signed this abdication:

"It is my sincere desire henceforth to live in absolute privacy and retirement from all publicity or even appearance of being concerned in the public affairs of the Hawaiian Islands, further than to express, as I now do, and shall always continue to do, my most sincere hope for the welfare and prosperity of Hawaii and its people under and subject to the Government of the Republic of Hawaii."

For eight months she was held a prisoner in her former palace; but on September 7, 1895, Liliuokalani and forty-eight leaders of the attempted restoration were granted conditional pardons. To show that no resentment was held against any of the revolutionists, the remaining prisoners were set at liberty on January 1, 1896, and the whole affair was forgotten by both sides. But annexation to the United States was still more than two and a half years in the future.

The Spanish American War undoubtedly brought about annexation sooner

LILIUOKALANI–THE ISLAND QUEEN

than would have taken place under normal circumstances. President McKinley realized the importance of the Hawaiian Islands, and they became American territory on August 12, 1898.

The ceremony of annexation, which took place in Honolulu, was important and rather pathetic; for it marked the passing of a nation that was old when the Pilgrims settled in New England. *Hawaii Ponoi* was played by the band for the last time as the national anthem of old Hawaii and the short-lived Republic. The mournful, long-drawn-out notes of *Taps* were followed by a salute of twenty-one guns. The old flag with its eight stripes alternating white, red and blue and the British Union Jack in the upper left corner, that had floated over imperial Hawaii these many years and later over the young Republic, was lowered, and the Stars and Stripes raised in its place. The islands were American territory at last. The old order was gone. Imperial Hawaii had died five years before, and the Republic that brought about a new order was no more. Two years later, July 14, 1900, the Territory of Hawaii was created; but statehood was still sixty years in the future.

One writer said that on that August day of 1898, "a nation died," and the old order was no more. But that was not quite true. There was one spot that was still Hawaii where the old order survived—the home of ex-Queen Liliuokalani. The flag of her native Hawaii still flew over the palace of its last imperial ruler, not to be replaced by the Star Spangled Banner for nearly twenty years. The American authorities respected her wish, and permitted that one spot of old Hawaii to live in complete isolation. The flag of the old order was never lowered until after the United States entered World War I. Then, when she heard that some Hawaiians had been killed in Germany's submarine warfare, the old ex-Queen hauled down the banner of her vanished island empire, and raised the Stars and Stripes.

For nearly a quarter of a century following the abortive attempt to place her back on the throne she lived in quiet retirement; not as a prisoner or "Uncle Sam's captive queen," as some sources dramatically asserted, for she enjoyed all the liberty of any American. Perhaps I should say of any *other* American. When she abdicated, the promise was made that her property would be respected. Owner of a million acres that had been seized by the white man, she relied upon this governmental promise. When no effort was made to restore her land she went to Washington to seek justice; but, as usual in such cases, she received scant consideration. From one department to another, from one official to another, she went begging for what was rightfully her own; but one million acres of rich Hawaiian land was a prize that the white man

LILIUOKALANI-THE ISLAND QUEEN

did not intend to give up. Like General John A. Sutter before her, she became just another pathetic figure of history.

An authoress of considerable ability in both the English and Hawaiian languages, the queen wrote many poems, some before she was queen and others after her retirement. During her imprisonment for a short period after the royalist failure to restore her to the throne, she believed that she would be banished from her beloved Oahu. It was then that she wrote *Aloha Oe* (Farewell to Thee), one of the most beautiful poems in any language, known over the whole world these many years. The most popular of all native songs, one always thinks of it whenever Hawaii is mentioned; and it gave its name to our fiftieth state—Hawaii, the *Aloha* State. Not only that, but many a regimental band played the haunting strains of *Farewell to Thee* as the boys marched along the street after tearful farewells, to fight and die on the battle-fields of France in World War I.

Although some authorities claim that the words of *Hawaii Ponoi*, the national anthem and now the state song, were written by her brother, King David Kalakaua, there are others who are just as certain that its composer was Liliuokalani. But regardless of who wrote it, *Aloha Oe* will always be Hawaii.

After her final renunciation of all rights to the throne, she held the love and respect of the native Hawaiians to the last day of her life; and when she died on November 11, 1917, a nation *did* die. That one spot in Honolulu that had been old Hawaii for almost a quarter of a century, was no more. The old order was dead.

The funeral of ex-Queen Liliuokalani, which was held in Honolulu almost half a century ago, was one of those pageants of barbaric splendor that we can hardly conceive of today—something that can never happen again. For it marked the end of an era, and was probably never surpassed in all its magnificent pomp and ritual. Other descriptions have been written, but I have not read one that describes all the brilliant details that are contained in this letter written on the spot to his wife by the Honorable Henry W. Temple, member of a Congressional committee visiting Honolulu at the time.

"I wish I could tell you about the funeral of Queen Liliuokalani in such a way as to enable you to see it, in which I may say, without disrespect, all its barbaric splendor. The services were held in the Throne Room of the Palace, where Governor Pinkham gave his reception in our honor a few days ago. About the coffin was the guard of honor, eight native Hawaiians, waving their feather *Kahilis*. At regular intervals they waved or dipped the *Kahilis* towards the coffin, while outside the windows could be heard the wailing

Officials marching in the funeral procession of Queen Liliuokalani.

chant of native men and women, generally old people who had not forgotten the ancient *meles* or poems suitable to the funeral of one of their sovereigns. Inside the Throne Room, but farther from the coffin than the guard of honor, were men of native race whose ancestry gave them a right to bear the large and bright colored *Kahilis* of their own families or those of the Queen's retinue. The *Kahilis* are carefully arranged, branching clusters of feathers, frequently arranged in designs of bright colors against dark. They branch about the top of a staff about the size and length of such a flagstaff as is carried by the color sergeant of a marching regiment. These *Kahilis* are the banners of the sovereign or his followers.

"Many of the Hawaiians (those whose ancestry entitles them to do so) wore feather capes or cloaks of exceedingly great value. The capes are worn about the neck and shoulders like an ordinary fur cape. The weather was very hot today, and the wearers must have been suffering, but there was never a sign of it in their behavior. The capes can never be duplicated, as the native birds from whose feathers they were made are extinct. They were always costly, for each bird furnished only a few feathers, taken from the soft and downy ones under the wing. They were fastened together by the quill end, if

Catafalque and Kahili bearers in front of Palace steps. Queen Liliuokalani's funeral.

these short fluffy feathers can be said to have a quill, and overlapped so that only the downiest part is visible. How many rows of them it takes to make a belt an inch wide I do not know, but the cape is evidently made from the skirt or border towards the neck, after a strip has been formed the whole length of the edge of the border.

"Only bright colored birds were used—yellow, like canaries, or red. The cape may be red, with a crescent of yellow, or yellow with designs in red, with sometimes a design also in black, but always the natural color of the feather. The capes, or cloaks, are among the most valued possessions of the families who have them, and the very, very few that are in museums are worth hundreds or even thousands of dollars. Even a feather *lei*, such as is sometimes seen on the street in use as a hat-band, is worth from twenty to thirty dollars, and it is made from the feathers of the Chinese pheasant, a common enough bird.

"The *Kahilis* carried by the marching nobles were most interesting. The multitudes that lined the streets, were no less so—Oriental faces, most of them, men, women and children.

"We were given places of honor in the Throne Room, in the procession and at the grave. Senator Poindexter and Mr. McLaughlin, the Senior Senator

IOLANI PALACE   (*All photos, Hawaiian Public Archives.*)

and Senior Representative in our delegation, were pallbearers. I regretted very much that I had not brought with me a frock coat and a suitable hat, but many Hawaiians of official position were dressed as we were.

"The funeral was an occasion of state. Regiments of the Regular Army, of the National Guard of the territory, and sailors and marines from a Japanese warship now in port, formed part of the procession. The guns fired the appropriate salute, the bugle sounded 'Taps' over the grave. The setting that made it strange was the Hawaiian ceremonial which almost made one lose sight of the service of the Episcopal Church, of which the Queen was a member.

"As the procession moved towards the cemetery an old man, a native of course, accompanied the hearse (or catafalque) and chanted in the Hawaiian language. Senator Chellingworth, of the territorial Senate, said that he was reciting the genealogy of the Queen and the victorious battles and other achievements of her ancestors.

"At the grave there was much chanting, a great deal of it by women. I recognized among the chanters a native woman whom I had met at Hilo and who came over from that place to Honolulu on the boat with us Friday. She was one of those who sang on the deck in the little company with Governor

LILIUOKALANI-THE ISLAND QUEEN

Baker in the evening. Governor Baker is a native and of high rank among them. He was governor of the largest of the islands in the old days under the monarchy, long before the native government was overthrown.

"It seemed to me that the chanting was easily to be distinguished from the peculiar wailing which burst forth at times, especially from older persons among the natives; though occasionally women, one who had spontaneously begun to chant would be overcome with emotion, the voice would break, and the chant become an inarticulate wail, indescribably sorrowful.

"I think I told you in a previous letter that the song "Aloha Oe," was the national anthem. I was so informed, but the statement is not correct. This song was composed by the Queen, and is probably the most popular and most beautiful of the native songs, but the national anthem is very different. I have them both, and some others for you to try on the piano when I get home. The national anthem is certainly very much like something I have heard and known long ago, but I have not yet identified it. Perhaps it will occur to me soon, or I may need to ask you about it:

> " 'Hawaii ponoi
> Nana i Kou moi
> Kalani alii
> Ke alii.' "

When Dr. Temple returned he brought back a book containing the words and music of fifty native songs, published in both Hawaiian and English. Two are *Hawaii Ponoi*, the old national anthem (now the state song), and the beautifully haunting and still popular *Aloha Oe*. Many of the songs were translated by Professor Henry Berger, who also wrote the music for most of them, including *Hawaii Ponoi* and *Aloha Oe*.

Farewell to thee, Liliuokalani.

BIBLIOGRAPHY

American Queen; Outlook, November 21, 1917.

Death of Liliuokalani, Hawaii's Dusky Queen; Literary Digest, December 8, 1917.

Emerson, Nathaniel B., A. M., M. D. *Unwritten Literature of Hawaii;* Bulletin 38, Bureau of American Ethnology: Washington, 1909.

Hart, H. H., of the Hawaiian Historical Society. *Aloha Oe, Liliuokalani;* Overland Monthly, January, 1918.

Last American Queen, The; Literary Digest, February 10, 1917.

Liliuokalani, The Last American Queen; Literary Digest, December 8, 1917.

Queen is Dead, The; Outlook, November 21, 1917.

Temple, Hon. Henry W.; letters dated Salt Lake City, Utah, October 31, 1917, and Honolulu, T.H., November 10 and 18, 1917.

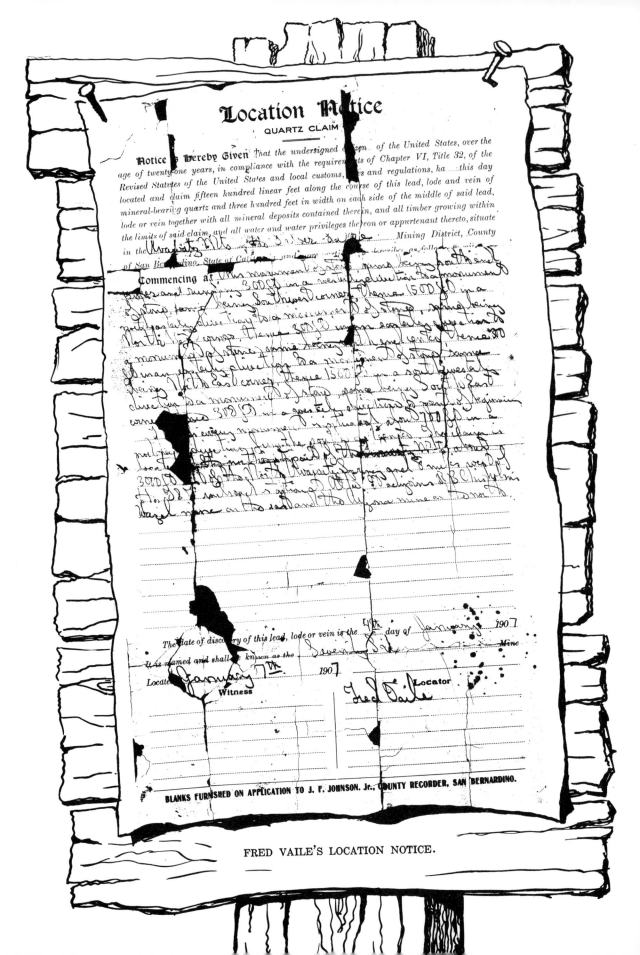

Location Notice
QUARTZ CLAIM

Notice is Hereby Given That the undersigned citizen of the United States, over the age of twenty-one years, in compliance with the requirements of Chapter VI, Title 32, of the Revised Statutes of the United States and local customs, laws and regulations, ha___this day located and claim fifteen hundred linear feet along the course of this lead, lode and vein of mineral-bearing quartz and three hundred feet in width on each side of the middle of said lead, lode or vein together with all mineral deposits contained therein, and all timber growing within the limits of said claim, and all water and water privileges thereon or appurtenant thereto, situate in the _____ Mining District, County of San Bernardino, State of California, and more particularly described as follows, to wit:

Commencing at _____

_____

_____

The date of discovery of this lead, lode or vein is the 4th day of January 190 7

It is named and shall be known as the _____ Mine

Locate January 7th 190 7

_____ Witness

Fred Vaile Locator

BLANKS FURNISHED ON APPLICATION TO J. F. JOHNSON, Jr., COUNTY RECORDER, SAN BERNARDINO.

FRED VAILE'S LOCATION NOTICE.

BURRO PROSPECTOR

By FRED VAILE

The late Fred Vaile, respected Westerner of the Los Angeles Corral, writes this article just as he would tell it to us in person. In a rambling, conversational style, Fred takes us over the trails with him; and at all stages of his narrative he holds us in complete captivation. This man was one of the West's best known prospectors, his experience taking him into Death Valley, the Dale mines, and other mining areas on the Mojave. The discerning reader will garner more than just passing entertainment from this saga of an era and an image that have all but vanished from our land.

As A NATIVE SON who grew up in Southern California around the turn of the century, I have always been interested in the history and development of the Southwest. But the constant struggle with the high cost of living has prevented me from doing any serious research work in this respect. In the absence of extensive research, this article will necessarily be based largely on personal recollections and this is almost certain to result in errors and omissions.

The impressions we have today of persons we knew and events that occurred fifty years ago are apt to be somewhat different than the impressions we had at the time. Our viewpoints change over the years; persons and events that didn't seem too important then have been forgotten or, at best, our memory of them is rather hazy. And the things we have remembered, that we have thought about and talked about over the years, we have probably glamorized in an effort to make better stories out of them and particularly to upgrade our own part in them. So today it is sometimes hard to determine what is fact and what is window dressing. If you take exception to any of my remarks, blame it on a faulty memory and not on any intent to mislead.

The burro prospector is no more, another victim of progress with his demise hastened by Henry Ford and the Model T. He was a colorful character and in my opinion has never been given proper credit for the part he played in the Winning of the West. Compared to the cowboy and the frontier sheriff, he is almost the forgotten man of Western America and yet his contribution to the exploration and development of the Southwest was very significant. He played no part in the discovery of gold in California but he was responsible for most of the important mining discoveries afterward from the Comstock to Oatman. He blazed trails across the desert and made it possible for this forbidding wasteland to become a rich agricultural empire and the winter playground of America.

BURRO PROSPECTOR

During the ten years I spent in Southern Nevada and Eastern California I met and knew many of these prospectors, most of them casually, some of them intimately. A few were old timers who had spent most of their lives searching for the pot of gold at the foot of the rainbow. Most of them had been attracted to the desert by the Nevada boom. But if a man survived for a year, he was no longer a tenderfoot but automatically became an old timer. There were miners from the Mother Lode, Virginia City and Cripple Creek— half the population of Cripple Creek moved to Nevada in the decade from 1902 to 1912; cowboys from the cattle ranches of Nevada, Arizona and Texas; hillbillies from the Ozarks; recent immigrants from Southern Europe; English remittance men and graduates from our American colleges. It was sometimes hard to tell just what a man's cultural background was; but I devised a rather simple test: if a man didn't eat with his knife, I assumed that he came from one of the old Boston families.

In spite of these differences in early training, most of these men had certain things in common.

Naturally, they had to be rugged physically.

They had to have a high degree of patience. They had to be patient to follow a burro all day at two and one-half miles an hour. If they started to press, to worry as to whether they would reach the next water hole by dark, they were putting themselves in jeopardy. Of the six men I knew who died of thirst, five of them could have reached water without serious difficulty if they hadn't become panic stricken. This attitude of patience, which I developed in those days, is a great help when I find myself on one of our freeways during the rush hours.

They had to be rather self-sufficient spiritually. An extrovert who depended too much on human companionship would have gone nuts in the solitude of the desert.

They had to have something of the pioneering instinct, the desire and ability to break new trails, to go out on their own without benefit of outside supervision.

They had to be optimists, believing that sooner or later they would make the big strike.

Most of them had a fair working knowledge of geology and mineralogy as it applied to the desert mountain ranges, although their technical vocabulary may have been somewhat limited. For example, Bunco Smith, one of the old timers, classified all rocks as quartz, porphyry or dogass.

While most prospectors came to the desert because of the lure of gold,

BURRO PROSPECTOR

to some of them it was a means of escape, perhaps from family troubles, from difficulties with the law, from broken love affairs, or merely an inability to adjust to the difficulties of living in a complex civilization.

It was not considered good form, and might be dangerous to ask a man about his past although some of them felt the need of unburdening themselves at times.

I remember one night I spent on the trail with a chap who apparently had held a rather responsible position in the Bay Area. We were attempting to make coffee on an open fire with the wind blowing thirty miles an hour and the temperature in the low thirties. In my growing disgust at finding myself in this situation, I finally asked him why he exchanged his former safe and presumably pleasant way of life for something like this. And he replied by quoting a few lines from the poem which is attributed to the notorious California highwayman, Black Bart:

"I've labored long and hard for bread,
For honor and for riches,
But on my corns too long you've tred
You fine-haired sons of bitches."

Men with that philosophy of life, who prided themselves on the fact that they wore no man's collar, would not fit very well into our modern society with its emphasis on security and conformity.

I missed the first years of the Nevada boom. I was still in High School when Jim Butler stumbled onto the Mizpah ledge at Tonopah. Five years later, when I had left the ivory halls of one of our leading educational institutions, to the evident relief of its faculty, Tonopah, Goldfield and Rhyolite were cities with banks, stock exchanges and plush hotels. I remember the mild shock I received on my first visit to Goldfield when I saw men wearing tuxedos in the lobby and the dining room of the Goldfield Hotel. It didn't seem to me that this was the proper attire for a frontier mining camp. My introduction to Rhyolite was a little different. I saw a poster in the Eye Opener Saloon at Silver Lake which said: "Wanted one thousand men to unload schooners at the Amargosa Bar." This sounded like an interesting job so I went up to Rhyolite and unloaded a few.

My experiences in Tonopah, Goldfield and Rhyolite, the three big camps of Southern Nevada, were strictly those of a visitor. My own activities were centered in some of the smaller towns, Skidoo, Ballarat, Silver Lake, Virginia Dale. The miners and prospectors I knew I met in these places, in neighboring mines or out on the trail. My memory in regard to most of them is rather hazy but a few incidents stand out.

Shorty Harris, one of the most famous of the burro men, came into Ballarat one evening from a prospecting trip in the Quail Springs country. When someone asked him if he found anything worthwhile, he replied, "I sure did, I found a brass mine." Now there probably wasn't anyone in the audience who didn't know that brass was an alloy of copper and zinc and was never found in nature, but that didn't prevent our having a wild celebration over this epoch-making discovery. Of course, it didn't take much to start a celebration in Ballarat where the natives boasted that the per capita consumption of whiskey was greater than in any other place in the world. After recovering from my hangover the next morning, I decided that Shorty had a more subtle sense of humor than he was generally given credit for.

One evening at Skidoo I met Bill Miller, who had some copper claims up near Tin Mountain at the north end of the Panamints. After a few drinks he invited me to come up and look at his claims and I agreed to do so. At the time, I was operating a little gold mine in Snow Canyon in the Argus Mountains. Instead of following the regular route via Harrisburg and Emigrant Springs, I took a short-cut trail from the north end of the Panamint Valley which joined the Tin Mountain trail at Cottonwood Springs. This trail passed by John LeMoigne's famous silver mine. I reached John's camp about noon and, in accordance with the almost universal custom at that time, he invited me to stay for lunch. After lunch he showed me his mine, which gave him a good living for many years. I learned later that this was something of a compliment as John didn't show his mine to everyone. A few weeks later, I ran into John at Darwin. We were eating lunch at the boarding house which was run by a very pleasant Irish woman whose name I don't remember. Her food was quite satisfactory but the coffee was a little on the weak side. During the course of the meal, she bustled over to where John was sitting and said: "Mr. LeMoigne, I understand that you make the best coffee of any one on the desert and I wish you would give me your recipe." And John replied: "Madam, to make good coffee, you use more coffee and less water."

One afternoon while travelling from Skidoo to Ballarat I stopped to see Frank Kennedy, the squaw man of Wild Rose Canyon. Frank was at loose ends at the moment because his squaw had become upset over something and had gone home to mother at Furnace Creek. Frank insisted that I stay overnight which I was glad to do. There was a bottle of Old Taylor in my saddlebag and we sat up most of the night killing it and discussing philosophy, all

BURRO PROSPECTOR

the way from Plato to Henry James. While I was fresh out of school then, and knew everything, I had to admit to myself, not to Frank, that he knew more about philosophy than I did.

One of my most interesting prospecting trips was with Jack Sweet, a competent prospector and a most agreeable companion. We camped for several days at Anvil Springs, near the south end of the Panamints, one of Death Valley Scotty's hideouts when he was attempting to avoid the men who wanted to buy his nonexistent gold mine. Sitting by the camp fire one evening I asked Jack if the Lost Gunsight Mine wasn't supposed to be in this general area. You may remember the story of the chap who left his party in Death Valley and struck out for the Coast. He had broken the front sight on his rifle and while going through a mountain range, presumably the Panamints, he found a vein of pure silver and fashioned a sight from it. After many hardships, he finally reached Newhall. When his attention was called to the home-made sight on his rifle, he remembered the vein of silver but his recollection was very hazy and neither he nor others who heard the story were able to find it.

In answer to my question, Jack replied that the Lost Gunsight was only a few miles from where we were sitting and that if I cared to take a day off from our prospecting chores, he would be glad to show it to me. Since I had never seen a lost mine, the idea appealed to me, and the next morning we filled our canteens and walked across Butte Valley through the herds of wild burros, whose descendants I understand are still there, and entered a canyon which led down to Death Valley. About halfway down, we turned up a side gulch for a short distance and there, sure enough, was a little gash vein of dirty white quartz and in it was a streak of pure silver two or three inches wide and perhaps ten feet in length. Of course, I don't know that this was the spot where the old timer had fashioned the sight for his rifle but it could have been.

And I think that a similar explanation might account for many of our lost mine stories. The desert is full of small pockets of rich gold and silver ore. A prospector finding one of these would naturally put a few specimens in his sample bags but, realizing that the deposit was too small to have any commercial value, he would not pay much attention to its exact location. Then he runs out of water and after many hardships stumbles into a camp or town in a semi-delirious condition. After recovering, he finds these high grade specimens in his gear and then vaguely remembers a large deposit of this high grade ore. As the story is retold, the ore gets richer and the vein larger, and men suffer great hardships and sometimes die searching for it, but it is never found.

I don't want to debunk our lost mine stories which are an interesting part

BURRO PROSPECTOR

of Western Americana but I can't help believing that many of them originated in this manner. And this could be particularly true of the most famous one of all, the Lost Pegleg.

No article of this kind would be complete without some reference to the most notable character of that period, Death Valley Scotty. Scotty was not a prospector nor a miner; he had been a cowboy and a trick rider and was, above all, a showman of the first water. I remember remarking to his older brother, Bill Scott, that I understood Walter was driving a tunnel on the Italy claim. Bill's reply was that there must be some mistake as Walter couldn't drive a tunnel through a hay stack.

No one on the desert, of course, thought that Scotty had a mine that turned out $100 bills. Most persons doubted that he had a mine of any kind or that he would recognize one if he saw it although his one time partner, Bill Keys, had some very promising claims in the Ibex Springs area. As far as I know, Keys, a real prospector and desert man, and Charlie Brown, now State Senator from Shoshone, are the only two remaining of the old timers that I knew well.

Before it became generally known that Scotty was being grubstaked by Johnson, the Chicago millionaire, there was much speculation as to the source of the money which he spent so lavishly. One of the widely circulated stories was that he had belonged to a group of train robbers and that after the others were all dead or in jail he had dug up the buried loot. There is no longer any mystery as to where Scotty obtained his money but to me there is still some question as to why. Johnson was a religious fanatic with a strong phobia against drinking, smoking and gambling; yet he furnished Scotty with considerable sums to spend on what Johnson must have considered a rather undesirable way of living. There must have been some reason.

A few years ago, I received a phone call from Bill Gates, one of our best TV engineers, who wanted to know if I was related in any way to the Fred Vaile who was prospecting in the Avawatz Mountains in 1907. It seems that Bill is something of a rockhound and a lover of the wide open spaces, and that he spends most of his spare time cruising around the desert in his jeep looking for rocks, lost mines, ghost towns and anything else of interest. On one of his trips he had left his jeep at Sweetwater, sometimes known as Mormon Wells, and had walked back into the heart of the Avawatz Mountains. In a rock monument near an old trail he found a tobacco can with a location notice which I had made out in January, 1907. Mrs. Vaile had the notice framed and it now occupies a place of honor in our library.

The Avawatz is a rather large mountain range, rising to elevations of about

BURRO PROSPECTOR

7,000 feet, which sprawls across the south end of Death Valley. State Highway 127, running north from Baker, skirts its eastern edge for some 25 or 30 miles. It is well mineralized in spots, but no mines of any importance were ever developed in the area in spite of a considerable amount of exploration work.

The Avawatz was a rather mysterious place when I first went there in the winter of 1906-1907. At times the night winds sounded like the music from a huge pipe organ and if you were at all psychic you could occasionally see strange lights on the mountain peaks. In a radius of ten or twelve miles in the heart of the mountains there were three springs: Arrastre Spring, North Avawatz Spring and Willow Spring, which were connected by wide, well graded trails. There was a small arrastre at each of these springs and good gold pannings could be obtained from the remaining tailings and the dirt under and around the arrastre stones. Arrastre Spring was at the end of the wagon road which connected with the road from Silver Lake to Cave Springs. There was a good size two room adobe there in habitable condition. A pool below the spring was a favorite watering place for mountain sheep.

In the bowl-like depression at North Avawatz Spring, which we called Poverty Hollow, there were five small stone cabins which a few years later were fixed up and used as bunk houses by the Avawatz Crown Mine. The hills surrounding Poverty Hollow were honeycombed with tunnels, several of them over 100 feet in length. Except for a few small pockets of silver ore, nothing of value had been discovered in any of these tunnels and it was apparent that no ore of any consequence had ever been taken out of them. I was rather intrigued by all this. Who had done all this work in an isolated part of the desert; why had they persevered so long with such meager results; where had they obtained their supplies? No one then in the area had any answers to these questions and most of them couldn't have cared less. Even Sam Francis (Amargosa Sam), who had been in this part of the desert since the beginning of time, could only mumble in his beard about some Spanish miners who were there during the eighties; but it was evident that he didn't really know anything about them.

The Avawatz was a good mountain sheep range in those days; it was not unusual to see bands of 20 or 25. When I revisited there in the thirties, there was no sign of sheep although the springs were full of water and the old cabins were still standing. Apparently for some reason the sheep had moved to another range. When I made a trip with Bill Gates a few years ago, the pond at Arrastre Spring had been overgrown with tules and the spring at North Avawatz, which had supplied a camp of 15 to 20 men for some years, was entirely dry. There were still no sheep, the adobe cabin had returned to dust and the rock cabins were little more than piles of stone. I didn't stay overnight on either of these trips so I don't know whether the winds still play organ music or the mystic lights still shine on the mountain tops.

Last year John Hilton, a corresponding member of the Los Angeles Corral, painted two pictures from snapshots I had taken in 1912. One showed the ruins of Old Dale and the other the town of New Dale, which was still active at that time. I am quite proud of these pictures and consider them a good example of the reason for the growing recognition of John as one of the really great desert artists. I started to call Dale the forgotten ghost town but that would not be quite accurate. Until it became a sight seeing trip for tourists from Twentynine Palms a few years ago, no one farther away than San Bernardino had ever heard of Dale.

This is somewhat strange since Dale lasted longer than most desert gold camps, from the time Hank Brown discovered the Virginia Dale Mine in 1883 until the Gold Crown and Supply finally closed down at the beginning of World War II. I presume that this is due to the fact that Dale lacked the glamor of the boom camps of Southern Nevada and the Death Valley country. Only one man was buried on its Boot Hill; it never had more than two saloons, and the Red Light District consisted of one small cabin separated from the main part of town by a rocky trail which could only be negotiated when one was reasonably sober. Still, Dale produced several millions in gold; and to the best of my knowledge is the only camp where placer mining with small hand dry washers ever paid off in a big way. I had hoped that someone would write the story of Dale, but now that all of the old timers are gone it would be a very difficult task.

The trouble with reminiscing is that it is hard to find a good place to stop. It would be easy to mention other times and other places, but there must be an end to all things. So I will close with the old slogan of the burro prospectors: "It's deep enuf."

LORDS AND TIN

By RAYMOND E. LINDGREN

Dr. Lindgren, in this scholarly article, introduces a surprising intruder into the field of early California mining history. The *British*, no less; and right at our geographical doorstep! This time it was not gold, nor silver, nor lead, nor tungsten, nor uranium. It was *tin*. And British Lords were jolly well in control of it. This all happened over at neighboring Riverside; but its peculiar and far-reaching implications transcended a mere Southern California interest. Dr. Lindgren gives a superb account of the incident in this paper.

HIDDEN FROM THE EYES OF MAN today in the folds of the Temescal Mountains is a hole in the ground which symbolizes the fate of most British investors in Riverside County. As one stands on the ridge of Cajalco Mountain, over-looking the blue waters of Lake Matthews, it is hard to imagine the twenty or more buildings once located there, and the feverish activity of the San Jacinto Estates, Ltd., in their mad search for tin.

Sobrante de San Jacinto, or the surplus of lands from the San Jacinto Nuevo and the San Jacinto Viejo, was a late grant in 1846 which was given by Pio Pico to Maria del Rosario Estudillo de Aguirre. Leandro Serrano had occupied and grazed herds of cattle on the rancho, but it was not notable for its profitable lands. Today it would be most desirable to have but a small piece of the property, for about 1500 acres lie within the city limits of Riverside and suburban expansion southward covers more and more of the old grant. About 1300 acres lie south and east of Riverside; another 2500 acres adjoin Arlington Heights and look toward Corona. To the east the hilly areas of the grant furnish grazing lands and the property now covered by the waters of Lake Matthews. In the original rancho were some 46,000 acres of land.

The San Jacinto grant also possessed valuable mineral property, for the Mexicans knew and used the gold of the Gavilan mine and silver deposits throughout the district. But it was only in the 1850s that tin, or the "magic metal" as the Indians called it, was discovered. A romantic fairy tale about the disclosure of the location of tin on San Jacinto usually casts a glimmer of mystery over the rancho and so why not repeat it? Daniel Sexton, a friend of the Indians and skilled in home remedy medicine, was called to attend a dying chief who, for reasons of this friendship and kindness, furnished Sexton with a guide to the mountain of tin. In exchange Sexton was to marry the niece of the chief in order to keep the secret within the family. So, the report continues,

LORDS AND TIN

Sexton went with his Indian guide to Cajalco Mountain and was taken to a hole in the ground where Sexton was shown an unusual ore which he identified as tin. In the next decade the discovery became widely known and mining claims were staked out by enthusiastic individuals who figured on getting rich.

Earlier than this reported romantic version, Abel Stearns, who was anything but a dreamer, purchased the entire rancho from the widow of Leandro Serrano, an Estudillo, for 200 cows. The cheap price and the willingness of Señora Serrano to sell is understood in light of the denial of the Land Commission to recognize the legitimacy of the grant, even though the other two San Jacinto ranchos were approved. Stearns then found himself involved in legal and financial troubles in fighting the claim through the various courts and in ousting the mineral squatters. He was able to interest the Phelps Dodge interests in the tin properties and other minerals, although Robert Cleland says that it is not clear just how they became involved or the amount of money furnished to Stearns. Later, in good Yankee fashion, Phelps Dodge attempted to extract money from a bankrupt Stearns and failed to secure any returns.[1]

With the grant in doubt, as decided by the United States Supreme Court in 1857, it was a shrewd stroke of business when Stearns sold the rancho to J. H. Ray of San Francisco for a stated price of $100,000. From 200 cows to a hundred grand is not bad business even though Stearns could not pay his debts some ten years later. The purchaser of the rancho did not succeed in achieving his aim of using mineral and other rights, for General E. F. Beale, the United States Surveyor-General, Edward Conway, H. Hancock and other associates of the land office patented the Sobrante de San Jacinto in 1867. From this date until 1888 the rancho was involved in incessant litigation through the interests of Stearns, acting for the Serrano heirs, and others. The cloud on the grant was complicated by accusations of fraud on the part of land office employees in using their position for private purposes. It was on this basis, and on the recognition of the validity of the original grant, that the United States Surpreme Court in March of 1888 declared the original grant, and thus the claims of the Serrano heirs and their agents, valid. In this case Senator William M. Stewart acted for the San Jacinto Tin Company against the interests of Colonel Robert S. Baker of Los Angeles and his associates who wished rights to the minerals on the rancho lands.

With the Sobrante de San Jacinto entirely quieted as to title, the owners through William A. Simmons attempted to sell the property in New York. Evidently Julius Lesznsky became involved and aided in the marketing of

---

1. Robert G. Cleland, *A History of Phelps Dodge, 1834-1950* (New York, 1952), 44-46.

LORDS AND TIN

the property in London. At least the rancho was again in the courts when Lesznsky sued for his ten per cent commission of $100,000 in U. S. Circuit Court. But the rancho was sold to the San Jacinto Estates, Ltd., and British lords and tin came finally together.[2]

The San Jacinto Estates, Ltd. was composed of British capitalists headed by Sir James Balfour and Sir John Stokes, the latter vice-president of the Suez Canal Company. The capital of the company consisted of £505,000, only partially paid-up, and the price paid for the rancho was reported to be $350,000 cash with another $50,000 in stocks.[3] Despite the rumor, reported by the South Riverside *Bee*,[4] that the property was purchased to prevent competition with Cornish mines, the company energetically, and with lack of good sense, started immediately in development work on the mines. Part of the reason for the early expansion and its flamboyant character was the American manager, Colonel E. N. Robinson, and the glowing reports of the British and American mining engineers on whose authority British investors plunged their gold. At the same time other English capitalists bought from New York and Boston investors the Harney Peak tin mine at Deadwood, South Dakota, so that the claim of monopoly might be more clearly indicated than first sight would reveal.

The reports of the mining engineers, whether American or British, glowed with praise and optimism and dangled prospective dividends of unprecedented proportions before the glazed eyes of British stockholders. Charles Craze, a Cornish mining engineer with considerable experience in British tin mines, visited Temescal for more than a month and kept as "dumb as an oyster" about his report. He flatly denied the possibility that the mines were purchased only to prevent production of American tin.[5] Charles Craze's favorable report was backed by those of George Grant Francis, Henry Mathey and William Williams who ecstatically reported on unbelievable riches underground. These four agreed, even though two were Cornish and two Americans, that the mines would make their British owners wealthy with assays of 5% to 80% tin from a solid vein of ore and 53 other lodes over some 15,000 acres of property. The total area equalled that of the Cornish mines which produced approximately 2 to 4% tin from their ores. These mining experts also reported on some 1200 feet of shafts and adits, an easy access to the deposits, and the availability of abundant water for the milling of the ore. They agreed fairly well on total costs of £50,000 to put the mines into operation and an estimated

2. South Riverside *Bee*, May 16, 1889.
3. *Engineering and Mining Journal*, L (1890), 174.
4. December 13, 1888.
5. South Riverside *Bee*, April 26, 1888.

daily output of 200 tons of ore which would more than pay the expenses of the development work. Evidently no wide exploration was made of the grant in their search for tin ore, as all four concentrated on the slopes of Mt. Cajalco where the richest ore could be found. Other traces in thin veins were reported over the total area but no assays were attempted and no exploration work undertaken. Tin still lies in these hills or under the waters of Lake Matthews; but its riches, compared to the world's resources, do not warrant exploitation because of the small amounts and the costs of operations.[6]

Befogged by their visions, the directors and stockholders proceeded to entrust the management of the mines to Colonel E. N. Robinson for almost the first year of operations. He built with lavish unconcern and wasted thousands of good British pounds on future prospects. Approximately $250,000 went immediately into the property in buildings, machinery, and development work, which was increased by an equal amount before closure of the mines. In brief, English investors sank almost a million dollars in purchase of the San Jacinto grant and its mining resources. To offset this investment, if no tin should be produced, the land, with irrigation and improvement into citrus orchards, was valued at more than four and a half million dollars.

Access to the mine from South Riverside, or Corona as it is today, was by Hoag Canyon Road. Across the mountains were adequate sources of water in Temescal Creek which Robinson immediately proceeded to dam with a towering structure 60 feet high and 450 feet long which, however, was never completed. Equipment shipped from London included a five stamp mill whose foundations and buildings were constructed under the supervision of Henry Mathey, one of the American mining engineers who had reported so glowingly on the mine resources of tin. Robinson built homes and bunkhouses for the workers "to make them happy" and furnished offices with plush equipment for the management. Before the end of 1891 a new thriving community occupied the foot of Cajalco Mt. in Hoag Canyon about six miles east and north of Corona, and the local citizens saw visions of profitable trade and the blossoming of a new industrial center for the West to rival Pittsburgh, Chicago, and New York.

By the spring of 1891 enough tin was produced to build a pyramid of tin bars to astonish visitors to South Riverside. President Benjamin Harrison and Governor Henry H. Markham praised this new product of California's mineral resources with rhetorical abandon, claiming that Temescal, in combination with the Harney Peak mines in South Dakota, would enable the United States

6. Prospectus, *Temescal Tin Mines*, Huntington Library.

LORDS AND TIN

to be self-sufficient in tin. Fed with such thin stuff, dreamers added California's coal, iron and tin as the main bases for a new industrial empire.

Development work on the mines consisted of a ninety-foot deep shaft which was intersected with two tunnels and numerous side adits for extraction of the ore. Heavy machinery was brought via the Santa Fé Railroad from either Los Angeles or San Diego where W. W. Stewart acted as agent for the company's purchases and its sales of tin bars when they were produced. No exploration or development was attempted beyond the immediate environs of Cajalco for the riches of these ores seemed inexhaustible. Lifts, steam hoists, tracks, and ore cars were hauled laboriously from Corona to the mine and rapidly installed. All during 1891 no clouds obscured the riches of the Temescal tin mine, now become the wonder of all the United States.

Yet skeptics repeated rumors of humbug and seriously doubted whether the tin from Temescal actually came from California. The company, and Colonel E. N. Robinson, issued small souvenirs of tin medals and small bars with Temescal tin stamped on them to prove their origin. A shipment of tin to Philadelphia by W. W. Stewart was so unusual that the New York *Tribune* borrowed the sizable shipment for exhibit at its offices to an amazed and unbelieving audience.[7] This doubt was charged as a deliberate plot of Democrats to prevent the passage of a tariff on tin; and Congressman W. W. Bowers of the district, fighting gloriously for his constituents and California, asserted that "Every Democratic organ and the party as a whole would rejoice over the utter failure of the tin mines . . . But however the heathen may rage the Temescal tin mines will continue to increase their output of tin for many years to come."[8] The injection of the tin issue into politics during 1891-92 caused no little conjecture because the Democrats refused to support a tariff favoring exclusion of British imports. In the long view the Democrats seemed to have been more farsighted than their Republican rivals who hoped to see the United States free of dependence upon foreign sources. So vehement did local pride become that tin was bought and cast into small blocks and, stamped with "Temescal Mines, San Bernardino County, California," sent to Democratic members of Congress and every prominent member of the party and the Mugwumps as well. Editors in the East who continued to ridicule the production of American tin were sent these small mementoes which were received by Democrats "pretty much as a sick man would receive a dose of quinine."[9] In the House of Representatives, when several speakers sar-

7. Riverside *Daily Press*, October 28, 1891.
8. Riverside *Daily Press*, October 15, 1891.
9. Riverside *Daily Press*, August 13, 1892.

castically referred to the new tin empire in California, Representative Bowers walked to the speaker's desk and deposited thereon a block of tin of fifty pounds weight, saying it was tin and was from Temescal and no more, letting those from Missouri believe. How Congressman Bowers carried a fifty pound piece of tin to the desk remains a mystery.[10]

Other doubting Thomases refused to take seriously the possibility of tin production amounting to much; but local editors boasted, as did the Redlands *Citrograph*, that the first shipment of Temescal tin to reach New York caused "tin dealers in London to telegraph New York dealers to lower prices on tin plate." Affidavits came with Temescal tin to prove its California origin and to allow some manufacturers in Ohio to advertise their product as wholly American.

More seriously, others commented on the black side of British interests who sought, in controlling both the Temescal and Harney Peak sources of tin, to prevent American production of tin plate. The serious purpose of the San Jacinto company was so doubted that Stephen Harris, the manager of the tin mines at Cajalco, issued a pronouncement denying that the production of tin at Temescal would soon fall off to suit the demands of British and Cornish interests. Later, however, the cessation of work allowed this rumor to take precedence; and South Riverside (Corona) and Riverside editors could state with conviction that the rich resources of the Temescal were being buried in order to prevent the breaking of the British monopoly on tin.

Complaints of local newspapers about the use of Cornish miners and their import to replace American laborers plagued local managers of the mines. They issued several denials and had them printed to stop the flood of denunciation of this typical British arrogance and blind egotism. The *Engineering and Mining Journal* of 1891, Los Angeles, Riverside and South Riverside newspapers printed denials with James Van Allen, the former editor of the *Scientific American*, stating flatly that at the time of his visit to the mine 163 American miners were employed with only 7 Cornishmen on the premises, and they long resident in the United States.

These complaints were minor clouds on the blue skies of optimism for the company when the stockholders heard the end of the year report in 1891. With Sir John Stokes in the chair the assembled group listened to an announcement of a change of management at the mine with the substitution of Mr. Stephen Harris for Colonel E. N. Robinson and the diversion of attention from extraneous work on dams and buildings to the exploration and development

10. Riverside *Daily Press*, March 28, 1892.

LORDS AND TIN

of the tin resources. To the enthusiastic "Hear, Hears" of the stockholders, Sir John continued by explaining the actual working of the mine. The one battery of stamps appeared to be sufficient for some time while below ground a great deal of work needed to be done to develop the property. The winze was carried 55 feet lower, a gallery driven to explore veins to the side of the main vein, the main shaft had been sunk deeper, and two new tunnels were being opened. The old furnace had proven inadequate and a new one was being built to reduce the ores which would, even without a new furnace, provide 25 tons of tin for the month of December.

Although work on the dam had been suspended, due to faulty engineering and miscalculation of the foundation rock, sometime in the future the dam would be finished to supply water both for the mine and for sale. Other sources of revenue were available, for grazing lands had been leased for a yearly rental of £1000 and the Gavilan Gold Mining Company had leased that property for a yearly rental and 20% of the gross income. The water supply was more than abundant for the mine and sales of surplus water could produce additional income; the completion of the dam and the sale of its impounded water would mean considerable cash return, perhaps sufficient to pay for the costs of construction of the dam itself.

Yet, Sir John continued, the company needed more capital to develop the mine. Without dwelling on the extravagance of Colonel E. N. Robinson, the chairman inferred that the magnificent outlay of moneys at the surface were responsible for the call for more capital. It was proposed to place on the market some £50,000 of the old debentures not yet offered to procure enough capital to put the mines into self-sustaining production. Sir John's statements were greeted with enthusiastic applause by the confident stockholders and approval was given unanimously to the proposed sale.

Despite this confidence, the management and directors betrayed some fears by having an American engineer, Gervaise Purcell, present to report about the properties. He estimated the tin lodes to number about 30, of which only one was being worked. Several assays showed an average of better than fifteen per cent tin and bodies of ores in sight outside the working lode for future development. Machinery at the mine was of the best quality and introduced a new type of milling technique into America. Plenty of water was available both in the tunnels of the mine and Temescal Creek for all purposes and even some excess which constituted a potential source of income. The fruit lands on the west side of the property, amounting to between 10,000 and 15,000 acres, must be irrigated to be profitable; but here again were potential sources of income.

In commenting upon the balance sheet for the year, Mr. Alfred Conder introduced a slight note of complaint by asking for the signatures of the directors on the report since the balance sheet showed an "enormous outlay on buildings, etc., and the very small outlay upon development of the mine. It is not my intention to cry over spilt milk. Mr. Robinson seems to have played ducks and drakes with the capital of the company and all the money that might have gone to develop this magnificent tin property appears to have been expended upon works that will return nothing for the present . . . That, however, is done, and we have to bear the brunt of it." Another stockholder inquired whether Mr. Robinson could be charged with misappropriation of funds and Sir John answered that it was misspent money and not misappropriation. He also noted that Robinson had come with the property as general manager and that the directors were not entirely to blame for this reason. In commenting later upon this meeting the Riverside *Daily Press* noted Sir John's remark that the directors and stockholders "would all have made your fortunes" in twelve months.[11] In closing the meeting, the attending stockholders voted a resolution of thanks to the board and chairman for their conduct of affairs.

Hidden behind this facade of affability and approval, however, was a struggle between London and Cornish interests for control of the mines. The debenture holders, most of whom were Cornish, sought to push exploitation of the tin resources rather than development in order to regain their monies and to have the mine pay dividends. The change of management, even without consideration of Robinson's evident mismanagement of funds, stemmed more from this fight than any doubts as to the mine or its potential income production for British stockholders. The policy of rushing extraction of ores and production of tin answered the hungry call for repayment of the debentures and dividends upon them.

During the first months of 1892 mine operations began a faster pace, and in February a shipment of more than 44,000 pounds of tin was made to Balfour, Guthrie and Co. of San Francisco which was followed by shipments in March, April and May. In addition other ore bodies were found by sinking new shafts and extending the tunnels, together with the uncovering of a new lode atop Mt. Cajalco which was rapidly utilized. Approximately twenty tons of tin were being produced per month during the first of the year and

---

11. January 4, 1892. The long report is taken from the South Riverside *Bee*, January 2, 1892, as printed in the *Mining World and Engineering Record*.

LORDS AND TIN

about a hundred men worked in the mine, mills and plant. The installation of new machinery improved the mine both as to quantity of ore produced and the efficiency with which it was extracted.

All this haste and activity cloaked the anxiety of both directors and managers of the mine. In April Stephen Harris resigned his position because he had become convinced that the property would not pay as a tin mine, and he carried his report to London. The output of the mine had fallen to 12 tons per month and the company was spending some $8,000 per month in excess of income. The new manager, Gervaise Purcell of San Francisco, who had given an optimistic report at the December, 1891, meeting of the board and stockholders, busily pushed ahead by installing new stamps and expanding and exploring new sources of ore.

No amount of exploration and good wishes could remedy the deficiency of ore. In the early summer experts reported, as did the manager, on the inability to find new veins. What happened is that the rich vein which had produced over 250,000 lbs. of tin ended at the 300 foot level, and no amount of work could find it again. Some laborers were laid off during extensive exploration, and the mines finally closed after the miners walked out on September 17 when paychecks were not presented on the regular payday. By then the ore had fallen to a quality of about 3 per cent tin and it was no longer economical with the higher cost of labor to produce tin in America. Despite these facts, Purcell continued to issue optimistic reports as to his confidence in the mine and his belief that further exploration would locate the new veins and prove the mine once more a valuable property.

The directors' and stockholders' meeting in October was a stormy argument between representatives of the debenture holders and the board of directors. An American expert, H. B. Varcoe, reported favorably as to prospects for he felt that other rich veins could be found elsewhere. To maintain possession of the properties the stockholders approved a vote to increase the stock by $200,000 in 5 shilling shares to pay off the debenture holders and keep the entire grant clear. But they also could not find any possibility for further working of the mine and no orders were given for re-employment of the discharged miners.

The London fight and decision to discontinue working the San Jacinto mine were seen locally as merely a suspension of operations and, as the Riverside *Daily Press* stated on September 28, 1892, most believed "that the shutting down has been done at the instance of the Democratic managers, who somehow seem to have an idea that tin mining developments will be detrimental to their party success [in the elections of 1892]." The *Daily Press* thought the suspension no serious loss because work would be resumed after the November elections and charged English free trade interests with having caused the temporary stoppage of work to assist in Cleveland's election. The Republican views of the editor of the *Daily Press* were not only evident, but they allowed him to gloss over an evident fact that Riverside and Corona had seen the last of tin operations.

The supporters of the San Jacinto mine could take some pride in their local claim to fame, however, in that the mines did produce the only American tin, except for scant amounts from Harney Peak and some later attempts at development of the Temescal properties. A total of over 250,000 pounds of tin had been produced at Cajalco and sold for about $60,000. Together with leases and income from the gold mine at Gavilan, this meant that British investors lost approximately $650,000 in their effort to furnish the United States with domestic tin. According to later mineralogical reports, it is evident that the San Jacinto properties were flukes with small quantities of high grade tin ore which could not be mined extensively. Rather than the fight in London between stockholders and debenture holders, Democratic opposition—whether real or imagined, or the desire of the Welsh and Cornish interests to keep American tin from the market, the real cause for cessation of the San Jacinto tin mines was the end of an ore vein and an inability to discover new ones.

Yet the San Jacinto Estates, Ltd., possessed a valuable property even if they little wanted to become real estate managers. During 1893 some movable property was sold, including the stamps, furniture, buildings and other assets in order to satisfy local debts and to realize as much from the property as possible. The Morongo King Mining Company purchased both the experimental and the unused new mill which had been shipped in the spring of 1892. No real property, however, was sold at this time.

The conversion of the property to real estate and agricultural purposes came in the reorganization of the company with leadership furnished by Sir Herbert Praed whose name still decorates a street in Arlington. Sir Herbert advanced money for the property and formed a company with M. Horner and F. E. Lander as other directors to manage the San Jacinto estate as an agricultural property. During the 1890s the dam was completed and water provided for the lands toward Riverside, which meant that the turn of the century saw the San Jacinto Estates launched on its twentieth century progress toward solvency. Varcoe, the last manager of the tin mine, continued to manage and operate the gold mine near Perris, after abandonment of the

LORDS AND TIN

Tin Ledge, Temescal Tin Mine. Riverside county, 1889.

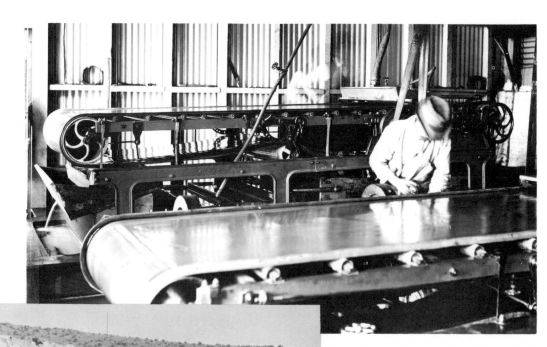

Concentrator—Temescal Tin Mine—1889.

"Control and office buildings, 1955."

Hoist at Temescal Tin Mine—1889.

LORDS AND TIN

lease by an American company.

Sir Herbert managed the San Jacinto much as a private estate and dispatched his nephew, Arthur S. Holden, to direct local activities. Holden's arrival in Riverside meant aggressive and positive leadership in an agricultural development although mineral properties were disposed of as the company continued to prosper during the booms in California and the growing demand for citrus products in the United States. The major development and sale of properties came during two periods, one prior to World War I and the other in the 1930s under Holden's management. About 30,000 acres of undeveloped land were sold in 1910 to a California company, leaving about 16,000 acres on the west side of the hills. In the rash of prosperity in 1927-28 an American company, the American Tin Corporation with G. H. Bryant as president, acquired rights to land and tin deposits in the mountains from American owners. But only a half ton of tin was produced and the tin resources were neglected until 1942 when Tinco leased the mineral properties to the Dodge Construction Company of Fallon, Nevada. Using bulldozers and earth moving machinery, the Dodge Company processed about 1400 tons of ore, recovering about a half pound of tin per ton of ore. However, before sympathizing too much with the Dodge Construction Company, it should be mentioned that all the work received government loans in a national effort to secure more adequate supplies of tin for war purposes. Thus the mill and equipment were actually paid for by taxpayers. When visited in September, 1959, other earth movers, trucks and bulldozers were active over and around the Temescal or San Jacinto tin mine, but this time moving earth to increase the height and width of the dam behind which lies Lake Matthews, a reservoir for the Metropolitan Water District. The District bought the land for this reservoir between 1937 and 1942 from many different persons.

In 1944 the San Jacinto Estates, Ltd., closed its American books with the sale of the last properties to a group of Americans among whom was Arthur Holden. R. A. Weeden and E. H. Gardiner (both of whom died in 1959) joined with Holden and others in the purchase of the properties. Apparently about 180 acres were still under the direction of Holden in 1944 and this acreage, reportedly sold at $3000 per acre, approximately paid for the original cost of the grant and a surplus of about $150,000. But neither British investor nor stockholder could recoup the losses of the only producing tin mine venture in the United States.[12]

---

12. My thanks should be expressed to Mrs. R. A. Weeden, John L. Holden and Mrs. Dorothy Cable for the information which they supplied about the operations of the company since 1893. Unfortunately the records of Arthur Holden and the reports which he sent to London are not preserved, and any complete story will have to await a visit to London and examination of the private materials there.

LORDS AND TIN

The Sobrante de San Jacinto had never been considered to be much as compared with the other two grants. It was accepted by Serrano in order to match the holdings of the Estudillo family into which he married. But its history of long litigation and the spectacular effort of the San Jacinto Estates, Ltd., management to develop a tin property brought notoriety to Riverside and the grant. And, if stockholders held their shares and the debenture holders were paid off, the sale of citrus groves and properties recouped all the losses sustained in tin. The lords could point with justifiable pride to their profits if not their sagacity.

"Remains of the old mill in 1955."

"Old central shaft as it appeared in 1955."

(Photos courtesy of Dr. James Mink, Special Collections
University of California at Los Angeles Library.)

This small chapter in British investment points up the importance of foreign capital in Southern California, and it is hoped that further exploration will reveal the magnitude of local investment. However great the value of British pounds proved to be for citrus groves, lands, mines, banks and other materials for California's twentieth century growth, they could never be as important as the introduction of cricket and polo on local grounds where, surrounded by the trees of the San Jacinto Estate, or what was once formerly its property, British emigrants, descendants of nobles, played those ancient and honorable games in complete ignorance of the story that lay behind either their coming or their lives.

DESERT GLIMPSES

By CHARLES N. RUDKIN

NOON

Below the fringe of dancing mountains,
Through the dull, uncertain sheen of the mirage,
A freight-train, grumbling, writhes its painful way.
Choosing his steps among the nearer bushes
Slowly lopes a solemn, stiff-eared rabbit;
Stops, and poised, looks blandly all about.
Close by, a slender lizard, shadowless,
Gray white-ringed tail erect, feet spread,
Skitters across the powdery loam. The sun,
A red-rimmed spot of black, straight overhead,
Burns at the end of a white-hot shaft—
Silence, gray sage-brush, loneliness,
And ragged buttes piercing the hot dead air.

THE DUST STORM

A gentle wavering air, as hot and dry
As the breath of fever, creeps from the west and grows
To a furnace blast, shrieking from Hell-mouth;
Laden with dust, brick-red and choking;
Smothering the sun, whose dull red disk
Glows murkily behind the gritty veil.
Stiff, stubby bushes lean far over and
Down the draft of the clutching wind;
A frightened rabbit in a flattened rush slips by.

NIGHT-FALL

Evening and calm—the great red sun
Poises a moment on the rim,
Stretching long purple shadows towards the east;
Then slips from sight beneath great blood-red cumuli.
Dusk deepens. The maniac yell of a lone coyote
Floats on the night-wind, shuddering, chill.
It is dark; and the cold hard stars
Shine with a steely glitter—
Bright points on a dead black velvet pall.

BRAND BOOK X TALLY SHEET

By Don Meadows

In every respect BRAND BOOK X has been assembled by members of the Los Angeles Corral of the Westerners. Writers, artists, editors, printers, distributors and publishers all belong to the Los Angeles outfit. The quality of the meat covered by the X brand indicates the range of interests and talents possessed by those who live around the town called the "Queen of the Cow Country." Not a single rider in the outfit has profited in dollars and cents from the roundup. The only compensation received was the satisfaction of knowing that they were taking care of their Western heritage. The whole Corral has done its share in keeping the book hog-tied, but a few waddies need to be cut out for special notice:

LYNN R. BAILEY

LYNN BAILEY grew up in an atmosphere of writing and research. Son of Ex-Sheriff Paul Bailey, he has been steeped in the lore of the West; and added book larnin', plus a degree in anthropology from the University of Arizona, has contributed to his background. For two years he was curator of collections of the Arizona Pioneers museum in Tucson; and as a research student he has delved into the National Archives and major libraries of the West, always in search of material on the Indians of the Southwest. His book-length study of the Navajo wars (1846-60), entitled *The Long Walk*, will be published in the Fall of 1963. Lynn is married and lives with his family in his native village of Los Angeles.

IRON EYES CODY

IRON EYES (OSCAR) CODY was born in Texas of Cherokee parentage. From his father, Thomas Long Plume, he learned the lore and customs of the first Americans. At an early age, with his father, he traveled with wild west shows, and in 1924 his career as a motion picture actor began when he appeared in *The Covered Wagon*. Since then he has been closely associated with motion pictures and television as actor, advisor and producer. For three years he was on a TV program with Westerner Tim McCoy, and later had his own show—*Iron Eyes' Tipi*. Iron Eyes lives in Hollywood with his wife Yewas and two sons. He is the author of a book on sign language, *HOW—Indian Sign Talk*, published in 1952.

EARLE R. FORREST

EARLE FORREST celebrated his eightieth birthday on June 29, 1963. For years his name has been associated with Western literature. During his early manhood he mixed a college education with punching cattle in Colorado, Arizona and Montana. From the range and college cloisters (Washington & Jefferson College and the University of Michigan) he drifted into newspaper work and for forty-eight years was a writer and publisher. Frequent interludes of browsing through the Southwest kept him supplied with historical material, and from his contacts he produced *Arizona's Dark and Bloody Ground*, *Missions and Pueblos of the Old Southwest*, *Lone Trail of the Apache Kid*, *California Joe*, and many others. His home is in San Marino.

JOHN B. GOODMAN, III

JOHN GOODMAN came to California from Colorado in 1904 when three years of age. Early in 1920 he entered the motion picture business with the old Famous Players-Lasky Company on Vine Street in Hollywood and progressed to be a distinguished Art Director in the motion picture and television field. At present he is creating the pictorial excellency of the *Rawhide* TV series. John says, "Because of my work I developed into a bibliophyle, collecting maritime books, early Californiana and overland narratives. I have been very fortunate in being able to recreate the interesting places and scenes of historical interest that my library includes. My business research and book collecting go hand in hand." His home is in Beverly Hills.

EVERETT GORDON, & ANNA MARIE HAGER

THE HAGERS, transplanted Easterners, have a shipshape home near Point Fermin in San Pedro overlooking the spot where Deadman's Island once reared its bulk above the sea. Authorities on the Long Beach-Los Angeles harbor area, they have recorded a great deal of history relating to the twin harbors that were created from a mud flat. Historians are indebted to the Hagers for compiling annotated indices to the publications issued by the Southern California Historical Society and the magazine *Touring Topics-Westways* issued by the Automobile Club of Southern California. For this outstanding work they were recipients of the Award of Merit given by the California Historical Society in 1962.

JOHN H. KEMBLE

JOHN H. (JACK) KEMBLE is Sheriff of the Los Angeles Corral of the Westerners. Modest about his accomplishments, he is a PhD. from the University of California, a full professor of history at Pomona College, was once a Commander in the U.S. Navy on the Staff of Admiral Nimitz at Pearl Harbor, is the author of several books and has an outstanding collection of books, paintings, lithographs, charts and ephemera dealing with maritime history. Some of his books are: *The Panama Route, 1848-1869; San Francisco Bay, a Pictorial Maritime History; Gold Rush Steamers;* etc. When this Brand Book appears Dr. Kemble will be on sabatical leave, making a trip around the world, and not by air.

GEORGE KOENIG

GEORGE KOENIG, native of Michigan (1918), spent four and one-half years with the U.S. Air Force in the Pacific. When World War II was over he headed for his home state, but got no farther than California. With senses unbiased by familiarity he caught the drama of California history and settled down to absorb some of it. The result was a *Guide Book of the Mother Lode Country.* Gold Rush research took him on the trails of miners who came by land, especially those who came across the southern deserts. He is now at work on a study of the Death Valley 49'ers. He is vice-president of the Geyer-Morey-Ballard Advertising Agency in Los Angeles, and lives with his wife, two children and a Siamese cat in San Fernando Valley.

RAYMOND E. LINDGREN

RAYMOND E. LINDGREN is Dean of the College and professor of history at Long Beach State College. A specialist in modern European history, he became interested in the migration of British capital and capitalists to California. In his studies he came upon the British purchase of the rancho San Jacinto de Sobrante on which the Temescal tin mines are located. Dr. Lindgren, a PhD. from UCLA, studied in Norway on a Full-bright scholarship. His recent book, *Norway-Sweden, Union, Dis-union and Scandinavian Integration,* was published by Princeton University. Another book, *Political Community and the North Atlantic Area,* was issued by the same press. Dr. Lindgren is married and the father of three children. His home is in Long Beach.

DON MEADOWS

DON MEADOWS arrived in southern California from Indiana more than sixty years ago and was soon on the trail of historical and scientific information. After corraling degrees at Pomona College and the University of California he tried newspaper work for a few years but gave it up for a more leisurely life of school teaching and research. He wrote a batch of scientific papers, a novel (fortunately not published), a stage play, two pageants (produced), two books on Baja California, several book reviews, *A History of Orange County* (Fall 1963), many historical articles; but no poetry. Becoming tired of teaching he built an adobe house around a library of Western Americana in. the hills east of Santa Ana.

HORACE PARKER

HORACE PARKER owns the Paisano Press and uses the Road-runner as a colophon. It personifies the man. Active, searching, astute, intense, ingenious and friendly he covers the brush country of the southwest in search of morsels for writing and publishing. A native of Boston, he was brought to southern California before he acquired a taste for beans and cod fish. A Doctor of Veterinary Medicine, ex-school teacher, author, publisher, desert explorer, bibliophyle and renovator of a ghost town hotel in Temecula, "Doc" gets around. His *Brush Country Journal* was long a feature in the *Riverside Daily Enterprise*. Several editions of his *Anza-Borrego Desert Guide Book* have appeared, and a revised edition is in the making. He lives on Balboa Island and in Temecula.

W. W. ROBINSON

ROBINSON, W. W. is a name attached to many books. A native of Colorado, he moved to Riverside, California while a young-ster; and, after graduating from high school, contributed to the lustre of the University of California by receiving a degree in 1916. An authority on the California ranchos he moved upward to become Vice-president of Title Insurance and Trust Company in Los Angeles. Along the way he wrote regional histories, children's books, poetry and technical papers. His bibliography would cover pages of the Brand Book. Outstand-ing titles in the list are: *Lawyers of Los Angeles*, *Ranchos Become Cities*, *Land in California*, etc. Now retired from executive activities, he gives his full time to writing.

Charles N. Rudkin

CHARLIE RUDKIN is Deputy Sheriff of the Los Angeles Corral. Retired as Manager of Procedures of the Southern California Edison Company, he has made available pertinent accounts of the southwest that have been hidden behind a foreign language. Translating from the French he unlocked the *Voyage of the Venus* by Petit-Thouars, *Voyage on the Colorado* by Francis Berton, and Camille de Roquefeuil's *Visit to San Francisco*. From the Spanish he translated the rare volume *Observations on California, 1772-1790* by Luis Sales. An outdoor man, he has hunted insects and history throughout the southwest. Charlie started his career by writing verse when a student in Wesleyan University where he got his B.S. degree in 1914. He lives in San Marino.

Fred Vaile

FRED VAILE was a quiet and kindly man who had little to say around the chuck wagon, but behind his reticence was a wealth of experience and knowledge. Born in Martinez, California, he entered Pomona College; but the lure of a Big Bonanza hidden somewhere in the wilds of the great Southwest took him away from the campus before he received a degree. For ten years he kept on the trail of a big strike, then settled down to become an expert on oil and mining taxation. In the waste land he did discover a golden philosophy. Fred left the Corral on September 22, 1963 at the age of seventy-five.

Harold & Lucile Weight

The names HAROLD and LUCILE WEIGHT conjure up the desert, for none has written so much about the dry country. Harold, a native of Los Angeles (1911), became a desert rat at an early age. He began tracing the Bradshaw Road early in the 1930's. After World War II he became an associate editor of *Desert Magazine*. (Lucile Harris was the other one, and Harold promptly married her.) After two years with the DM they started their own publication, the unique *Calico Print*. With a four-wheel drive vehicle they covered completely the Bradshaw Road, a deed that was an adventure even when mules pulled the wagons. The Weights have contributed articles about the desert to many national publications. Their home is in Twentynine Palms.

To Those Who Made It Possible -- *Our Thanks*

Principal credit for *Brand Book Number Ten* must go to its contributors. These writers not only have provided a welcome diversification of subject matter; they have supplied definitive material concerning important historic episodes about which little or nothing has heretofore been recorded. Among these contributors are those recognized as authorities in the subjects of their choice. Happily, the Los Angeles Corral is privileged to claim all these capable writers in its membership.

Members of the *Brand Book* Editorial Staff served loyally and well. To this fine group of trained, accomplished men who gave so willingly of their time and energy, go our sincere thanks for a job well done. Special appreciation is merited in the instance of Committee members Paul Galleher and Arthur Clark, Jr., of The Arthur H. Clark Company, who—over the years—have conducted the Sales and Distribution program of our Brand Books. Not only have these men given freely of their time and effort; they have generously absorbed a substantial portion of the expense involved. To Arthur Clark, in particular, we express gratitude for his excellent contribution to this *Brand Book*—the preparation of its Index.

There are others, not members of the Committee, who deserve mention. Lonnie Hull assisted in providing necessary photographs from his files and in preparing reproductive prints of the Ellsworth paintings; Iron Eyes Cody cheerfully cooperated in supplying information, photographs, sketches and paintings relating to the late Clarence Ellsworth; and Bert Olson—he who holds diligently the purse strings—at all times kept the Editor informed of our financial position, and thus aided in bringing this project to completion without deficit.

Of those who served, there are two whose contributions to this *Brand Book* proved indispensable to its successful accomplishment. John Goodman assumed responsibility for the art program, not only for its actual creation but for the planning and direction of it. Homer Boelter, who over the total life of our Los Angeles Corral has produced these lovely Brand Books, once again consented to give us the benefit of his guiding council, his creative talent, and his personal supervision of the designing and printing of the book. The Editor personally, and in behalf of the Committee and the Corral, extends to them his thanks.

E. I. EDWARDS

INDEX

INDEX

INDEX

INDEX

INDEX

INDEX

INDEX

INDEX

INDEX

INDEX

INDEX

INDEX